Historical Perspectives on Business Enterprise
Mansel G. Blackford and K. Austin Kerr, Series Editors

UNEXCEPTIONAL WOMEN

*Female Proprietors in
Mid-Nineteenth-Century Albany,
New York, 1830–1885*

Susan Ingalls Lewis

THE OHIO STATE UNIVERSITY PRESS | COLUMBUS

Library of Congress Cataloging-in-Publication Data
Lewis, Susan Ingalls, 1949–
Unexceptional women : female proprietors in mid-nineteenth-century Albany, New York, 1830–1885 / Susan Ingalls Lewis.
    p. cm.—(Historical perspectives on business enterprise)
Includes bibliographical references and index.
ISBN 978-0-8142-0398-9 (cloth : alk. paper)
1. Self-employed women—New York (State)—Albany. 2. Businesswomen—New York (State)—Albany. 3. Entrepreneurship—New York (State)—Albany. I. Title.
HD6072.6.U52A43 2009
338.09747'4308209034—dc22
                    2008038410

This book is available in the following editions:
Cloth (ISBN 978-0-8142-0398-9)
CD-ROM (ISBN 978-0-8142-9178-8)

Cover design by Janna Thompson-Chordas
Text design by Juliet Williams
Typeset in ITC Galliard
Printed by Thomson-Shore, Inc.

*This book is lovingly dedicated to the memory of my beautiful and
talented friend
Patricia Ann Doran (1948–1996)
Artist, Ceramicist, Teacher, and
Dean of Graduate and Continuing Education,
the Massachusetts College of Art*

CONTENTS

●

Contents

ILLUSTRATIONS

PREFACE

In this book we describe the ways of knowing that women have cultivated and learned to value, ways we have come to believe are powerful but have been neglected and denigrated by the dominant intellectual ethos of our time.

—*Women's Ways of Knowing*, 1986[1]

IN THE LATE 1980S, I WAS a graduate student whose embryonic ideas about women and gender—shaped largely by my own family background and personal experiences in the "real world" of working women—seemed to conflict with standard interpretations of women's history. Before returning to school in 1988, I had been employed as a picture researcher, a medical secretary, and a museum curator for nearly twenty years. Once enrolled in a program of public history with an emphasis on local and regional studies, I immersed myself in a series of intensive "readings" courses. Although I had not originally intended to concentrate on women's labor history, it bothered me that the female models then current in both women's and labor history failed to reflect my own experiences and those of the women I had known. In contrast to paradigms of middle-class domesticity and male support, generations of women in my family had worked for a living outside the home. And while most historical analyses stressed the powerlessness and exploitation of female workers, the women I knew had found satisfaction, if not great wealth or authority, through their employment. Was my own experience, and that of my female friends and family members, so unique?

The project that eventually turned into this book began with a term paper on milliners, written for a labor history course during my second term in graduate school. Little did I suspect that the paper would lead to a fifteen-year research project on mid-nineteenth-century businesswomen in Albany, New York. Very early in this project, I had the opportunity to take part in an informal panel discussion, "Women in Communities," as part of an annual New York State Women's Studies Conference.[2] This was my introduction to the wide scope of women's studies and the manner in which it integrates a broad range of academic disciplines. The theme of the conference was "Women's Ways of Knowing," and psychologist Blythe Clinchy presented the keynote address. In retrospect, I realize that many of my ideas about both scholarship and teaching—what had been rather inchoate and unsophisticated "feelings" up to that point—crystallized while listening to Clinchy's talk. In her discussion of "women's ways" I was able to recognize the validity of using my own life experiences, and the stories of women in my own maternal family as passed down through the generations, as models against which to check historical hypotheses.

As I began the research for what I planned to be my master's thesis, I assumed that I might find fifty or so millinery entrepreneurs active in mid-nineteenth-century Albany. I took for granted that these would be rare and exceptional women, and that finding out everything I could about each one of them would be a fairly straightforward and limited task. To my surprise, using city directories and credit records, I quickly uncovered more than two hundred female millinery proprietors within a far more numerous population of businesswomen who were *not* milliners. Eventually, my research on this single American city during a fifty-five-year period (1830–85) revealed that the population of women in business exceeded two thousand individuals. When I decided to expand my study to include all mid-nineteenth-century businesswomen in the city of Albany, I was intrigued by a subset of women who—like the women in my own family and those I had met while working—did not seem to fit comfortably into the paradigms presented by feminist historians of the 1970s and '80s. That is, I was discovering women who were (to draw on the wording of Gerda Lerner's well-known article) neither "ladies" nor "mill girls."[3]

One benefit of allowing any project to unfold over time is the opportunity to reassess one's original assumptions, to test theses, and to explore important questions from many angles as one's views develop. While exploring the scope of businesswomen's enterprises in mid-nineteenth-century Albany, my interpretations have gone through a series of stages. The first stage of my work was simply a reaction to what I thought of as the "victimization" school of women's labor history. Considering milliners as entrepreneurs and artisans as well as downtrodden workers, I argued for a richer, more complex, and more heterogeneous model of nineteenth-century working women.[4] As part of my continued resistance to the "exploited and oppressed" characterization of nineteenth-century women, my early explorations of Albany's female entrepreneurs might well be seen as a contribution to the "women were there, too" school of feminist history.[5] In presentations, I stressed not only the ways in which business was open to mid-nineteenth-century women in Albany but also the size and variety of the community of businesswomen who took advantage of this option. In addition, I focused my research on the most prominent and successful of the hundreds of female proprietors in the Albany business community, and particularly on those whose commercial, artisanal, or industrial efforts had been investigated and recorded at length by the credit examiners of the R.G. Dun Mercantile Agency.[6] Although I realized that such exceptional businesswomen constituted only the "tip of the iceberg" in terms of women's economic activity in the marketplace, initially I found little to say about the mass of women either neglected or dismissed by the R.G. Dun investigators.

The second stage of my thinking came when I recognized the need to uncover the rest of that iceberg—the women who remained to be excavated through painstaking research in city directories and census listings. Mid-nineteenth-century Albany did support a few relatively successful female entrepreneurs, who built up flourishing business concerns from relatively modest capital investments. However, to understand the vital role played by business in the lives of the vast majority of Albany's enterprising women, one must move beyond the concept of mid-nineteenth-century entrepreneurial "success" based on traditional male models. The celebrated stories of Andrew Carnegie and Horatio Alger find echoes in the careers of relatively few of the women who engaged in business ventures in Albany during this period, and even the most successful rarely managed to build up establishments worth more than $10,000 (about $1 million in today's currency). In order to understand and appreciate the careers of the vast number of businesswomen who were not exceptional, it became necessary to problematize definitions of entrepreneurship, success, and even business proprietorship itself, since standard definitions essentially negated the contributions of most women in the marketplace. Instead of looking at only those female entrepreneurs who significantly increased their means, earned large profits, invested in real estate, and gradually increased their commercial size and worth, I realized that a thorough study of businesswomen demanded that I focus on the role of small businesses (capitalized at $50 to $1,000, the equivalent of $5,000 to $100,000 today)—concerns that *did not* dramatically expand or remain even profitable—in the lives of the women who owned and operated them. This reassessment appeared especially important since such microbusinesses provided the majority of ventures in which Albany's women were involved. What did these enterprises mean to their individual proprietors, and what part did they play in the mid-nineteenth-century urban marketplace as a whole?[7]

Yet reaching this second stage almost immediately required me to embark on a third level of conceptualization—how to develop new models of business, proprietorship, success, and entrepreneurship that would "fit" the experiences of nineteenth-century businesswomen. After some consideration, I decided to view female business enterprises in the context of the opportunities and limitations of women's, rather than men's, actual lives during the mid-nineteenth century itself. Similarly, it made sense to compare women's business careers to the range of female employment available during that period rather than to opportunities available to women today. Much of this book is devoted to that project.

Although part of me (and most of my family) feels that this project took a long time to come to fruition, another benefit of allowing my work to mature over time is the current opportunity of locating my discussion within the emerging subspecialty of women's business history. When I started my research on nineteenth-century businesswomen, there was little scholarly research and no significant historiography in the field. Today there is a growing recognition of the importance of women's business history from the early modern period through the present, and an exciting wave of new publications. As will be shown, many of my discoveries and conclusions have recently been echoed in the work of other scholars.

One's own experiences inevitably shape one's research interests and historical interpretations. When I began this project in 1989, my personal identity was bound up in my work, the series of careers described earlier, and I thought of myself as a relatively independent economic actor. As a graduate student, mother, and adjunct instructor for the next ten years, however, I became more dependent on my husband as the family breadwinner. While I started this project looking for independent and ambitious career women (like the person I used to be), I actually discovered a population of working women who were personally and economically interdependent within their families (like the person I had become), with all the conflicts and rewards such mutual dependence inevitably creates. As I complete the present stage of my work, it is these interdependent women—mothers, wives, sisters, daughters, and friends—who appear to me as most typical of working women, past and present, and thus the most intriguing subjects of my study.

To conclude this preface, I would like to offer an insight, a principle, and a metaphor—each of which has been fundamental to the understanding and interpretation of my research. First, the insight: it has become clear to me that when nineteenth-century social commentators spoke of "woman" or "women," they did not define those terms as referring to all female members of their society. Rather, most descriptions of "woman" in nineteenth-century writings (whether social commentary, journalism, or literature) portrayed societal attitudes *only* about white, middle-class, native-born women—not women of color, immigrant women, or women of working-class backgrounds. Thus, I would argue that sweeping nineteenth-century pronouncements on women's nature as fragile, passive, and defenseless creatures were neither meant nor understood to apply to African-American laundresses, Irish factory operatives, or native-born proprietors of saloons. Therefore, statements taken from mid-nineteenth-century prescriptive and proscriptive literature that seem to take for granted that women never trafficked in the marketplace must be understood as applying to a different segment of the female population from that which engaged in industry and commerce—at least in Albany.

Second, the principle: I have deliberately avoided the use of the word "public" to describe the marketplace activities of businesswomen. Although scholars often use the term "public sphere" as synonymous with "outside the home" or "in the street," I prefer to use the definition employed by Jürgen Habermas in *The Structural Transformation of the Public Sphere.*[8] Habermas uses the term "bourgeois public sphere" to describe the rise of public discourse about politics and the state in such settings as the urban coffeehouse and public press. According to his definition, this public space contrasted directly not only with the intimate domestic sphere, but also with the private sphere of individual business ventures. Thus, in Habermas's terms, "private enterprise" would not be defined as an activity located in the "public sphere." Obviously, such an understanding of public/private contrasts directly with—even contradicts—both our "common sense" understanding of the term public and the public street/private home dichotomy used by many contemporary historians. His definition works far better, however, in an analysis of nineteenth-century businesswomen, who had little role in the public sphere of shaping governmental policy yet remained active in *both* private spheres—the home *and* the marketplace. Indeed, the term "private enterprise" accurately describes the vast majority of these female ventures in two additional ways. Research reveals that most of their businesses were home-based, located in their dwelling places. In addition, during this period and throughout the entire United States, hardly any female-operated companies ever went "public" by offering stock—they remained privately held concerns. Thus, as I discuss the marketplace and the domestic sphere and their intersections in the business careers and personal lives of female proprietors, no simple dichotomy labeled "public" and "private" will be drawn.

Third, I would like to propose a metaphor to describe nineteenth-century women of all races, classes, and ethnic origins. It is evident that these women did not have the freedom to grow up as strong and straight as trees in an open field. Their potential as individuals was not encouraged and nurtured to that extent. Nor were they free to strive equally in a "battle of the fittest" like the trees in a forest, pushing their way up to the light and air. Still, this does not mean that the aspirations of nineteenth-century American women were all shaved off like blades of grass in a mown field, or that their lives were stunted like a collection of dwarf trees. Instead, I envision nineteenth-century American women as shaping themselves against obstacles and impediments, like the twisted trunks that grow out of windy rocks by the sea, or the branches of espaliered trees, trained into decorative patterns against garden walls. That is, whether of the upper, middle, or working class, women tended to expand into areas where opportunities were present and to exploit the openings that existed. It was only the most exceptional who pushed against the barriers that stood in their way rather than working their way around them.

This incontrovertible fact seemed problematic to feminist historians of the 1970s and '80s, who searched for radical and reforming women to study and even attempted to explain the choices made by some women of the past as the result of what they labeled "false consciousness."[9] To me, the project of social history requires that we look at the lives of not only women who were "ordinary" women in terms of their fame, wealth, and class but also women who were "ordinary" in terms of their consciousness. We need to study women who were neither prominent enough to leave extensive records nor exploited enough to become the subjects of investigative exposés. I believe that reliance upon sources such as the prescriptive and proscriptive literature described above, or the writings of middle-class reformers and investigators, has tended to obscure both the prevalence of businesswomen and the real conditions of their lives. To understand the mid-nineteenth century, we need to find women where they were and look at what they were actually doing, to study them as human actors shaping their own lives and careers within the context of nineteenth-century American ideologies and material conditions. I present this book as a contribution to that greater project.

ACKNOWLEDGMENTS

IT IS A PLEASURE TO FINALLY have the opportunity of acknowledging all those who assisted and inspired me over the many years it took to complete this book. From the beginning of my career as an academic, I have been unusually fortunate in my opportunities to receive guidance from gifted historians. My graduate courses with G. Barker-Benfield, Robert Dystra, Gerald Zahavi, Warren Roberts, Thomas Dublin, Katherine Kish Sklar, Jean Quataert, Deborah Hertz, Sandra Peacock, and the late Warren Wagar, all shaped my thinking and held me to the highest standards. Gerry Zahavi, who first suggested that I look at millinery entrepreneurs in Albany and use the R.G. Dun & Co. credit records, deserves the credit for pointing me in the direction of an exciting topic and fruitful source. While Gerry led me to my dissertation topic, Tom Dublin provided the consistent guidance that made it possible for me to complete my dissertation. It would be impossible to thank him adequately for the years of painstaking reading, editing, rereading, proofreading, critiquing, and encouraging that he performed with unfailing attention. Other professors provided insights at crucial junctures. Jeffrey Ravel inspired a key turning point in my thinking when he suggested that I needed to "problematize" the concept of business success for women.

Colleagues met at conferences were equally important in furthering my ideas. Carole Turbin was a participant in my first professional roundtable discussion; Alice-Kessler Harris asked challenging questions after my first

paper presentation. Mary Yeager served as the Chair and Mansel Blackford as the encouraging Commentator at my first business history session.
Over the years, I have continued to benefit from the comments of many
historians, most notably Ruth Crocker, who urged me to focus on stories
rather than statistics. Co-presenters and colleagues whose papers I myself
commented on have also influenced and enriched my thinking, especially
the work of Jocelyn Wills, Susan Yohn, Barbara Balliet, Bettina Bradbury,
and Edith Sparks.

Two outstanding scholars in the burgeoning field of women's business
history—Angel Kwolek-Folland and Wendy Gamber—have not only been
supportive but consistently treated me as a valued colleague. Wendy, whom
I met at the very beginning of this project, has been a gracious source
of information and inspiration, as well as an adviser and sympathetic ear
from time to time. She also reviewed the entire first draft of this manuscript, making numerous constructive suggestions. Although I was not able
to incorporate all of her excellent ideas, this book is significantly better
because of her comments.

No researcher can function without the assistance of librarians and
archivists, and I have been fortunate to work with enthusiastic and supportive staff members at several institutions, most notably Mary Osielski of
Special Collections at the University at Albany and Geoffrey P. Williams,
the University Archivist, as well as the entire staff of the Baker Library of
the Harvard Business School, in particular Laura Linard, and the staff of
the New York State Library, especially Paul Mercer. The time they spent
helping me was greatly appreciated. In addition, three institutions sponsored conferences that contributed significantly to my intellectual development: Exeter University, whose conference on "Women Trade and
Business" spanned centuries and introduced me to British scholarship; the
Center for Historical Analysis at Rutgers University, where I participated
in a stimulating conference on "The Widows' Might," and, of course, the
Business History Conference, whose annual meetings both educated me
and exposed me to the cutting edge of business history.

I have also appreciated financial support in the form of fellowships and
grants that were vital to completing my research and writing. In particular,
I would like to thank Sherry Penny and Barry Kramer for funding gradu-
ate student awards at Albany and Binghamton, respectively; my union, the
United University Professionals, for the Nuala Drescher award; the New
York State Library for the Cunningham Research Award; the Baker Library
for a Chandler Traveling Fellowship; and SUNY New Paltz for a Creative
Research Award.

I must give special thanks to those individuals who provided me with
personal as well as professional support over these years. Two are academics:

Warren Roberts of the University at Albany and Pamela Laird of the University of Colorado at Denver have both offered me the kind of unlimited, unfailing, positive support one finds so rarely in any area of life, but particularly in academia. Pam also read much of this manuscript twice and provided invaluable comments and suggestions. Wonderful graduate school colleagues, especially Allyn Van Deusen, Suronda Gonzalez, and Penelope Harper, helped balance the anxiety of the stressful years where I attempted to juggle school, work, and family. My dear friends Harriet Temps and Elizabeth Ann DiPippo also shared all the ups and downs of this project, while Lynn Street and Donald Margulies always expressed a genuine interest.

My family has lived through this process with me, not always to their benefit. For all the times I couldn't do something fun because I was "working on my book," I must apologize to my son Rob. His zest for life and great sense of humor have kept me in touch with the real world. I thank all the others for their understanding. Joan and Henry Lewis have been wonderful in-laws, as have Debbie and Mike Biltonen. My father, James Warren Ingalls, Jr., was always a strong supporter of my academic career, though he clearly believed that I could have—and should have—finished both my dissertation and this book sooner, and did not live to see the book published. My mother, Flora Salvador Ingalls, is a great lover of both reading and history and clearly passed her passions on to me. My sister Vicky has been called upon to fill in for me innumerable times—sacrificing her own priorities and projects, and I am truly grateful. Nor have I had as much time as I would have liked to spend with my sister Patsy, or my nephews James, Ryan, and Mathew.

Of course, the person who made the most sacrifices for this project was my husband Richard. Not only did he read (and often reread) every paper I wrote over my entire academic career, every chapter of my dissertation, and every part of this book manuscript, but he always asked the most pertinent question for all non-historians: "is it really interesting?" He happily moved with me so that I could pursue my graduate studies, provided a charming companion when he accompanied me to conferences, and put up with a commuting spouse for about a decade and an overworked junior faculty member for the past seven years. I know that he expected none of this when we were married over 25 years ago, yet he adjusted and I believe has almost forgiven me for starting over and going to graduate school at the age of 38.

It has been pure pleasure to work with The Ohio State University Press, particularly director Malcolm Litchfield, copyediting coordinator Maggie Diehl, copyeditor Kristen Ebert-Wagner, and designers Juliet Williams and Janna Thompson-Chordas. Their professionalism, patience, and enthusiasm for this project have been extraordinary. Most especially, my series editors Mansell Blackford and Austin Kerr provided both support and constructive criticism at crucial junctures.

Finally, I would like to thank the three institutions in the SUNY system that nurtured me from Master's candidate to a Ph.D. to an Associate Professor of History: first, the University at Albany, where I was inspired to become a scholar and a teacher; second, Binghamton University, which provided me with outstanding training, vital financial support, plus several gratifying awards; and finally SUNY New Paltz, whose history department took a chance on someone who had not yet finished her dissertation. My colleagues Lee Bernstein, Kathleen Dowley, Andrew Evans, Katherine French, Kristine Harris, Amy Kesselman, Stephen Kitsakos, David Krikun, Joel Lefkowitz, Heather Morrison, Abigail Robin, Reynolds Scott-Childress, and Steve Vinson have each provided me with vital advice and encouragement at important points in my career. In particular, I would like to thank my Chair, Louis Roper, for keeping me on track to complete this manuscript and earn tenure. Dean of Liberal Arts & Sciences Gerald Benjamin, Provost David Lavallee, and President Steven Poskanzer have all assisted me in numerous ways. Above all, Professor Laurence Hauptman has been my faithful mentor and constant supporter. Although Wellesley College provided me with an excellent undergraduate education, it was the State University of New York that changed my life and made me the scholar that I am today and hope to become in the future.

Portions of this book appeared in slightly different form in "Female Entrepreneurs in Albany 1840–1885," *Business and Economic History,* Second Series, Vol. 21, 1992; "Beyond Horatia Alger: Breaking Through Gendered Assumptions about Business Success in Mid-Nineteenth-Century America," *Business and Economic History,* Vol. 24, 1, Fall 1995; "Businesswomen in the Land of Opportunity: Immigrant Proprietresses in Albany, New York, 1880," *Hudson Valley Regional Review,* Fall 1997; "Business or Labor? Blurred Boundaries in the Careers of Self-Employed Needleworkers in Mid-Nineteenth-Century Albany," in *Famine and Fashion, Needlewomen in the Nineteenth Century,* ed. Beth Harris, Ashgate, 2005; and "Business Widows of Mid-Nineteenth-Century Albany, New York," in *Women on Their Own, Interdisciplinary Perspectives on Being Single,* ed. Rudolph M. Bell and Virginia Yans, copyright © 2008 by Rutgers, The State University, reprinted by permission of Rutgers University Press. I am grateful to Dun & Bradstreet for granting permission to cite the R.G. Dun & Co. records.

INTRODUCTION

Traditionally, the achievements of women have been defined in other than
economic terms whenever it is possible.

—Caroline Bird, 1976[1]

FROM THE MID-1850S through 1876, Sarah Denmead ran a small business selling trimmings, fancy goods, and millinery in Albany, New York. The
credit records for 1857 note that although the Denmeads' "trimmings"
shop was in John's name, his thirty-one-year-old wife had "for many years
carried on the business" (this despite the fact that their son Zacharias had
been born just seven years earlier). Regular entries in the R.G. Dun &
Co. credit records make clear that Sarah, not her husband John, was the
real head of the concern, referring to her as "the principal business man
of the concern," "the boss," "the man of the house," "the active man,"
or simply "the man," as well as "a smart shrewd woman." In contrast, her
husband John appears in the credit reports as a stock character—drunk and
dissolute—but Sarah's reaction to his behavior was far from the long-suf-
fering, hand-wringing, genteel stereotype passed down in nineteenth-century female fiction. According to the reporter, Sarah "several times desired
him"—her husband—"to leave her forever, but like a bad cent he always
returns. He lately, pistol in hand, drove her from her store, threatened her
life and took all her goods and is selling them out." This kind of problem
with drunken and abusive husbands is what supposedly kept women from
committing themselves to business enterprises in the nineteenth century.

Five months later, however, Sarah was still in business and making
money, while John continued to drink and run after women. It seems that
she attempted to rid herself of the problem in a unique way—"she hires

him to go away every once in a while and when he comes back again she hires him to go away again." Mrs. Denmead's remarkable business drive and resourcefulness are illustrated time and again over the more than twenty-year period in which she and her husband were evaluated for credit. Though John eventually sobered up, he was never a good businessman. After several changes of line (from trimmings, to millinery, to the manufacture of cords, fringes, and tassels, to fancy goods), expansions, failures, changes of proprietorship (from John to Sarah and Zacharias) and business reorganizations, in 1876 Mrs. Denmead took her stock and moved to Buffalo.[2] However, she suddenly reappears in the city directories in 1885, as Matron of the City Homeopathic Hospital, while John, who had lost his sight, is listed as an inmate of a different institution—the Home for Aged Men.

Although Sarah Denmead's career biography is one of the more dramatic tales uncovered by research on businesswomen in mid-nineteenth-century Albany, Denmead's experience in business was not exceptional. Her story, like that of thousands of women in nineteenth-century Albany, was a story of entrepreneurship on a small scale. Making business decisions, investing time and money, considering the marketability of her products, working most often from her home, she supported herself and her family, sometimes alone, sometimes with the assistance of her husband or son. She survived, prospered, failed, relocated, and finally established herself in a different field. Yet microentrepreneurship had dominated most of her adult life.

We most often imagine and study nineteenth-century women in the United States in domestic roles within the middle class, as struggling working-class women, or as feminists in their quest for citizens' rights. Yet tens of thousands of women (or perhaps hundreds of thousands) across the country engaged in endeavors that fit into none of these categories—like Sarah Denmead, they ran their own businesses and supported themselves (and often their families) from the profits. In fact, businesswomen abounded in the nineteenth-century United States. Rather than exceptional pioneers, these women were unexceptional contributors to their family economies and local communities. Neither notorious nor particularly notable, the vast majority were home-based microentrepreneurs who faced many of the challenges that today's working women assume are unique to the late twentieth and early twenty-first centuries. For instance, their ranks included wives in dual-income marriages, working mothers, and single parents struggling to support themselves and their dependents.

Exploring women's economic contributions makes it possible to build a fuller picture of American history from the colonial period through the present, and historians are filling in our pictures from multiple directions. As producers and consumers, as debtors and lenders, as unpaid domestic laborers or wage workers, as contributors to the family economy and independent economic actors, as exploited piece-workers or munificent philanthropists, women must be present at the center of any complete understanding of the American economy. Conversely, an appreciation of the role of economic forces on women's lives is equally central to our understanding of women's history. Notable women reformers and professionals were as much influenced by economic forces as were the mill girls of Lowell, the seamstresses in the Triangle Shirtwaist factory, or female entrepreneurs such as Madame C. J. Walker.

Much exciting work has emerged within the field of women's economic and business history, broadening our understanding of the ways in which women have been integral to production, consumption, and monetary exchange in colonial North America and the United States. Whether the goods and services produced by women (including Native American, African-American, and women of European descent) were consumed within the tribe, household, or plantation, or offered for sale or barter, their daily activities supported the colonial economy. Similarly, North American women took an active role in consumption, the motor of capitalism. In the late-eighteenth- and early-nineteenth-centuries' transition from a subsistence to a market economy, women were once again players, as both producers for cash and consumers of manufactured goods. Their paid and unpaid labors produced personal, familial, and community wealth; their demand for manufactured goods completed the economic cycle that fed national prosperity.

By the second half of the nineteenth century, independent investigators such as Virginia Penny and Caroline Dall, reforming women such as Helen Campbell, and female intellectuals such as Charlotte Perkins Gilman began to study the impact of women on the economy and vice versa.[3] More than a hundred years ago, women scholars stressed the importance of women's economic history. Yet, as Caroline Bird so aptly observed in one of the first studies of American businesswomen to emerge from the new women's history of the 1970s, "Traditionally, the achievements of women have been defined in other than economic terms whenever it is possible."[4]

The study of women in business should be at the forefront of contemporary efforts to place women within the economic history of the United States, yet this potentially vast area of study has until recently attracted few scholars. From colonial times to the present, female proprietors provided a constant stream of goods and services to their largely local clientele. Their stories are as multifarious as the women themselves, the periods when they did business, the communities where they operated, the merchandise and services they provided, and the customers they served. Female proprietors in mid-nineteenth-century Albany, New York, worked in just one of the many locations and times when small business offered women a better opportunity than most other available employment, and where businesswomen formed a vital piece of the local economic puzzle.

The study of nineteenth-century businesswomen has important, broad applications for both the research agendas and the theoretical frameworks of business, women's, labor, family, and urban history. In the towns and cities of industrializing America, business (particularly self-employment and microentrepreneurship) provided a far more common, and important, occupation for nineteenth-century women and men than most historians have recognized. The stories of such small business ventures, run by "penny capitalists," bridge historical specialties, and can be integrated into the narratives of each field. Moreover, a serious consideration of the impact of female microentrepreneurship on the local economy and business networks calls for a reconceptualization of nineteenth-century business and economic history, one that places small, home-based businesses at the center of market daily exchange, and no longer at the periphery of our historical attention.

The Story So Far

After a long period of benign neglect, the history of businesswomen in the United States is currently engaging serious scholarly interest. Within the past decade, a new subdiscipline of gender in business history—and business in gender studies—has emerged as a previously untapped frontier of women's history. Until the late 1990s, the sole volume produced by a generation of women's historians remained Caroline Bird's *Enterprising Women*, published in 1976. A pastiche of brief, isolated biographies of both entrepreneurial and professional women from colonial times through the twentieth century, this text provided a perfect example of the "women worthies" school of feminist scholarship. What Wendy Gamber has labeled the "women were there, too" approach to history was also evident in Elisabeth Anthony Dexter's *Career Women of America, 1776–1840*, first published in 1950 (reissued in 1972), which devoted one chapter to female shopkeepers and another to needleworkers, including millinery and dressmaking proprietors.[5]

For the historian of businesswomen, Bird and Dexter at least provided a welcome antidote to the conviction that women were *not* there in the competitive marketplace of nineteenth-century America. Through the 1960s, '70s, and into the '80s, most historians assumed that nineteenth-century business had been—by definition—the province of men. The standard narrative of women's history described colonial businesswomen ("deputy husbands" and widows) at some length, yet suggested that respectable nineteenth-century wives who wished to produce income for their families had to choose between taking in boarders or doing putting-out work (usually needlework) at home for local, male merchants. Like everyone else, historians subtly defined these occupations as domestic rather than entrepreneurial.[6] The continuity of female proprietorship was generally ignored in favor of a story of declension away from economic opportunity, independence, and valued contributions.

Significant evidence that nineteenth-century women entered business, ranging from broad economic analyses to research on Irish immigrants to local histories, appeared to have little impact on nineteenth-century women's, labor, or business history.[7] Even those few studies that acknowledged the presence of female proprietors in this period argued that women entered business rarely, went in-and-out quickly, very seldom met with success according to standard masculine notions of success, *and* were limited to a few uniquely "feminine" enterprises.[8] In local and regional studies, references to women in business remained a fraction of the whole, rarely the focus of an entire monograph, and research on businesswomen was most often split into the pre– and post–Civil War eras.[9] Finally, historians who investigated nineteenth-century American businesswomen tended to concentrate on a single notable individual (such as Lydia Pinkham), a single trade (such as millinery), or a single segment of the population (such as Irish or African-American women).[10] It was hard, it seems, not to think in terms of exceptions without detailed evidence about the mass of unexceptional female proprietors, the kind of evidence I have compiled.

During the 1980s and early 1990s, labor historians continued to define their populations in such a way as to ignore and exclude women engaged in business pursuits, for example, focusing solely on "wage-earning" women.[11] As late as 1991 the most prominent historian of American working women, Alice Kessler-Harris, stated unequivocally in a popular one-volume encyclopedia of American history that only "a handful" of women in nineteenth-century American communities "ran their own businesses."[12]

It was business historians, seeking to integrate small enterprises into a narrative that had previously stressed the nineteenth-century evolution of big business, who proved most likely to propose female proprietorship as an area worth exploring. In the same year that Kessler-Harris dismissed female proprietors as a mere "handful" of nineteenth-century working women, Mansel Blackford called for research into female entrepreneurship, especially "the roles that small businesses have played for women over time."[13] Beginning in the 1990s organizations such as the Business History Conference, institutions such as the Hagley Museum and Library, and journals such as *Business History Review* welcomed "gender as a category of analysis," to quote Joan Scott's famous phrase. Suddenly and rapidly, the analysis of women in business moved beyond the contributory approach and provided a variety of sophisticated insights. In the late 1990s two pioneering studies established the subfield of women's business history: Wendy Gamber's tightly focused monograph *The Female Economy: The Millinery and Dressmaking Trades, 1860–1930*, and Angel Kwolek-Folland's sweeping overview *Incorporating Women: A History of Women and Business in the United States*.[14] Gamber's examination of needlework proprietors (along with their employees and customers) provided the depth of an intensive examination, while Kwolek-Folland's synthetic text offered breadth by spanning the colonial period to the present. The challenges inherent in integrating gender into American business history were addressed by Wendy Gamber, Kathy Peiss, and Joan Scott at a 1996 Hagley Symposium on gender and business. Subsequently published in a special issue of *Business History Review* (1998) titled "Conceptualizing Gender in American Business History," their papers still present one of the most far-reaching explorations of the multiple issues faced by historians attempting to develop a new business history that not only includes women as actors but also incorporates gender analysis.[15] In 1999 Mary Yeager contributed a three-volume collection of previously published articles with an international scope, *Women in Business*.[16] Dramatically updating the scholarly study of women in business, these publications took businesswomen from the fringes to the forefront of women's, labor, and business history.

Since 2000 major encyclopedic and bibliographic projects on businesswomen have been published, spanning the colonial period to the present.[17] Scholarly and popular biographies of such noteworthy businesswomen as Elizabeth Murray, "Mammy Pleasant," Martha Matilda Harper, and Hetty Green have appeared to enrich our understanding of individual female entrepreneurs.[18] Beginning in 1999, the Baker Library of the Harvard Business School undertook a major survey of resources on women in their Manuscripts Collection, resulting in an article for *Business History Review* in 2000, and a Web site, *Women, Enterprise, and Society*, which was launched in 2002 and includes an important scholarly bibliography on businesswomen.[19] In addition, a new business history journal, *Enterprise and Society*, sponsored by the Business History Conference and first published by Oxford University Press in 2000, produced two special issues in 2001 highlighting women and gender analysis in business history, both edited by Kwolek-Folland.[20] Also in the early 2000s, The Schlesinger Library at Radcliffe created a national, traveling exhibit titled *Enterprising Women: 250 Years of American Business*. Sponsored by the Ford Motor Company and AT&T, and touring the United States from 2002 through 2005, this show represented the most prominent public portrayal to date of the history of women and business in the United States. In 2005 Margaret Walsh reviewed the impact of gender on contemporary scholarship in business history for the British journal *Women's History Review*.[21] Finally, Edith Sparks's *Capital Intentions: Female Proprietors in San Francisco, 1850–1920* (2006) recently provided the first community study of businesswomen in one city, and, following her previous groundbreaking work on milliners and dressmakers, Wendy Gamber has now offered a complex and intriguing picture of boarding-house keepers in a new volume on *The Boardinghouse in Nineteenth-Century America* (2007).[22]

Reconceptualizing Enterprising Women

As popularizing works, academic articles, and scholarly monographs begin to shape the field of women's business history, it is important to consider their theoretical frameworks and assumptions. Examining the range of offerings described above, two approaches are troublesome, while several appear unusually promising. One misleading approach, the celebratory, was perfectly represented by the *Enterprising Women* traveling exhibit. Covering 250 years of American business through the biographies of forty individual female entrepreneurs, this project described itself as "a major national exhibition that reinterprets the history of American women and of American business."[23] Along with a companion Web site and book of the same title by Virginia Drachman, the show focused on the remarkable achievements of entrepreneurial leaders, conveying the impression that the story of such prominent individuals *equals* the story of women in American business.[24] Particularly for the nineteenth century (just twelve of the forty businesswomen featured were active in the 1800s), the viewer was left with an impression that only a few extraordinary women were able to break through Victorian gender barriers to engage in business careers. This theoretical approach (or lack thereof) represents a throwback to Caroline Bird's individualistic, exceptionalist narrative of the 1970s. Although it could be argued that museum exhibits are rarely expected to provide cutting-edge historical analysis, the failure to set selected remarkable businesswomen within the context of the much larger population of unexceptional female proprietors resulted in a lost opportunity to educate the public on the multiple contributions of businesswomen to the American economy over time. Once again, the "women worthies" and "we were there, too" approach triumphed over a more nuanced analysis.

Much of the problem with previous scholarship—just as much as with popular stereotypes—has been the lack of evidence. The stories of Sarah Denmead and the multitudes of other ordinary women operating their businesses left few traces. Even at the time they operated, their home-based microentrepreneurships were mostly invisible as "businesses." Their very ordinariness made them unnoteworthy and kept them out of the historical record. Unlike Lydia Pinkham, they left only a few faint traces through advertisements or patent medicine bottles. Unlike Hetty Green, they left no trail in the nation's financial centers. Unlike Rose Schneiderman, they made no inspirational speeches to stir public opinion in response to a disaster of the magnitude of the Triangle Shirtwaist fire. They didn't even leave volumes of published poetry, as did some of the women who toiled in the Lowell mills. Instead, most of them left only minute traces in city directories, the credit reports of the R.G. Dun Mercantile Agency, entries in the census, or tiny ads in local newspapers. By tracking down those slight remains of their hard work, I have rebuilt their stories. In some cases, such as Sarah Denmead's, I have been able to reconstruct a satisfying account of their lives. In too many cases, however, the evidence is thin; I have, instead, been limited to constructing composite stories.

The "great woman" bias in the study of businesswomen is relatively easy to see and critique, but a second scholarly framework, with more subtle assumptions and biases, also has misdirected us. "Explaining away" the importance of women in business, or business enterprises for women's history, remains surprisingly common. This tendency recognizes that many women were small proprietors but dismisses the significance of women's participation in nineteenth-century business. That is, while it seems normal and "natural" that nineteenth-century men would enter business, female proprietorship remains a choice that requires an explanation.

Even scholars who have advanced our historical appreciation for women's economic roles have missed how unexceptional was female proprietorship. For instance, Kenneth Lipartito made this disclaimer in the foreword to Kwolek-Folland's 1998 *Incorporating Women:*

> What remained a constant for businesswomen, however, was the link between their participation in the economy and their role in the family. . . . They have historically brought values beyond those of profit and individual success to their enterprises. . . . Whatever the case, women could never assume that business was simply a means of individual upward mobility.[25]

And, as Kwolek-Folland herself has written, "Women have traditionally operated businesses because of their status as relatives of men. As widows, wives, and as mothers women held the family properties intact."[26]

Similarly, in her study of gender, law, and the market economy in colonial New York, Deborah Rosen echoes these assumptions by claiming that businesswomen did not function "as people expressing independent entrepreneurial motives but as family members," and she cites other scholars who describe businesswomen as "trustees" or "conduits" for passing a business on to future generations.[27] This suggestion, that women undertook business only as part of a family strategy, presumes that male business enterprises were solely individualistic, as if men were not equally interested in their wives, siblings, children, and descendants. Although unstated, the assumption is clearly that males were perfectly independent economic actors, choosing between an infinite range of possible options. However, a cursory study of nineteenth-century biography (or a look at the world we live in today) demonstrates the multiple fallacies inherent in this assumption. Much as male-dominated history naturalized nineteenth-century women as domestic, dependent, middle-class wives, women's history has had a tendency to naturalize men as ambitious, single, middle-class entrepreneurial individuals. Yet we know that nineteenth-century fathers, like those today, struggled to take care of their families, while sons and brothers supported their mothers and siblings, and grandfathers considered how to best preserve their property for those who followed.

A similar argument advanced in the interpretation of female proprietors is that women ran businesses only because they were forced into entrepreneurship by hard times, or by the failure of male relatives to provide adequate support. For example, when presenting my research at conferences, I have often encountered questions about whether women started businesses because of the Civil War. Again, how many men in the nineteenth century had the luxury of not working at all? Surely most men, as well as most women, felt the financial necessity of earning a living. An additional claim in the "dismissal" mode of understanding women's business history suggests that since women's businesses generally remained small and short-lived (an assumption that will be challenged in following chapters), they were relatively unimportant and hardly worth mentioning. Again, weren't many—if not most—men involved in small businesses that failed? In his survey of the history of small business in the United States, Mansel Blackford points out that small enterprises were "the norm" before 1880, and concludes, "Small businesses have always led perilous lives, with relatively few lasting more than about five years."[28] Similarly, Rowena Olegario argues in her study of the evolution of credit reporting in the nineteenth century that "the mortality rate for women-owned establishments appears to have conformed to the average for all businesses."[29]

The argument that women were not really ambitious and entrepreneurial is also potentially dismissive. For example, in the introduction to her three-volume collection *Women in Business,* noted business historian Mary Yeager argues that business was "more often than not simply 'work'—a way to make a living and survive." Based on the evidence from Albany, I would agree that this statement accurately reflects the attitudes and motivations of most, though not all, nineteenth-century female proprietors. Yet there is a danger (not for Yeager herself, who has demonstrated a strong interest in businesswomen) in interpreting such statements. Scholars should beware two assumptions—one, that unless proprietorship is ambitious and entrepreneurial it doesn't really count as business, and second, that men who started businesses were not simply trying to make a living and survive. Although it may well be true that businessmen were more entrepreneurial and ambitious than businesswomen, it is not clear why this would discount the experiences of those proprietors (male or female) who were less so. Moreover, women's lack of risk-taking in business relative to men, if proved, requires analysis rather than acceptance as a reason to discount their experiences and importance.

Unfortunately, not valuing the skills women learned inside their homes on a par with men's skills can result in another subtly dismissive claim, because the businesses in which women engaged were often related to skills they developed in their domestic roles. For example, Kwolek-Folland concluded that "Women tended to dominate in business areas related to their role as housekeepers, mothers, and wives—food preparation, textiles, and women's and children's clothing."[30] The use here of the word "role" versus "skill" could reinforce a common, if unstated, assumption that domestic activities such as cooking, sewing, and housekeeping were unskilled compared to male activities such as carpentry, masonry, or blacksmithing. Yet we know that in a period before gas stoves and electrical appliances, the work of food preparation, laundering, and making clothing was both time-consuming and complex. Even today, massive volumes on the intricacies of housework become bestsellers. In the mid-nineteenth century, a large market flourished for such skills, defined as feminine, even if for far less remuneration than male-associated skills.

Ideally, the history of businesswomen should engage the most recent historiographic trends in business history, and the history of businessmen. For example, the model of a single, ambitious, independent male entrepreneur may be largely a mythical creation, as suggested by Pamela Laird's work on male mentoring and social capital.[31] Nor is male success the "norm" against which female failure should be measured, as illustrated by Scott Sandage's study of (mostly male) business failures and Edward Balleisen's work on bankruptcy.[32]

A vast area of potential scholarship remains in the fertile middle ground between the celebratory and the dismissive approaches to women's business history. Without romanticizing nineteenth-century female proprietors as "exceptional" women, both the potentials and the limitations of their careers deserve exploring. We should question and test our assumptions about the rise and fall of women's participation in the business sphere over the course of the nineteenth century; variations by region remain to be researched and analyzed. Work by Susan Yohn mapping the locations of women's businesses in nineteenth-century Brooklyn, and by Barbara Balliet linking newspaper advertisements and personal papers to trace the stories of female artists and printers, show exceptional promise of fresh approaches to the field.[33]

My interpretation of research findings on Albany's businesswomen owes much to, and supports, the innovative work of Wendy Gamber and Angel Kwolek-Folland. Both agree that historians of women, labor, and business had neglected the history of women and business in America. Both have also stressed the need to rethink the definitions, standards, and categories used by historians to examine businesswomen. Finally, both Gamber and Kwolek-Folland argue that notable female entrepreneurs should not be categorized as "exceptional" individuals but rather seen as representing points on the wide spectrum of women's business activities and contributions.

I hope that *Unexceptional Women* will make a significant contribution to the field of women's business history. As I write, only one monograph on businesswomen in a single community, Edith Sparks's study of female proprietors in San Francisco between 1850 and 1920, has been published for *any* location or *any* period in U.S. history.[34] Her work offers a counterpoint for my investigation, particularly on the question of whether the West provided more opportunity for female entrepreneurship than eastern cities such as Albany. My study of Albany's mid-nineteenth-century businesswomen also offers a useful contrast to Gamber's detailed investigation of milliners and dressmakers in Boston, providing a comparison with a slightly earlier period (1830–1885 versus 1860–1930), a less populous urban center with a different local culture (Albany versus Boston), and a wider scope of business ventures (all proprietors versus milliners and dressmakers). Finally, the detail provided by my study both supports and challenges some of the conclusions in Kwolek-Folland's survey, particularly her chapter "Mills and More: Women's Business and the First Industrial Revolution, 1830–1880."

While other scholars have been approaching the conceptual problems of integrating women into business history nationally (Gamber, Kwolek-Folland, and Drachman), or even globally (Yeager and Scott), I, like Sparks, am approaching them locally. That is, while other scholars have been analyzing the whole range of business history to determine how women fit into—and change—the picture, my work focuses on using a specific population of nineteenth-century businesswomen as a case study against which to test current theoretical questions. Based on the study of Albany, it is clear that running a small, home-based business was a relatively common occupation for women in the mid-nineteenth-century United States, particularly for immigrant wives and widows, and that businesswomen formed a small but integral part of local business networks. Rather than identifying a declension in women's business opportunities from colonial times through the nineteenth century, I reject the concept of a golden age for businesswomen of the colonial period in New York. In fact, in Albany it appears that women's business opportunities increased as the nineteenth century progressed, the result of commercial development, industrialization, urbanization, and immigration.

Research on businesswomen in mid-nineteenth-century Albany suggests that while small businesses provided a vital economic resource for female proprietors and their families, and while women were certainly contributing to the commercial life of the growing city, their entrepreneurial experiences—in terms of earnings, business growth, and long-term survival—paled when compared to those of their most successful male counterparts. In fact, the very model of "entrepreneur" hardly seems to fit the reality of most mid-nineteenth-century businesswomen, at least in Albany. These dry goods, notions, and variety dealers, these makers of hair jewelry, lace, fringes and tassels were rarely risk-taking capitalists but were far more often "self-employed" artisans, shopkeepers, and petty manufacturers. Most labored as well as supervised, and minded the store as well as ordered the goods. Even the most successful of Albany's businesswomen, including those who operated ventures at more than one location, supervised numerous employees, and continued in business for over forty years, never managed to build up establishments worth more than $150,000 (the equivalent of approximately $15 million in today's money) or to expand their enterprises beyond the regional market.

Instead of assuming that women were unable and unwilling to take advantage of the booming business climate we associate with mid-nineteenth-century America, it is possible to look beyond gendered assumptions about what constitutes a successful business, to discover the ways in which women used businesses within the scope of their particular needs and life cycles. In nineteenth-century Albany, it appears that women used business as a method of self-employment and survival, as a means of family support and mobility, and as a strategy for immigrant assimilation into an urban economy and middle-class lifestyle. Understanding differing goals should translate into new measures of success. In order to begin a fruitful study of businesswomen, we need to explore and develop new paradigms for business success in mid-nineteenth-century American cities for women and men. As suggested above, developing these new models will require not only modified research priorities but also a reassessment and reinterpretation of familiar patterns.

This study proposes and tests revised definitions of "business" itself, as well as "proprietorship," "success," "entrepreneurship," and "opportunity" as these terms might be applied to mid-nineteenth-century American businesswomen. The definitions I present have evolved gradually out of patterns evident in my research findings. In each case, I have attempted to develop categories applicable to the entire range of women's business experiences, paralleling the range in size, scope, and purpose of women's commercial and industrial ventures. Most important, I propose to measure women's business experiences in terms of the experiences, needs, desires, and motivations of Albany's population of *female* workers—not according to those supposedly "universal" paradigms of success, enterprise, and entrepreneurship that I have come to see as essentially "male" models. In fact, typical masculine paradigms may not even have applied to most businessmen.

THE FIRST FOUR CHAPTERS of the book provide detailed evidence on Albany's mid-nineteenth-century female proprietors from different angles. Chapter 1 focuses on businesswomen themselves and argues that female proprietors were not exceptional individuals by presenting an overview of women's business activity in Albany between 1830 and 1885. The second chapter incorporates a statistical analysis of female proprietors active in Albany between 1875 and 1885, and offers portraits of typical businesswomen in Albany by trade. Women's participation in the marketplace is surveyed in chapter 3 by focusing on their motivations for entering business, the size and longevity of their concerns, how they obtained capital and credit to start their ventures, and descriptions of the types of enterprises in which women were engaged. Chapter 4 locates Albany's businesswomen within their working families, neighborhoods, and local business community, exploring the ways in which these networks both supported and limited female entrepreneurship, as well as the ways in which female proprietors contributed to and at times caused problems for the local economy.

The next four chapters (chapters 5–8) offer a dialogue between the research findings presented in the earlier chapters and broader issues involved in interpreting this evidence. Chapter 5 suggests that for many women, especially female artisans, there was no clear boundary between business and labor. Gendered definitions of success and failure for businesswomen are proposed in chapter 6, which evaluates female business success in relation to other moneymaking opportunities open to women during the period. Chapter 7 presents a definition of entrepreneurship for nineteenth-century female proprietors relative to possibilities open to businesswomen, rather than nineteenth-century businessmen or women in business today. In chapter 8 the respectability of female proprietors is assessed through the attitude of the local business community (represented by the reports of credit evaluators) rather than the writings of middle-class commentators and reformers. Finally, the conclusion briefly relates my findings back to the wider context of women, trade, and business from medieval times to the present, concentrating on Western Europe and North America. It draws connections with contemporary patterns of female business enterprise and microentrepreneurship, exploring the ways in which businesswomen of the mid-nineteenth century appear to resemble—and yet remain different from—the much-hailed female entrepreneurs of the late twentieth and early twenty-first centuries. Most of all, I hope to impress other scholars with the exciting potential of this underexplored subfield of women's business, labor, and economic history.

CHAPTER ONE

Unexceptional Women

Female Proprietors in Albany, 1830–85

American women never manage the outward concerns of the family, or conduct a business, or take a part in political life.

—Alexis de Tocqueville, 1840[1]

IT IS NO DOUBT BECAUSE of convictions such as those expressed here by Tocqueville that it has taken historians so long to investigate the role of women in business in the nineteenth-century United States. Yet a study of nineteenth-century Albany, New York, reveals that, far from "never" conducting a business, more than two thousand individual women joined with their male counterparts to engage in commerce and industry between 1830 and 1885. Indeed, merely scratching the surface of nine-teenth-century history exposes the roles that numerous female proprietors played across the nation. To focus on a single historical episode—the assas-sination of President Abraham Lincoln in 1865—the theater troupe per-forming that night was owned and managed by a woman, Laura Keene, and a female boarding-house keeper, Mary Surratt, was later convicted of helping plot the assassination. At the time, Mary Todd Lincoln's closest female companion and confidante was her dressmaker, Elizabeth Keckley, a former slave who had previously used the proceeds of her business to purchase her own freedom.[2] As this example suggests, once one is looking for evidence of businesswomen, even a cursory study reveals broad par-ticipation by ordinary women in the business economy of the nineteenth-century United States.

A glance at the Albany city directory listings of 1830/31 (the very time that Tocqueville visited that city), discloses 60 female proprietors doing business in their own names—as boarding-house keepers, milliners, grocers, dressmakers, dry goods merchants, confectioners, a baker, and the operator of a corset warehouse. Although they made up only about 7% of the approximately 800 businesspeople in the city, such individuals openly operated in the supposedly "male" marketplace. Who were these women, seemingly invisible to Tocqueville and other contemporary commentators on the nineteenth-century American scene? What part did they play in the business community of their city, and in the local community of working women? As their existence is recognized and explored by scholars of women's, labor, and business history, how can it best be retrieved, reconstituted, and conceptualized?

Most historians of nineteenth-century American working women have stressed limitations to success in the entrepreneurial field. Indeed, historians often assumed that the cult of domesticity and women's "separate sphere" largely precluded not only women's engagement in business activities but also any desire for commercial careers among respectable females. Until recently, American business in the nineteenth century has been seen as an exclusively male preserve. We pictured women nesting at home, soothing and supporting the entrepreneurial male. Nineteenth-century women appeared on the pages of our histories as consumers, not merchants: often buying, rarely selling. The mid-nineteenth century in particular has long been assumed to represent the height of the cult of domesticity.[3] One might have expected to find few respectable women engaged in business pursuits: perhaps a widow, or a couple of spinster sisters, eking out a bare living in a subterranean shop; perhaps an immigrant wife of loose morals running a bordello alongside her drunken spouse.[4]

To correct these images, we need to descend from the broad overview to the eyewitness view, from the city panorama to the city street. Focusing on female business activity in Albany, the capital of New York State, from 1830 to 1885 reveals that thousands of women (single, married, widowed, divorced, and separated—yet most of them perfectly "respectable") were involved in business activities, operating as owners and managers, conducting business under either their own names or the names of male relatives. Had we strolled around the city's commercial neighborhoods any year between 1830 and 1885, we would have passed dozens—later hundreds—of enterprises run by women. As the years went by, we would have observed such female-managed businesses move from location to location, expand and decline, change focus, prosper or perhaps fail, often to be replaced by similar female-owned or operated concerns.

The Place, the Period, and the Population

At the outset of this study it is reasonable to ask, "Why Albany?" Why select Albany, New York—an insular, provincial, and relatively small capital city—as the site for a study of businesswomen in the mid-nineteenth century? Less well known to historians than Troy, its industrial sister city across the Hudson River, Albany has inspired only a single study of its mid-nineteenth-century labor history, a single dissertation in women's labor history, and no monographs within the field of business history.[5] Although the Hudson and Mohawk Valleys have been the focus of numerous community studies based on river towns such as New York, Poughkeepsie, and Troy, or canal towns such as Kingston, Utica, and Rochester, the chronicles of nineteenth-century Albany seem to have been left to the pen of novelist William Kennedy.[6]

Yet the question "Why Albany?" would probably not have been raised a hundred years ago, and would certainly not have occurred to the mid-nineteenth-century inhabitants of the city itself. Geographically, Albany was important as a crossroads, a linchpin, and a hub. The original settlement, Fort Orange, erected as a trading post by the Dutch West India Company in 1624, had replaced a previous series of makeshift "forts" established since 1614. As a colonial crossroads, its location on the north-south line between French Montreal and British New York, as well as the east-west axis between Boston and the Great Lakes, gave it great strategic value. During the Early Republican period, Albany—capital of the rapidly expanding state of New York from 1797—was connected by northern, western, and eastern stage lines to Burlington and Rutland, Vermont; Cooperstown and Buffalo; Hartford, New Haven, Boston, and Hanover, New Hampshire. Stages, steamboats, packet boats, and sloops ran down the Hudson to New York City, the steamboats on a regular schedule three days a week.[7] In the antebellum period, Albany became the linchpin in a Hudson River–Erie Canal transportation network. As the eastern terminus of the Erie Canal (opened in 1825), Albany was a commercial hub and transshipment point for goods traded between the Great Lakes, New York City, and the rest of the world. In terms of passenger travel, it was linked by regular steamship service with Manhattan, the voyage taking only 12 to 13 hours as early as 1830. The Albany directory of 1830/31 waxed rhapsodic over the city's potential:

> Albany is remarkable for its commercial situation, being nearly at the head
> of sloop navigation, on one of the noblest rivers in the world. It . . . is the
> natural emporium of increasing trade of a large extent of the country west

and north. . . . The canal, finished about five years since . . . is a work of prodigious magnitude and perseverance, by which the various merchandizes of the western world find their way to every part of the civilized globe; and as the western part of the state rises in population so is there reason to believe Albany will increase in magnitude and splendor, equal if not superior to most cities of the United States.[8]

When railroads began to replace rivers and canals in mid-nineteenth-century commerce (the first rail travel in the United States began with a trip between Albany and Schenectady in 1831), Albany continued to be an important transit hub, with tracks stretching in all directions, complementing the steamship and canal services still in operation. At the same time, immigrants from Europe—especially Ireland and Germany—transformed the ethnic and religious character of a city previously dominated by a native-born, Protestant elite of Dutch and English ancestry.

Though Albany never rivaled the port city of New York in size or importance, during the half-century covered by this study its population more than quadrupled, growing from more than 24,000 in 1830, as the impact of the Erie Canal began to be felt, to an estimated 98,000 in 1884. In 1786 Albany had been the sixth-largest city in the new nation, with a population of over 3,000 individuals.[9] At the turn of the nineteenth century Albany was the largest inland city in the new nation, and the tenth-largest city in population overall by 1810. The censuses of 1830 and 1840 ranked Albany as the ninth-largest city in population in the United States, slightly smaller than Cincinnati but larger than Washington, DC. While its sister city across the Hudson, Troy, became a center of manufacturing, Albany engaged primarily in commerce and politics. On the eve of the Civil War, it ranked thirteenth in population (after Louisville but still larger than Washington, DC) and twenty-first in manufactures among all American cities, placing it "roughly on a par with Chicago and Pittsburgh."[10]

As in other American cities of this era, residents were self-consciously proud of Albany's prominence. Politically, it housed the government of the most populous and richest state in the Union. In the realm of culture, Albany regularly hosted national lecturers such as Emerson and Dickens, and performers such as Lola Montez and Jenny Lind. Famous travelers, among them Fanny Wright, Alexis de Tocqueville, Harriet Martineau, and Frances Trollope, included Albany in their American tours. Trollope was particularly impressed by shops that were "large, and showily set out" but disappointed by the shoddy cheapness of the goods sold. By 1834 traveler Charles Augustus Murray described Albany as "a busy and prosperous town," "a place of much commercial activity," and "the greatest emporium of internal trade in the United States," while in 1854, Isabella Bird found

Albany a "very thriving place" with an "enormous" river traffic between the capital and New York City.[11]

By 1870, however, Albany had slipped to twentieth in population among U.S. cities, directly behind Milwaukee and Detroit; in 1880 it had fallen out of the top twenty largest urban places altogether. Despite continued dramatic growth, New York's capital never became a major industrial center. Still, as it celebrated the 1886 bicentennial of its incorporation—"an occasion of great historical importance in American municipal history, and of pride to Albany, the oldest city in the Union"—leading residents of the city remained confident of a "still more glorious future."[12] As late as 1891 Henry Phelps, author of *The New Albany: A Record of the City's Progress,* boasted that "Albany is the Center of the Wealthiest Commercial Quadrilateral in America" with "Buffalo, Montreal, Boston, and New York the Angles."[13]

Because the New York State capital was a relatively large, prosperous, and important urban center, the city's population and business enterprises were carefully recorded during the mid-nineteenth-century period. Albany offers the nineteenth-century historian an ideal venue for the examination of businesswomen in the urban context—well documented at the time, but investigated by few previous scholars.[14] Available records make it possible to recover a wide range of information about the vital statistics and life cycles of businesswomen, who can be named, traced, and matched in a variety of sources. Mid-nineteenth-century Albany presents a location large enough to offer a wide range of economic activities but not so large as to pose insuperable research obstacles. Thus, Albany provides a rich (but not overrich) site for a case study.

The analysis presented in this book is based specifically on the population of women who owned or operated businesses in the city of Albany, capital of New York State, between 1830 and 1885, and includes an intensive statistical examination of those active between 1875 and 1885. In order to study such a population, however, it is first necessary to define precisely what constitutes a business. If we consider business enterprise as identical with "the firm," then few women in nineteenth-century America—including Albany—would qualify as being in business. But if we consider business as encompassing all forms of proprietorship and self-employment, many more women qualify. I propose that for mid-nineteenth-century Albany, most cash-generating ventures exclusive of wage work qualify as business ventures. That is, female peddlers should be included along with the owners of large dry goods stores, and the owners of basement grog shops in addition to the proprietresses of elegant hotels. I am defining as a "business" any commercial, artisan, service, or manufacturing venture that provided self-employment (versus wage work) and generated cash (versus unpaid domestic labor). Specifically, I am defining women as "in business" who (1) were listed under their own names in the business sections of city directories, (2) were identified as having business occupations (for example, grocer) in the individual listings in city directories, (3) were identified as running businesses in their own names or in the names of male relatives in the credit reports of R.G. Dun & Co., and/or (4) were identified as having business occupations in the manuscript census of 1880. This definition encompasses capitalists employing up to twenty workers, small shopkeepers whose staff was made up of their own relatives, and microentrepreneurs who worked alone.

Since the definition of small business has traditionally included firms with up to 250 (or even 500) employees, the term "small" business itself seems a misnomer for most of Albany's businesswomen.[15] As grocers and saloonkeepers, boarding-house operators and confectioners, as the owners of fancy goods and variety stores, these "penny capitalists" operated concerns that have usually been conceptualized as the very edge of the thriving nineteenth-century marketplace. Falling as they do into the interstices between women's, business, and labor histories, the experiences of nineteenth-century female entrepreneurs and microentrepreneurs do not fit neatly within the definitions and categories developed by historians in each of these subspecialties.

Joan Scott has critiqued such a broad definition of entrepreneurship as obscuring "the workings of capital" through a desire to demonstrate "something about women's empowerment through work," suggesting that the inclusion of very small enterprises represents "pushing these women into business history."[16] Yet the category of "business" is not necessarily equivalent to "evil big business." If we see business as a descriptor of women's economic activities that may have either exploited women or empowered them (or both), we broaden our view to observe more fully what women were actually doing in the nineteenth-century economy. Just as it would be a mistake to limit evaluations of men's work to their work for wages, women's paid work ranged well beyond wage work. Therefore, a wide and inclusive category for business allows us to recognize the economic contributions of many more women who were working and generating cash—though not in the form of wages.

Although I wish to cast a wide net into which I can draw the majority of Albany's female-owned and managed businesses, I would like to avoid drawing so many female occupations under the umbrella of business that the term begins to lose its meaning and usefulness. Therefore, I have eliminated a number of occupations from consideration, occupations that (although they fit the definition of self-employment) fall into what I consider gray areas. First, there are several types of female professionals who have been defined as businesswomen by other scholars but whom I have decided not to include in this study. I have not included any waged or salaried workers—and therefore I will not be considering women who worked as managers for business firms as being "in business." That is, a woman managing a family business in her husband's name, who presumably was not working for wages, I consider to have been "in business"—the supervisor in a department store or millinery shop who worked as an employee would not be included. I have also decided to exclude self-employed teachers (both proprietresses of their own schools and freelance teachers of such skills as music, dancing, languages, and needlework) as well as self-employed nurses, midwives, and physicians. Women writers have also been eliminated from my population, though one might easily argue that female journalists, novelists, and reformers of the nineteenth-century exhibited entrepreneurial characteristics.[17] In addition, I have included only the owners of commercial laundries—not laundresses (though they may well have been self-employed)—as part of my business population. I have also attempted to distinguish between dressmakers and milliners who were in business for themselves, and needleworkers (including tailoresses and seamstresses) who worked for others or by the job, although many of these might also be described as self-employed. That is, in the "gray areas" of women who took in washing and ironing, or dressmakers not listed as having a place of business, such occupations are discussed but the women themselves have not been "counted" as businesswomen in my analyses. Finally, my population of businesswomen includes only women who were identified by at least one source as boarding-house keepers or those who took in three or more boarders, not women who housed two boarders or less but were never listed as boarding-house keepers in the city directories or manuscript census.

The reason for eliminating these trades from my population of female proprietors is twofold. Had I included women engaged in such occupations, the ranks of Albany's businesswomen would certainly have swelled. However, since teachers, writers, nurses, laundresses, freelance needleworkers, and women who took in only a few boarders do not fit most scholars' definition of being "in business," I feared that to incorporate them might allow others to dismiss the importance of my findings. Also, in all these areas—teaching, school-keeping, nursing, writing, laundering, and boarding-house keeping—other researchers have already provided, or are currently developing, significant research and insights.[18]

There are other categories of women involved in business dealings whom I think it important to recognize, but who also fall outside my definitions and have not been included in the study's statistical database. Although I will discuss the subject of women's investment in business ventures in Albany, I am not including as part of my population female capitalists who funded, but did not participate in, the enterprises of their relatives (male or female). Similarly, although they will be acknowledged, I will not be counting as female entrepreneurs women who served as legal "principals" for male relatives dodging bankruptcy, unless they themselves became involved in business management (although the actual involvement of women in such a position is often impossible to determine, as discussed in chapter 4).

Given these parameters, what size population are we dealing with? For the entire period of 1830 to 1885, I have located over two thousand women who were listed with their trades in city directories, listed by their business occupations in the federal census of 1880, or identified by the R.G. Dun & Co. credit ledgers as either owning their own concerns or managing a family business. The histories of these women provide a vivid portrait of female activity in the business sphere.

The selection of starting and ending dates covered by this study, 1830 to 1885, is logically related to Albany's history and available sources, beginning in 1830 as the impact of the Erie Canal became evident, and ending on the eve of Albany's bicentennial celebration of 1886. This period also offers the advantage of superseding the traditional pre- and post-1865 division of American history, replacing a war-based periodization with the more economically based "industrializing" period sometimes used by labor and business historians. Interestingly, these dates closely correspond to dates chosen by the authors of the most recent scholarly overviews of American women in business for chapters on mid-nineteenth-century businesswomen: Kwolek-Folland's "Mills and More: Women's Business and the First Industrial Revolution, 1830–1880," and Drachman's "'To guide and encourage other women in business,' Profit in the Service of Women, 1830–1890."[19]

Sources and Methods

Most important, the years 1830 to 1885 correspond to the availability of important records. Three sources were essential to this study: Albany's annual city directories, the credit ledgers of R.G. Dun & Co., and the 1880 federal manuscript census for the city of Albany. In general, business longevity and changes of trade were best conveyed by the city directories; character and financial worth were assessed only in the credit reports; age, ethnicity, marital status, and family structure were recorded most clearly in the manuscript census. Linkage between and comparison of information gleaned from each of these sources, plus research on specific female proprietors in the state and federal manuscript censuses of 1855, 1860, 1870, and 1875, made it possible to compile detailed databases recording evidence on individual businesswomen. In addition to providing different types of information about individual female proprietors, each source also identified a somewhat different population of businesswomen.

Albany's city directories, published yearly by a series of editors and presses from 1813 on, provided an alphabetical listing of names, addresses, and trades for household heads. City directories indicate the names of individual businesswomen and their trades, as well as their business and home addresses (and thus, whether businesses were located at home), plus names and occupations of adult male relatives living at the same address. Unfortunately, as noted by its compiler William Cammeyer in 1829, the standard Albany city directory is "but a Book of Errors."[20] Nevertheless, it provides the only available overview of women's occupations and business activity, the longevity of their concerns, and a snapshot of change over time. The manuscript census offers an invaluable source for the study of businesswomen. Although women's occupations began to be recorded only in 1860, and then not always consistently or reliably, the census is the only source that includes detailed demographic evidence on individual women. Census records provide each woman's age, marital status, and nativity, as well as information on family size and structure. The directories and census records provide important data for constructing individual and group biographies, demographic profiles, and quantitative analysis.

The surviving credit reports of R.G. Dun & Co., housed at the Baker Library of the Harvard Business School, provide detailed information on many of Albany's business enterprises from the 1840s through the early 1880s. Entries in handwritten ledgers not only support and enrich the quantitative data from other sources but also provide a very human glimpse into the commercial world of mid-century Albany as described by professional credit examiners. Credit assessments were entered as frequently as every month or as rarely as every few years, depending on the size and activity of each business. In most cases, reports were generated every few months, or even on a daily basis in the cases of business crises such as a fire, legal judgments, bankruptcy proceedings, or the death of the proprietor.

These credit reports include information on nearly eight hundred of Albany's female proprietors, including most of those who remained in business for several years or more. Indeed, the histories of some businesswomen span a period of twenty to forty years (though for smaller businesses operated by women, a single entry often appears to have sufficed). Inclusion in the Dun ledgers is a fair indication that a woman's business might be "small" but was not "microscopic," while multiple entries over many years indicate a venture that had achieved at least a modest visibility within the mercantile sphere. Thus credit entries provide a unique source of information for hundreds of small female-run enterprises as well as a rich source for medium-to-large scale commercial endeavors directed by women.

The credit reports are also an exceptionally fertile historical source because the exclusively male investigators evaluated character as well as finances. These records provide a fascinating glimpse into the lives of individual women: their status in the business community, their personal reputations, their work habits, their successes and failures, their family relationships, even their motivations and aspirations. At the same time, the reports are themselves evidence about the attitudes of the mid-nineteenth-century (predominantly male) business community toward female proprietors, allowing one to discern the lenses through which businesswomen were viewed and judged.

The weight of material available from these three sources alone—city directories, the census, and credit records—is remarkable. Based on their evidence and linkages between them, one learns not only about the enterprises in which the women of Albany were engaged but also the proportion of businesswomen within the community of working women. We can investigate business success and failure (although these very concepts will need to be problematized, as previously discussed). These sources also make possible an inquiry that expands outward from a study of individual lives to an analysis of the business patterns of Albany's female proprietors and their families. Although there are significant differences between the data provided by each source (as discussed in Appendix 2), their evidence is additive, and the disparities are themselves revealing.

Unfortunately, beyond the quantitative record little in the way of traditional historical sources survives for the women on which this study focuses. The paper trail left by more than two thousand women entrepreneurs appears to consist merely of an advertisement here, an invoice or trade card there. No letters or diaries, standard sources for women's history, no commercial ledgers or company records, the most common sources for business history, and no investigative reports or union records, typical sources for labor history, appear to have survived. Nevertheless, the city directories, credit records, and manuscript censuses do illuminate both the size and shape of this underexplored area of female activity in nineteenth-century America. Records linkage permits the reconstitution of at least the outlines of the careers of Albany's businesswomen. With the careful integration of quantitative evidence with the qualitative credit reports, as well as the few advertisements, receipts, and contemporary descriptions that survive, one can weave portraits of individual female proprietors. Incorporating nineteenth-century journalism, fiction, and material culture, one can suggest the texture of businesswomen's lives and the overlapping communities in which they worked and lived as well.

Businesswomen in Context

One might be tempted to label all of Albany's businesswomen as exceptional individuals. Certainly, these female proprietors constituted a small minority of all business owners and a minority of working women. According to the information that can be gleaned from city directories and census records, most women in Albany at mid-century did not work, and most of those who worked were not in business. Indeed, most mid-nineteenth-century working women in this city were probably either domestic servants or needleworkers, as in other American communities.[21] Yet the number of businesswomen in Albany in any year far exceeded the "handful" that has been suggested by an eminent historian of American working women.[22] Between the time that 32 individual female proprietors were recorded in the first city directory of 1813, and the year 1885, when 495 were listed in the annual directory, far more than two thousand Albany women embarked on business careers.

Annual city directories reveal that businesswomen in mid-nineteenth-century Albany generally became proprietors either of small artisanal and manufacturing concerns (particularly those associated with the making and trimming of clothing) or of small retail shops (especially those providing food, clothing, or household goods), as well as boarding houses and saloons. This focus did not necessarily mean catering to women alone. Female shirt and collar manufacturers, proprietors of commercial laundries, dealers in gentlemen's furnishing goods or boots and shoes, piano and furniture dealers, grocers, brewers, and confectioners, the keepers of boarding houses, hotels, saloons, and restaurants—all served a mixed or even primarily male clientele. A few women in Albany even went beyond these boundaries and engaged in businesses associated with masculinity and the male "sphere." For instance, during the second half of this period, city directories regularly list female manufacturers of cigars and proprietors of tobacco shops. Similarly, although few female proprietors were active in trades dominated by men, it was not impossible for women to enter such fields. In Albany, women became proprietors of plumbing establishments and livery stables; rare females headed undertaking, blacksmithing, or cooperage operations. And, while women monopolized only a tiny number of trades, in particular millinery and dressmaking, they represented a significant share of proprietors whose trades were associated with clothing and shelter—such as dealers in fancy goods and boarding-house keepers. Concerns owned and operated by businesswomen also made up a consistent, if small, share of businesses dealing in food and drink—such as confectioneries, groceries, and saloons or liquor stores.

Taking into account the limitations of sources on businesswomen, it is possible to reach some broad conclusions about the prevalence of female proprietors within the business community as a whole as well as within the population of Albany's working women. Between 1830 and 1885, women represented a mere 10% of all listings in Albany's city directories, and the proportion of women identified by trade or occupation represented only from 15% to one-third of the total number of women listed. Most individuals listed in the city directory were men, and these men were far more likely to be listed with occupations than were women. Taken as a group, men enjoyed a far wider range of general occupations *and* operated a greater variety of business enterprises than did their female counterparts. Whether one considers blue-collar, artisan, commercial, or white-collar occupations, most of the trades practiced by men were hardly ever practiced by women—and many never were. Although many men were classified simply as "laborers" in the city directories and census records, many others were engaged in a wide variety of specific crafts and skilled trades, from carpenters and masons down to such minute categories as gold beaters and pianoforte tuners. Men also operated a far broader range of business ventures than those run by female proprietors, from lumberyards to hardware stores to flouring mills. During this period, businessmen in Albany also became manufacturers of everything from stoves to plows to steam engines to gas meters. In terms of professional careers, during the mid-century period only men were listed as lawyers, engineers, ministers, or clerks in government offices.

The majority of businesswomen in Albany engaged in a very limited field of occupations relative to those practiced by their male counterparts and relations. Yet, although women did not enter most trades, several types of businesses were operated by both sexes. Women as well as men operated boarding houses and hotels, groceries, fancy goods shops, confectioneries and bakeries, commercial laundries, restaurants, saloons, liquor stores, and retail shops selling everything from drugs to dry goods, and from boots to books. Female proprietors dominated in only two major fields: dressmaking and millinery. And in Albany, almost no women ever became wholesale dealers, even in those fields where female proprietors were well represented, except for a few dealers in "millinery goods." For example, no wholesale boot and shoe dealers, wholesale dry goods dealers, or wholesale grocers were women. As the commercial sector in Albany expanded, women did not become major suppliers.

Most enterprises run by women in nineteenth-century Albany were associated with the domestic sphere. In addition to the provision of food, shelter, and clothing, a few women sold wigs, artificial hair, and Victorian hair jewelry as well as flowers, china, crockery, and furniture. Only a few trades practiced by women in mid-nineteenth-century Albany clearly fell outside the female sphere, and these occupations engaged relatively few female proprietors. For instance, producers of cigars and dealers in tobacco products never amounted to more than 1% of the total number of businesswomen in the city (and no women were listed as selling either cigars or tobacco before 1870). Finally, a very few female proprietors engaged in such idiosyncratic ventures as fortune-telling or selling fishing tackle, or previously mentioned masculine trades such as plumbing and blacksmithing. Such types of trades consistently made up a mere 1% to 2% of all women's business ventures during this fifty-five-year period.

Yet although most businesswomen in mid-nineteenth-century Albany were engaged in a limited number of fields, over the years Albany's female proprietors were involved in over ninety specific trades (see Appendix 1). For instance, although the majority of needleworkers were either dressmakers or milliners, businesswomen also made or sold children's clothing, collars, corsets, ladies and gentlemen's furnishing goods, gloves, men's hats and caps, hoop skirts, shirts, trimmings, umbrellas, and underwear. Women manufactured bandboxes, lace, root beer, rubber goods, umbrellas, and wax flowers; they sold coal, coffee, fish, gloves, and notions. Although their ventures fell largely into areas associated with female domestic skills, they also operated express wagons, news depots, livery stables, and undertaking establishments; they published newspapers and financed opera houses.

Business as a Female Occupation

Although businesswomen in Albany represented only a small proportion of the entire business community, they represented a substantial proportion of the population of working women listed in city directories and the manuscript census. According to the directories, running a home-based business was the most common "white collar" or professional occupation for women in nineteenth-century Albany, and certainly the most common recorded form of moneymaking employment for female heads of household. Logically, since the city directory listed (at least in theory) all heads of household, male and female, and since business was the most common occupation recorded for women in city directories, and since some of the women in business were not heads of household, the majority of females who were household heads with occupations were clearly proprietors.

Women with occupations listed in city directories from 1830 to 1880 can be loosely divided into four groups: business proprietors, professionals (primarily teachers and nurses), needleworkers (seamstresses and tailoresses in the early years, dressmaking and millinery wage workers in the later period), and "other" (including domestic and clerical workers). Throughout this period, business proprietors always made up the largest group of women whose trades were recorded in directories—reflecting the purpose of the city directory as a business and professional guide rather than a census of female trades. The major trend in female occupations reflected by Albany's city directory listings between 1830 and 1885 is that the percentage of needleworkers (not in business for themselves) decreased, while the percentage of clerical and professional women increased.

Most surprisingly, at any time during these years, the number of Albany's women engaged in small business greatly outnumbered those pursuing the teaching profession. In 1830, for example, over 60% of women with directory-listed occupations were in business for themselves, as compared to less than 5% who were identified as teachers.[23] This differential is perhaps not remarkable, since we know that the feminization of teaching was just beginning to take place early in the century. But as late as 1885 the figures are almost as striking—out of 1,055 women identified by trade or occupation in the individual listings of that year's city directory, almost half were in business for themselves, as compared to the 25% employed as schoolteachers or administrators.[24] That is, in Albany in 1885 (at least according to the city directory), there were about twice as many female proprietors as schoolteachers.[25] This picture is confirmed by the federal manuscript census, which as late as 1880 suggests that in Albany small business provided the third or fourth most common occupation for women after domestic service and needlework, ahead of all white-collar occupations, including schoolteaching.[26]

Confirmation of this rather surprising finding can be found in Anita Rapone's statistical analysis of female occupations in Albany based on the census of 1875: using a sampling technique, Rapone concluded that businesswomen made up 49.7% of the female white-collar workforce in Albany, while teachers made up only 30.7%, saleswomen 6.3%, nurses 5.2%, and clerical workers 4.9%. Even using the 1880 federal census (where married businesswomen were systematically undercounted, as discussed in Appendix 2), Rapone found that businesswomen made up 37.3% of white-collar female workers, teachers 36.3%, saleswomen 13.9%, clerical workers 4.7%, and nurses 2.6%.[27]

Challenging Victorian Stereotypes

Many noted scholars have exploded the myth that women conformed to the ideal pattern of domestic isolation described by Tocqueville and prescribed by advice literature of the period.[28] We know that working-class women labored in factories, that farm wives and daughters assisted their husbands and fathers in the fields, and that middle-class women went out into the world as teachers and reformers. Scholars have stressed the ways in which women achieved a measure of independence, autonomy, and sometimes power within the family and domestic sphere, as well as through religion, wage work, labor protest, and movements for abolition and women's rights. The resistance of servants and enslaved women has been investigated, as well as women's efforts to limit reproduction and control their own bodies.[29] Business, however, has not been highlighted as an important sphere of ambition or success for nineteenth-century American women.

Research on female proprietors in Albany suggests that these assumptions need to be modified. Despite the limitations to women's business success in the mid-nineteenth century, there can be no doubt that females were part of Albany's business community. As such, they set up stores and workshops, hired and fired, supervised workers, bought and sold, asked for and extended credit. According to profitability and business cycles, these women moved locations, expanded, and changed lines. In a commercial climate marked by cutthroat competition, they competed with both male and female entrepreneurs in the same field. Those who worked in the realm of fashion also competed to satisfy their customers' desires for the latest styles. On the streets of Albany, in full public view, nineteenth-century businesswomen played a role that required, and rewarded, both ambition and enterprise. It seems that at least some of these women acted from self-interest and a personal satisfaction derived from their success in the business world.

Among the female capitalists and microentrepreneurs of Albany, the familiar nineteenth-century female stereotypes of the dependent daughter, the starving spinster, the wilting wife, the woebegone widow, and the self-sacrificing, moral mother must make way for new characters. Indeed, the very existence of businesswomen in itself confounds the image of helpless dependence conjured up by the term "Victorian woman." In direct contrast to this well-worn model, one finds instead an opposite series of archetypes—ambitious daughters, self-sufficient spinsters, independent widows, and enterprising wives—even domineering mothers and shifty madams! Although such characters can be inferred indirectly from career biographies reconstituted through record linkage, it is easiest to find them in the stories recorded by R.G. Dun's credit examiners.

To replace the stereotype of the shrinking ingénue, let us consider the ambitious daughters and self-sufficient spinsters among Albany's population of businesswomen. In 1870, for instance, twenty-five-year-old Miss Ellen J. Simmons became the proprietor of a fish market previously owned and operated in turn by her father, then brothers, then mother. The original Elijah Simmons ran a fish stall at Albany's central market for many years, although he was reported by credit examiners to be "a fast man" who "drives fast horses" and should be required to "pay cash" for his purchases. After Miss Simmons's father's death in 1867, her brothers inherited the business, but a year later her mother assumed control of the concern. (The boys were called "wild," and by the time their mother took charge of the family enterprise were said to have "ruined it.") Mrs. Simmons herself died soon afterward. Ellen Simmons, however, was commended as "a smart young woman" who "attends to financial matters," and continued in business until her own death in 1883—thirteen years later.[30]

In addition to independent single women such as Ellen Simmons, numerous widowed female proprietors in Albany managed to support families on their own, without the assistance of charity. For instance, in 1868 fancy goods dealer Margaret Armstrong was described as a "widow with family of small children whom she supports by her industry," while another such dealer, Barbara Doctor, was said to be making "a living for herself & 4 children."[31] By 1880 Doctor's three daughters had become a saleswoman, a milliner, and a schoolteacher.

Instead of starving sisters and dependent wives, the study of Albany's female proprietors reveals sisters and wives capable of supporting themselves and assisting their families. One remarkable set of sisters belonged to the Springhart family of German immigrants, who came to the United States sometime before 1860. Their mother, Philopina, had been a millinery proprietor; their father, Carl, was the "steady" owner of an apothecary. The family, immigrating from the German state of Württemberg, raised five milliner daughters: Louisa, Augustina, Amelia, Julia, and Paulina, as well as one son, Edwin. By 1870 the parents owned property worth several thousand dollars. When Carl died in 1874, Edwin inherited his father's business, worth approximately $5,000. This the young man managed to run into the ground within a brief period. Edwin was rescued from financial ruin by loans from his sisters Julia and Amelia (the first single, the second married)—now millinery entrepreneurs in their own right under the style (legal business name) of "Springhart & Miller." In 1876 Julia took over the apothecary business until a buyer could be found and packed her brother off to New York City to "complete his studies." The last credit entries for "Springhart & Miller," in 1881, characterized them as "satifac[tory] & good for eng[agemen]ts," "indust[rious] h[ar]d w[or]k[in]g" with "good char[acter] & cr[edit]," praising them as "close and careful buyers" with an estimated worth of about $5,000.[32] Their business was still listed in city directories as late as 1897. Another set of sisters, Sarah Anderson and Alida Mesick (one widowed, the other single), operated a successful confectionery establishment for more than twenty years, from 1857 through 1878. Described in 1863 as "upright, square women d[oin]g a good bus[iness]," by the time of their retirement they owned their business premises, advertised in the city directory, and were said to be worth $20,000. The thriving enterprise was then passed on to Anderson's sons (Mesick's nephews).[33]

Among Albany's businesswomen, the Victorian "type" of the helpless wife is replaced by the supportive helpmeet. Evidence from credit reports reveals that not only were many businesswomen members of dual-income couples but the profit from female-run business could be used to support the commercial endeavors of their husbands as well. For instance, in 1869 one William J. Gearon, "formerly in stove bus[iness]," who had also "practiced a little in law" and been "a kind of associate 'Editor' for one of the papers," opened a millinery shop. According to credit reports, "this bus[iness] is new to him, but his wife understands it," and Mrs. Gearon was described as "v[er]y atten[tive] to the bus[iness]." By 1871 Gearon himself had acquired "a situation in the custom house in NY wh[ich] yields him quite a g[oo]d salary," while his wife, with her "good bus[iness] capac[ity]," attended to and managed their millinery establishment. In 1874, however, the Gearons advertised "to sell out," after he and a partner had purchased "The Catholic Reflector"—at least partly, one assumes, with the profits of his wife's millinery business.[34] In a second case, when George Robinson "resumed" his business in steam- and gas fitting in 1879, credit examiners noted that he was operating in the name of his wife. "Mrs. R.," they reported, had been "engaged in the hotel bus[iness] for past 3 seasons" in Ocean Grove, New Jersey, "& is said to have made some money." Two years later Robinson was "still doing bus[iness] in name of his wife who owns everything."[35] Similarly, in 1880 credit examiners said of Mrs. Ferdinand Lange, a manufacturer of hair jewelry, that "ab[ou]t her entire m[ea]ns are invested in what is known as the 'Langes Garden' . . . the prop[ert]y is leased to her husband who pays a small rent." Thus it appears that Mrs. Lange's hair goods business, with "but small am[oun]t of Cap[ita]l invested," served to underwrite her husband's saloon and volksgarden.[36]

Rather than descending into poverty and depression when their husbands failed to provide, Albany's entrepreneurial wives took over and ran businesses by themselves. For example, in 1873 Elizabeth Zeller continued the hotel and saloon formerly listed in her husband Ernest's name while he was judged "not exactly right in the head" after a trip to the Utica Asylum. Called "a smart woman" who "attends closely to bus[iness]," by 1876 Mrs. Zeller was "d[oin]g a very good bus[iness]" and "m[a]k[in]g money." After her husband's death that same year, she continued to prosper, and by 1882 was reported by the credit examiners to own real estate worth $8,000, to have a capital of $7,000 invested in her business, and more "money at interest" as well.[37]

Instead of the self-sacrificing mother so dear to the heart of Victorian moralists, one discovers among Albany's community of businesswomen mothers who could only be described as domineering. A striking example of such a woman would be Mrs. Jacobina Tietz, who was said to be "the head of the conc[ern]" (a business repairing and manufacturing pianos) even before her husband Frederick (the nominal head) was "cut to the pieces by the cars at the Union Depot" in 1872, leaving an estate of $30,000 in trust for their children. Three years later this "very shrewd businesswoman" was marketing "a great number of cheap class of pianos m[anu]f[actu]r[e]d in N[ew] Y[ork]" with sales "principally on the installment plan" to people "in modest circ[umstance]s." By the end of the decade she was described as owning property and as having a personal worth of up to $20,000, yet Tietz continued to manage the business herself, employing her sons as assistants. Credit examiners consistently described Jacobina Tietz as "close," "careful," and "sharp," commenting on her "very peculiar ways" and "exceedingly quick temper." Indeed, Tietz gained the reputation of "taking severe measures to enforce payments" and of being "a hard woman to deal with," having "many disputes about the correctness of Bills &c." When she and her son Frederick proved "unable to agree" in 1880, the "hardworking young man of good habits" went into business for himself—just down the street. Whether for this or other reasons, by 1883 Mrs. Tietz's business had fallen on hard times, and she began legal maneuvers such as transferring her assets into the name of another son and her daughter. According to the credit report of that year, "She is up to all the technicalities of the law & is shrewd enough to take advantage of any point that might be in her favor."[38] This fascinating vignette of a businesswoman remaining at work despite comfortable circumstances and competition with her own child, hounding debtors and evading creditors, flies in the face of many presuppositions about proper female behavior in the nineteenth century. Indeed, these sketches of Albany's female entrepreneurs suggest a desire to hold onto money and exert power over their grown children that reminds one more of Puritan fathers than Victorian mothers.

However, one can discover in Albany at least one Victorian type who appears to have played her role to the hilt—the shifty madam. In the 1850s credit examiners characterized Sarah Creswell as an "English lady, age 60" who "likes beer." According to the entry of 1854, Creswell was "a woman of large 'amativeness'" who "loves to sport w[ith] strange men either for money living or pleasure." Not only were Creswell's personal habits immoral, but in 1855 she was running a cheap "bawdy ho[use]!!" described as "a 25 cent concern more or less!" In fact, the credit reporters suggested that she "causes old Dr. Geo[ge] Cooke a g[ood] deal of bus[iness] in the way of curing certain complaints." (Dr. Cooke was Albany's specialist in venereal diseases, and advertised as such in the city directories.)[39] Despite her unsavory reputation, however, Creswell's "corset warehouse" was listed in the city directory as early as 1830, and she continued "in bus[iness] a great many y[ea]rs" before her death in 1856.[40]

In confronting these industrious and resourceful businesswomen, whatever their trades and reputations, we discover a previously "hidden" segment of mid-nineteenth-century women: neither completely downtrodden nor totally protected, neither exploited nor leisured. That such a group may have existed is of interest. To what extent they reflect values of a working-class community (as opposed to the middle-class values sometimes assumed to have been hegemonic) is of even greater interest. Albany's enterprising women provide what one might call a multicultural model to replace the bipolar paradigms—men as "self-interested and aggressive," women as "self-sacrificing and tender"; good women as "sexless," bad women as "carnal"; domestic women as "normative" and working as "abnormal"— that dominated Victorian discourse and continue to inform much of our discussion about American women of the mid-century period.[41] In looking at their life stories, their business strategies, and their work culture, we can begin to move beyond images of cultural hegemony, dominance, and victimization. And, although we can never truly recreate the complexity of their lives and the world in which they lived, we may avoid the trap of forcing them into simplistic stereotypes that actually hinder our understanding of nineteenth-century American women.

CHAPTER TWO

●

Female Microentrepreneurs

Linking Stories and Statistics

She sold small stores, candy, kindling wood, and so on, but there was no great income from this and we soon became poorer than ever. Dear me! I can see the small shop now, with its jars of striped candy, its loaves of bread, the room at the back where we all lived, and my oldest brother sawing kindling wood which we sold to the neighbors.

—Harriet Hanson Robinson, 1898[1]

IN 1950, ELISABETH ANTHONY DEXTER published *Career Women of America, 1776–1840,* describing the occupations available to women in the Early Republic, including teaching, nursing, midwifery, preaching, performing, writing, tavern and boarding-house keeping, shopkeeping, needlework, farming, speculating in real estate, and mill work. Dexter's book, like her earlier *Colonial Women of Affairs,* was based on research in primary sources such as newspapers, magazines, memoirs, travel writings, and local histories. Her chapter on shopkeeping, "Behind the Counter," includes the quote above from Harriet Hanson Robinson, later famous for her description of life as a mill girl in Lowell. Here Robinson recalls the tiny store her widowed mother opened in an attempt to support herself and her four young children after Harriet's father's death in 1831. Dexter follows this quote with the comment, "Little information is available about this type of shop."[2]

Research on Albany demonstrates that it is possible to find intriguing—if incomplete—evidence on small shops and their owners. Since self-employment through running such small, home-based businesses was a relatively common occupation for nineteenth-century women, particularly for wives and widows with children, their stories represent an important part of American women's history. In addition, businesses run by women, while relatively minuscule compared to those run by some (not all) men, contributed to the expanding commercial economy of the United States, often providing the final link on a chain that stretched from raw materials to suppliers to customers. These home-based enterprises fed and housed urban workers, provided liquor and comradeship in leisure hours, and provided working-class neighborhoods with necessaries such as needles and shoelaces, as well as cheap luxuries such as ribbons, beads, toys, and candy.

"Vital" Statistics

This chapter describes the most ordinary of Albany's female proprietors, those whose stories challenge the assumption that nineteenth-century women in the United States could not or would not conduct businesses—whether because of legal restrictions or the ideological power of middle-class domesticity. Moving from the wide-angle view of female proprietors in the period from 1830 to1885 presented in chapter 1, the discussion focuses on a more detailed view of businesswomen active between 1875 and 1885. Linking evidence from city directories, credit records, and the 1880 federal census, it is possible to identify more than 1,500 female proprietors who were active in Albany at any point during this decade, more than 600 of whom have been located in the census to provide a population for demographic analysis (see Appendix 2 for a more detailed description of sources and methods used). Although the term "vital statistics" is commonly used to refer to birth and death dates, the heading above is meant as a play on words, stressing the importance of a statistical analysis to our understanding of businesswomen. Statistics are vital because they provide a method of describing ordinary women—women who were once alive, not businesswomen as mere images, constructs, or heroines, or even a few individual women who happened to leave personal records. The impersonality of such statistics, however, led me to develop portraits of average proprietresses by trade, and to match these to individual Albany businesswomen. Yet because the original statistics are based on evidence from sources that were themselves influenced by nineteenth-century cultural norms (such as the belief that married, native-born women did not engage in business, while immigrant widows did), the statistical portrait itself must be interrogated. Thus the chapter includes a section on "Interpretive Challenges" that raises important questions about the validity of a purely quantitative approach to the study of nineteenth-century businesswomen.

The statistics reported here are based on a population (not a sample) of female proprietors active in Albany at any time between 1875 and 1885,

linking data from city directories and credit ledgers to the federal manuscript census of 1880. The most common type of business venture for the
more than 1,500 businesswomen identified as active in Albany between
1875 and 1885 was dressmaking (representing 402 individuals or 27% of
the total), followed by running a small grocery store (17.5%), keeping a
boarding house (14%), or keeping a saloon (11.5%). Enterprises practiced
by under 10% of the total were dealing in dry and fancy goods (9%), millinery (5%), making or selling confectionery and candy (5%), owning a
variety store (4%), and selling liquor (4%, or 64 individuals). Peddlers, bakers, and hairdressers or dealers in hair and hair goods each made up only
about 1% of the total population of businesswomen in this decade, and
cigar dealers represented less than 1% (see figure 2.1).

Such trades have been long recognized, by both observers at the time
and scholars today, as those in which nineteenth-century women in America were able to operate on a small scale in other American localities. For
example, nineteenth-century investigator Virginia Penny observed female
proprietors in "mercantile pursuits" as merchants, booksellers, dealers in
china, and grocers, while historian Elisabeth Anthony Dexter described tavern and boarding-house keepers, as well as small retail dealers, dressmakers,
and milliners in her study of "career women" in the period between 1776
and 1840. Contemporary scholar Wendy Gamber has found that "more
than four-fifths of the women who advertised their services in the *Boston Directory* of 1876 were purveyors of food, clothing, or lodging," and
Angel Kwolek-Folland's overview of American women's business history
concludes that in the mid-nineteenth century women "tended to dominate" in domestic fields such as "food preparation, textiles, and women's
and children's clothing" and that they operated shops and ran boarding
houses.[3]

Albany businesswomen identified in the census of 1880 were most
likely to be middle-aged, widowed, white, foreign-born mothers with several children living with them in the same household. The evidence shows
that they were significantly different from the young, single women who
made up most of the wage-earning female workforce in the nineteenth
century.[4] Their demographic profile suggests that opening a home-based
business not only was an important opportunity for mature women but
may have represented a choice related to a specific period in their life
cycle. That is, although it has commonly been assumed that fewer mature
women "worked" in this period, their work may simply have shifted from
wage labor to work at home—as either outwork or a modest business
venture. In fact, considering also the underreporting of businesswomen's
occupations in the census (28% of women whom we know from other
sources were conducting businesses were identified in the 1880 census

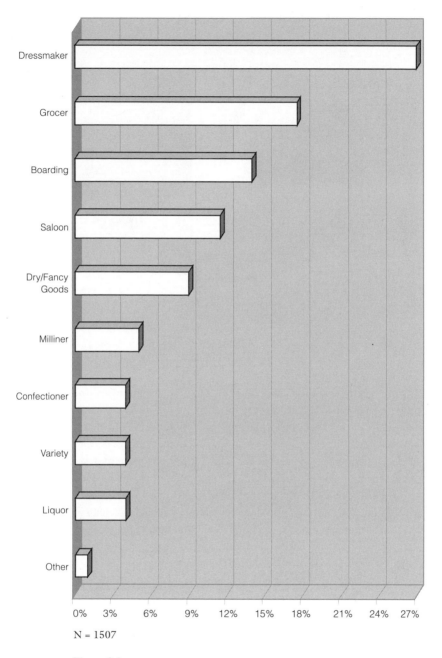

N = 1507

Figure 2.1
Trades of Albany businesswomen active at any time between 1875 and 1885.
Source: Albany City Directories, 1875–80, 1882–85; R.G. Dun & Co. Credit
Ledgers, New York, Vols. 7–14; 1880 Federal Manuscript Census.

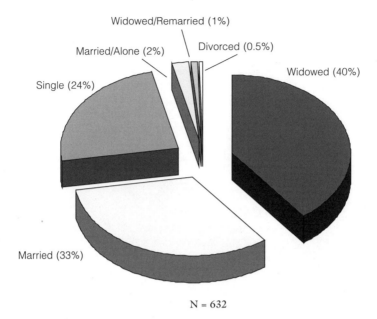

N = 632

Figure 2.2
Marital status of female proprietors in Albany active at any time between 1875 and 1885.
Source: 1880 Federal Manuscript Census.

without trades, as simply "keeping house," or "at home"), these findings suggest that suppositions about the dearth of mature working women for this period need to be reexamined. (See Appendix 2 for a full discussion of the census undercounting of businesswomen.) However, although most active businesswomen in Albany were middle-aged, embarking on their careers at the median age of 37, the ages of female proprietors identified in the 1880 census in Albany actually ranged from 16 to 79.

The marital status of Albany's female proprietors was also more diverse than one might imagine based on Victorian stereotypes of desperate spinsters or widows forced to shoulder the burdens of the "male" marketplace by economic woes. Although the largest group of businesswomen in Albany *were* widowed (40%), a substantial proportion were also married (about one-third) or single individuals (almost one-quarter). Of the remainder, 2% were listed as married but had no mate living with them, 1% can be identified (from other sources) as widowed and remarried, and only one-half of 1% were divorced (see figure 2.2).

In terms of nativity, fewer than half of Albany's female proprietors identified in the census of 1880 were born in North America (45%); of those the vast majority were from New York State. Most businesswomen in 1880 were immigrants from Europe—33% had been born in Ireland,

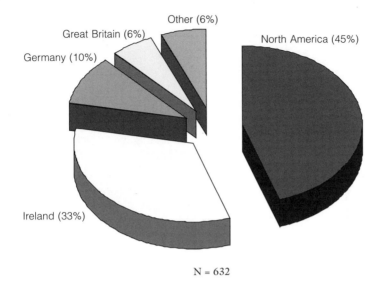

N = 632

Figure 2.3
Nativity of businesswomen in Albany active at any time between 1875 and 1885.
Source: 1880 Federal Manuscript Census.

about 10% in Germany, approximately 6% in Great Britain, and most of the rest in Western Europe—Holland, Luxembourg, and Switzerland. Immigrants from Great Britain were from England, Scotland, Wales, and the Isle of Man (see figure 2.3). Of those businesswomen born in the United States, fewer than half were second-generation immigrants.

Racially, almost all of the businesswomen located in the 1880 census were identified as white; only three individuals were recorded as either mulatto or black. These included the proprietress of a hotel identified in the census as "mulatto" (Catharine Blake, whose career will be described in chapter 7); a married woman, Adaline Douge, labeled by the census as "black," who was listed in city directories as a dressmaker and later "janitrix"; and a single "black" dressmaker, Celia Willard. It is likely that other African-American women were acting as freelance laundresses (in fact, Willard was boarding in a household of black laundresses), but since they did not appear in the business section of the city directories and were never evaluated for credit, they have not been included among the female proprietors analyzed here.

As with many businesswomen today, married female proprietors were often members of dual-income couples. Almost all spouses of Albany's married businesswomen were themselves working, according to the census enumerators; fewer than 10% of female proprietors would have been "forced" into business because their husbands were elderly, disabled, or unemployed. (Only a tiny portion—2.5%—of husbands were listed with no occupation in the census, only 4% were disabled in any way, and only 1% of husbands were unemployed for as long as 12 months.) Instead, the husbands of female proprietors included wage earners, artisans, businessmen, and professionals; such couples almost appear to presage modern dual-career, double-income marriages. According to the census of 1880, the most common single occupation of the spouses of women who were in business at some time between 1875 and 1885 was that of laborer (15%), followed by grocer (7%), carpenter (5%), baker (4%), and moulder (3%). Businesswomen's husbands were engaged in a wide variety of other occupations as well. Many were self-employed, skilled craftsmen such as shoemakers, chairmakers, and umbrella makers. This confirms evidence from the credit records. However, the largest segment of female proprietors' spouses (40%) were actually in business for themselves—as manufacturers, shopkeepers, and proprietors of taverns, hotels, and other commercial enterprises. Of these businessmen, 40% were in the same business as their wives; the most common trades thus "shared" by husband and wife included (in descending order) those of grocer, baker, confectioner, liquor dealer, and fancy goods dealer. Either these couples were partners during their lives, or the wives continued the same line of business after the death of the husbands (suggesting that they had previously been involved in the home-based, family business). Businessman-husbands not in the same type of venture as their wives engaged in almost thirty different lines of trade. They included a contractor and a commission merchant, dealers in items ranging from kindling wood to musical instruments, the owner of a livery stable, the proprietor of a barbershop, a manufacturer of bluing, and a photographer.

Based on the prescriptive and proscriptive literature of the mid-nineteenth century, one might assume that businesswomen—flouting the conventional norms of true womanhood and domesticity—were a controversial or even "outcast" group. Yet research shows that Albany's female proprietors were certainly not isolated individuals living on the fringes of society. The overwhelming majority (about 89%) of Albany's businesswomen lived with relatives. Forty-five percent of women doing business in 1880 who lived with relatives were widows living with their children, 30% were wives living with their husbands and children, and 17% were single women living with their parents and/or siblings. Very few businesswomen—less than 10%—were living in a different type of family configuration, either alone or as boarders in households of nonrelatives. Again, few would have been lonely or marginal figures in their communities.

The Average Proprietress

Statistics are useful in providing a broad overview of Albany's business-women and their households. Nevertheless, such numbers fail to establish a human connection with one's subjects, the "stories" that make up history. Happily, this basic statistical analysis of Albany's female proprietors can be enriched with short biographies of "typical" women in each important trade, created by linking evidence from the manuscript census, city directories, and the R.G. Dun & Co. credit records.

If it is possible to construct a composite, "ordinary" Albany proprietress from the preceding statistics on 1880, what would she look like? Taking the average characteristics from each category (trade, age, marital status, nativity, and household structure), such a businesswoman would be a widowed, foreign-born dressmaker in her forties who headed her own household, which would include at least one working son, one adult daughter, and one additional relative, plus perhaps a boarder. This description does roughly match the profiles of two businesswomen who have been located in all three sources. Both Mary A. Woods and Regina Held were born in 1838, the first in Ireland, the second in Baden, Germany, and thus both were 42 years old in 1880. Both were widowed dressmakers living with their adult children in the same household. Both, in fact, lived with four children: dressmaking daughters who were in their twenties (Helena Held was 23, and Annie Woods was just 20), one working son (George Held was an 18-year-old printer, while William Woods was a 17-year-old store clerk), one daughter described by the census as "at home" or "keeping house" (Hattie Held was 21, while Margaret Woods was only 14), and one child still in school (Henry Held was 14, Cathrine Woods just 10). Both women had also entered business in the 1870s, when they would have been in their thirties and their children significantly younger. In fact, Mary Woods was listed as a dressmaker in city business directories beginning in 1871, when her four children would have ranged in age from 1 to 11 years. According to the credit ledgers, Woods had come to the United States via Canada, where her children were born, in 1871—apparently to be near her brother, Pat McHugh, who was said to assist her. Held, on the other hand, had started business in 1875 as a married woman; her husband, Christian, was a retail liquor dealer who did not die until 1880, leaving her half of his property, including her business premises worth about $2,500 but mortgaged for more than half that amount. Perhaps because of Held's stronger financial base, her business lasted far longer (some twenty years), until 1895. Meanwhile, Woods's dressmaking and millinery establishment may have closed even before the 1880 census was taken. Although she had been described as "d[oin]g v[er]y well" upon opening in 1871, she was actually reported as dead by the credit examiners in 1873, "worth 00" in 1874, "m[a]k[in]g only a living" in 1875, and as having opened a laundry in 1878. Both women, however, were typical in being described as "honest" and either "worthy" (said of Held) or "h[ar]d w[or]k[in]g" (reported of Woods) by the credit examiners, and each remained in business for more than seven years.[5]

Yet, in several ways the composite figure described above and illustrated by Regina Held and Mary A. Woods is not really typical. For instance, although dressmakers made up the largest single group of businesswomen in the decade from 1875 to 1885, and although the majority of businesswomen in Albany were foreign-born, most dressmakers were actually native-born women. A more accurate and sensitive approach to the search for an average proprietress is to develop a series of typical portraits of businesswomen depending on their trades. A representative dressmaker or milliner, for instance, was far different from the average female grocer or saloonkeeper. The demographic data for Albany presents us with a picture of a business community segmented by trade and nativity (and thus by class), with diversity in marital status and age dependent on these variables. Therefore, it is most accurate to create "models" for each major business in which women were engaged in mid-nineteenth-century Albany. Here, then, are snapshots of a range of "typical" businesswomen: a single native-born dressmaker, a married Irish-born grocer, a remarried German saloonkeeper, and two widowed British-born proprietors: one the keeper of a boarding house and the other of a fancy goods/variety store.

The average dressmaker in Albany was single, native-born, and somewhat younger than other female proprietors. (More than half—56%—of all single female proprietors were dressmakers, and 65% of dressmakers were single.) One dressmaker who matches these parameters was Sarah Tygart, born in New York. Like many other single proprietresses, Tygart lived with her widowed mother, Phebe.[6] She entered business in 1860 at the age of 33, and left business fifteen years later in 1880. Despite this relative longevity, Tygart's business was "v[er]y limited" according to credit examiners, who called her a "careful prudent woman" but a "slow pay" who should "pay cash." Nevertheless, suppliers in Albany granted her a "small credit." That Tygart's business provided less than a comfortable living is suggested by the fact that, according to the census of 1880, she and her mother (then aged 73) housed a family of five boarders—a machinist, his wife, and their three children aged 2 through 6. In fact, Sarah Tygart at age 48 was caring for her dependent mother and carrying on two small businesses as both a dressmaker and boarding-house keeper.[7] In contemporary terms, Tygart was working a double shift—but working both shifts simultaneously in the same location.

Female grocers in Albany were usually Irish women in their forties, either widowed or married. (Sixty percent of Irish businesswomen were engaged in providing food and drink—in groceries, saloons, liquor stores, breweries, restaurants, and related enterprises—as compared to only 21% of American-born proprietresses.) A grocer of 1880 can be represented by 43-year-old Mary Convery, an Irish immigrant who operated a small store from 1875 to 1886. Although Convery's husband, George, was identified as the proprietor of their grocery in the 1880 census, credit records reveal that he actually worked "at his trade"—as a bookkeeper—while she ran the business and "attended" to the store. This, according to credit examiners, was quite small; although the business premises, worth $3,000 to $4,000, legally belonged to Mary, the building was mortgaged for $3,400—"its full value at a forced sale." Indeed, her entire worth was estimated at only about $300, and the ledgers warn "she is not regarded as a very desir[able] cust[omer] tho' she gets a little cr[edit]." The census records suggest that Convery was assisted in her business by her 19-year-old son William (listed as a grocery clerk) but give no occupation for her 17-year-old daughter Mary. Nevertheless, since the store was located at home (in a dwelling shared with at least two other families), one can assume that daughter Mary was also engaged in the family business. The youngest child, George, was still in school at age 11; his mother had been running the store at least since he was 6.[8]

One boarding-house keeper of 1880 who can be identified and linked in city directories, census records, and credit ledgers is Mary A. Lamb. Lamb was typical in the sense of being an older widow. Her business career spanned forty years and included some variations of trade, yet she appeared in only a single credit entry, where she was described in 1873 as "an honest woman" running a saloon and boarding house, having "purchased the property where she does bus[iness]," worth about $5,000 and "worthy of cr[edit]." Lamb was born in 1810 in England; her first business listing can be located in the 1855 city directory, when, at the age of 45, she was operating the elegantly titled "Hudson River House." It appears that Lamb continued in the same line through 1871, and although her venture did not appear in the business sections of the city directory after that year, both the credit records of 1873 and the census of 1880 confirm that she was still running a boarding establishment. Between 1883 and 1885, city directories listed Lamb as the keeper of a refreshment saloon; from 1886 to 1891 she was said to be running a retail liquor store, and in her final listing—1895—she was identified as a boarding-house keeper once again. In 1880 Lamb (whose occupation was listed as "Boarding house" in the census) was living with six relatives, including an adult daughter identified as a "housekeeper," a son-in-law stove mounter, and three grandchildren ranging in age from 13 to 19. Her grandsons were categorized as a laborer and student, while her granddaughter of 17 was listed simply as "at home." In addition, Lamb's 35-year-old son, James Lawrence, appears in the household identified by the word "saloon."[9] It makes sense to conclude that son James helped run Lamb's saloon, while her married daughter Mary (aged 48) and granddaughter Susan (aged 17) assisted the 70-year-old Lamb in the care of a household that included 18 male boarders in addition to the seven family members. It is typical of the census, however, that the trades of all male relatives and the male boarders—maltsters, stove mounters, blacksmiths, laborers, a boat captain, and a plasterer—were carefully enumerated, while Lamb's female relatives were not clearly identified as assisting in the family business. Much like the unpaid, hidden work of caring for one's own family, the domestic work of caring for 18 boarders was not recognized as either a job or a business by the census enumerators.[10]

Many saloonkeepers in Albany were German-born widows; one individual with these characteristics located in all three sources is Lena Huttner. Born in Prussia, Huttner was widowed around 1878 and left with a family of four children aged 3 to 13 by the time she entered business in 1880 at the age of 35. According to the census of that year, Huttner was assisted in her business by a brother, who acted as a clerk in the saloon, but lived with no other servants or employees. Despite the challenge of juggling family and commercial responsibilities in a home-based business, Huttner by 1881 was said to be "d[oin]g a f[ai]r bus[iness]" and even "credited with m[a]k[in]g a little something over her expenses which are small." In 1884 Huttner was remarried to brewer Fred Mattman; although the saloon was now listed in his name (according to both credit records and city directories), credit entries reveal that Lena Huttner Mattman "gives the bus[iness] her usual attention & looks after the establishment altogether." Although this was the last credit entry for either Huttner or Mattman (who had previously been employed "at good wages," was said to be worth $4,000 to $5,000, and was "fitting up a brewery" in a neighboring town), Lena Mattman's own name reappears as a retail liquor dealer in the Albany directories from 1891 to 1900, and as a saloonkeeper as late as 1915—almost thirty-one years after her last credit entry.[11]

Albany's female shopkeepers were most commonly native-born or immigrants from the British Isles. A rather typical fancy goods or variety dealer (the terms often seem to be used interchangeably in the records) located in all three sources is Mary McAllister, an "honest atten[tive] & indust[rious]" widowed Scottish immigrant who operated a store from 1871 (when she was 53 years of age) until her death in 1883. Although McAllister does not appear in the city directory business listings until 1875, a credit entry of 1874 indicates that she had already been in business for three years.

Her shop was called a "small place" at that time, with a stock worth only $300 and doing only a "small trade." Four years later in 1878, however, she was said to be "d[oin]g well in a small way" with a worth estimated at $1,000 to $1,500. By 1879 McAllister was "credited with doing the best business in her line on 'Arbor Hill'" (a city neighborhood); in 1881 she was described as "d[oin]g good bus[iness] & m[a]kin[g] a little money" as well as owning real estate, while her estimated worth had risen to $2,500. When she died in 1883, McAllister passed the business to her married daughter, Mary Roseboom, who as "the only heir to her estate" inherited "all told" $3,000. Although Roseboom (also born in Scotland and then aged 33) was identified as married in the 1880 census, no husband was present in the household or mentioned in the credit records. Also in the household were Roseboom's young daughters (McAllister's granddaughters), 9-year-old Mamie and 7-year-old Jennie, both in school. That Roseboom had assisted her mother is made clear by the sole credit entry under her name, which explains that "she has had management of the bus[iness] for sometime & understands it well." The census of 1880, however, had listed Roseboom without any occupation. Had her mother not died, her contribution to the business might never have been recorded in the credit ledgers, and the store would not have appeared under her name from 1884 to 1888 in the city directories.[12]

This series of brief business biographies for typical trades demonstrates that most female proprietors in Albany were neither wealthy nor destitute, neither domestic goddesses nor wage slaves. They appear as respectable, working-class women enmeshed in family relationships and engaged in ventures that generated modest profits and sustained their families, but rarely served as the sole support of all family members. (We might note, for instance, that dressmaker Sarah Tygart—without wage-earning relatives and with a dependent mother—found it necessary to take in boarders as well as practice her craft.) The image that emerges is one of continuous effort for modest rewards—business as a source of self-employment and family survival, rather than an entrepreneurial venture in search of fortune or fame.

Interpretive Challenges

Significant interpretive challenges face the historian of nineteenth-century businesswomen, problems that arise largely from the type of data on businesswomen available to researchers of this period. For example, sources providing evidence on Albany's female proprietors disagree about such fundamental information as the prevalence of trades in which businesswomen were engaged and the identity of individual businesswomen.[13] That is, individual women identified as doing business in one source, such as the city directories, may never be mentioned in the credit records, and may be named without any occupation in the census. Or, a woman identified as an grocer in the directory may be called a saloonkeeper in the credit records and a liquor dealer in the census! Beyond such factual discrepancies, the more deeply one investigates the careers of female proprietors the more forcefully one realizes ways in which even seemingly objective sources were actually biased by societal assumptions about women and their proper roles.

The apparent specificity of figures determined by counting individual businesswomen—such as the statistical analyses presented in this chapter—is appealing. Neat statistics, however, obscure the constant quandaries facing a historian who attempts to identify and count all the businesswomen in a nineteenth-century city or neighborhood. In order to generate a useful statistical analysis, for instance, one must be able to identify such basic information as whether an individual should be considered the actual proprietor of a concern, her particular line of business, and the dates when she entered and left the commercial arena. Yet for many—if not most—of Albany's female microentrepreneurs, proprietorship may be hidden by the presence of male relatives, evidence on trades may be ambiguous or even contradictory, and the length of business activity may prove extremely difficult to determine with accuracy.

Let us consider specific cases that illustrate the difficulties outlined above. First, what constitutes a business? For women in Albany, "business" was not synonymous with "the firm" or incorporation, much less with the type of "big business" that emerged in the mid-nineteenth-century. Instead, most businesswomen fall into the categories of what one might call "self-employed" workers or "petty" retailers. They were, as previously noted, far more likely to be microentrepreneurs than "classic" entrepreneurs, and far more likely to be running a home-based business than operating a separate store, workshop, or factory. In fact, the vast majority of Albany's mid-nineteenth-century female entrepreneurs were engaged in trades that appear, in terms of size and structure, little changed from the types of businesses that engaged American women in the colonial and early republican periods.

Once a historian of businesswomen has decided which types of endeavors should be classified as businesses, the next vital question becomes, Who was the proprietor? Although this might seem to be a straightforward question, the study of Albany's microentrepreneurs reveals many murky areas. For example, in 1884 the credit entry for one James H. Connors, the keeper of a grocery and saloon, reads, "The bus[iness] is carried on in his name, but his mother-in-law Mrs. John Eagan[14] frequently buys stock for the place in her own name & the concern seems to be *somewhat mixed as to proprietorship*" [emphasis added].[15] Interestingly, a Mr. John Egan had run a grocery at the same location as Connors's store for "a long time" according to the credit reports, although these never mention his wife.[16] However, the activity of *Mrs.* John Eagan (the mother-in-law of James H. Connors, above) at the same site immediately after *Mr.* John Eagan's death in 1883 suggests that she had been a hidden partner in her husband's concern all along. In fact, credit examiners argued that Connors was good for whatever he ordered if *she* would "indorse for him" rather than vice versa, since she was "worth fully $10,000 in unencumbered R[eal] E[state]," while he was "worth but little if anything over debts." Evidence of such situations abounds in the entries of the R.G. Dun & Co. credit examiners, and proprietary complications may have been common in Albany's small business ventures. But, as noted previously, credit entries for smaller concerns tend to be nonexistent or quite limited. Thus, the R.G. Dun & Co. credit records cannot be solely depended on to provide complete information on proprietorship for the owners or operators of Albany's most modest business ventures.

It is possible, however, to use census entries to extrapolate information about female involvement in commercial concerns. For instance, the 1880 census describes Irish immigrant Cornelius Droogan as keeping a grocery store at 15 Morton Street—his family's place of residence—while the occupation of his Irish-born wife Marie was given as "keeping house." Yet Cornelius was a 65-year-old who suffered from rheumatism, according to the census, while his wife was only 44, with no recorded physical ailments. Thus, in addition to caring for five children ranging in age from 5 to 12, it seems likely that Marie Droogan took part in the grocery business—along with Cornelius's daughter Katie, 24, who was described simply as "at home." Shall we count Marie Droogan and Katie as businesswomen—or not?[17] In the case of the Droogans, a credit report of 1882 indicates that "the bus[iness] is managed by his wife in his name," confirming that Marie not only "took part" but in fact personally "managed" the grocery. But how can we know at what point Marie assumed this responsibility, and to what extent she was involved in the business all along?[18] How should her contribution be assessed for statistical analysis?

In another case, the manuscript census for Albany lists John O'Connell, Jr., as a "Hotel Keeper"; his 29-year-old wife Bridget (a second-generation Irish immigrant) was identified merely as "keeping house." Yet her household included 28 individuals besides herself and her husband, 24 male boarders and 4 live-in female servants. Are we to conclude that her husband "ran" the hotel while Bridget remained in the "domestic sphere" of their private suite? It seems far more realistic—and accurate—to assume that Bridget O'Connell was involved in the daily operation of the hotel officially recorded under her husband's name.[19] As Wendy Gamber has argued in her excellent study of nineteenth-century boarding houses, "boarding-house keeping was women's work. Even when husbands and fathers styled themselves proprietors, wives and daughters, sometimes assisted by female servants, performed the labor that keeping boarders entailed."[20] An even stronger case can be made for identifying married women as the proprietors or managers of boarding houses and hotels when their husbands were carrying on a separate trade or business. Thus, although Irish-born Bridget James received a notation of "keeping house" next to her name in the 1880 census, the fact that her husband James was running a retail liquor store suggests that Bridget played a vital role in taking care of the 7 boarders listed in their household.[21]

Once one has determined proprietorship, an additional unexpected question arises when doing research on Albany's businesswomen—how to identify, and differentiate between, their trades. Although we may assume that there is a clear difference between a grocery store and a saloon, for instance, in the mid-nineteenth century the divisions between these common business enterprises appear to have been ambiguous. In fact, women identified as grocers in one source were often described as saloonkeepers or retail liquor dealers in another, and vice versa, while several businesswomen named in the census were given the double designation of "keeping a grocery and bar room." One specific example was Mrs. Philip Stein, a widow who in 1870 was said to offer "a few vegetables and fruits" as well as to keep a bar.[22] The dividing lines between needleworkers and fancy goods dealers, and between different types of needleworkers (such as dressmakers, milliners, and corsetmakers) can also be confusing, and once again numerous proprietors were listed as one or the other depending on the date or the source, and sometimes as both at once. The solution here requires research into a variety of sources—including fiction and reform literature—to elucidate the nature of those trades in which nineteenth-century women were engaged. (For instance, Virginia Penny observed with concern that most small groceries in New York City sold liquor, while, as we will see, fiction on fancy goods and millinery shops reveals numerous ways in which such businesses were "mixed" together).[23]

Determining the length of time in which a woman was engaged in her business can also be difficult. How should one record the commercial activity of, say, a female confectioner such as Sophia McFarlane, who took over a business on the death of her husband Andrew and then, as a widow, ran the concern from 1883 to 1897 in her own name? The obvious answer would be 14 years, and this indeed was the number used for the earlier statistical analysis. However, we can also determine through records linkage that Andrew McFarlane had been in the confectionery business from 1860 through 1882, that Sophia had been born in 1830, and that (since their eldest child was born no later than 1854), they had probably been married since at least 1853. Although Mr. McFarlane was the official business proprietor for the years before his death, one can assume that this home-based business was a family concern based on the evidence that Mrs. McFarlane was able to continue operating after her husband's death and that their son Archibald was listed as a confectioner in the city directory of 1885. Would the correct length of Sophia McFarlane's business career, therefore, be 14 or 37 years—more than twice as long?

Conclusion

With all these caveats, is it possible to reach any conclusions about Albany's mid-nineteenth-century female proprietors, or must we just throw up our hands in despair? I believe that an exploration of these contradictions, questions, and ambiguities reveals as much as it obscures. Although it is evident that any statistical analysis of this population must be understood as approximate rather than absolute, it is also clear that exploring the contingencies suggested above actually assists us in the project of reconceptualizing mid-nineteenth-century businesswomen in the United States.

For instance, many widows were *not* newcomers to the business world, bravely shouldering new burdens. Research in credit records reveals that numerous women were active in family-run businesses before their husband's death. The death of male spouses simply exposes to the light of history the contributions their wives had been making all along, by removing the official, male name under which the company had been operating. Indeed, I would propose that the very fact that a wife continued in "her husband's" business suggests that she was familiar with that business already. Thus, it seems most probable that when women such as Margaret Burt, confectioner, and Elizabeth McAneny, variety and toy store proprietress, "took over" their husband's trades, they were experienced individuals continuing, *not* suddenly beginning, their business careers.[24]

Similarly, it seems clear that family businesses listed under male names, but located within the household, were not "individual" concerns with sole proprietors. Resident wives, mothers, sisters, and daughters who were not otherwise employed contributed to, and sometimes managed, these concerns. In the case of those home-based trades where we know that widows regularly carried on businesses after their husbands' deaths—such as bakeries, confectioneries, groceries, saloons, fancy goods and dry goods stores, for instance—surely it would be *most* accurate not only to include the years before the husband's death as "years in business" for widows but to count the wives of men engaged in such home-based ventures as businesspeople, too.

Lest this obsession with the accurate counting of female proprietors or years in business seem to be grappling with an issue of minor importance, consider how the adjustments suggested above would change the profile of the female business community as presently understood. Dressmaking and millinery have often been seen as the enterprises with most female participation. Yet could this be simply because these were the fields in which women would be far more likely to be running businesses in their own names, and thus be recorded as such in city directories and census records? If one goes back and adds to a list of female proprietors the wives of men who were recorded as operating boarding houses or small shops in their own homes, specifically in those trades that were often carried on by women after their husbands died (such as bakeries, confectioneries, and fancy goods stores), would the predominance of the female-dominated needle trades hold up? Would we still believe that married women were only rarely involved in business enterprises, and that fewer married women were in business than widows?[25]

As Wendy Gamber has pointed out, a precise accounting of the number of nineteenth-century female entrepreneurs in the United States is not possible. Nevertheless, when one adds together the approximate numbers offered in this chapter with an understanding of the comprehensive undercounting that skews our understanding of women's real contributions to local business economies, we can begin to understand the specific ways in which women *were* active participants in the nineteenth-century marketplace.

Albany's businesswomen were not all stamped from the same mold. The diversity in their stories presents a series of variations on a theme and reminds us that "real life" tends to escape from the organizational categories historians attempt to impose on a chaotic past. Interestingly, after creating composite types for each trade commonly practiced by Albany's businesswomen, one discovers that few real women actually fit into their precise demographic outlines. And, just as businesswomen varied in their demographic profiles, the outlines of their business careers—the size, worth, and longevity of their concerns, as well as their motivations for entering and leaving business—also differed significantly. The parameters of this variation will be discussed in the next chapter.

Doing Business

Patterns and Parameters

Mrs. Maidment was a dumpy little woman with a kindly smile for us, and she talked as if she had a hot potato in her mouth. She would lift up her hands and say, "God bless you my dears. I have been waiting for you, all Mrs. Parker's grandchildren. Now, what will you choose?"

—Huybertie Lansing Pruyn Hamlin[1]

BEGINNING IN THE 1920S, Huybertie Lansing Pruyn Hamlin (1873–1964), a descendant of several elite local families, wrote a memoir of her privileged childhood in late-nineteenth-century Albany, later published as *An Albany Girlhood.* Her social class can be established from the fact that she was presented to Queen Victoria, and that her mother had been so presented on three separate occasions. Among her early memories of shopping she included a visit (which can be dated to the early 1880s) to "Mrs. Maidment's bakery." According to Hamlin:

> There were large raisin buns, cream puffs, eclairs, sheets of fresh ginger bread, cookies, jumbles, doughnuts, and all kinds of pies. We knew we must not be too greedy, but it was hard to choose one thing out of so many. Generally there was a large order for Grandmother, and Mrs. Maidment would seriously consider which one of us could be trusted to carry out the fairy ginger bread without falling down and breaking it.[2]

We actually know quite a bit about Harriet Maidment, who was listed under "Bakers" in the city directories (sometimes as "Harriet" and sometimes as "Mrs. Edward") from 1877 through 1892. Unlike other female bakers who appear in the directories only after their husbands' deaths, Maidment was in fact not a widow; her husband Edward was still alive until at least 1885. According to credit entries, Edward Maidment did a "large bus[iness]," was "doing very well," and was estimated to be worth

$15,000 to $20,000 in the 1860s. In 1869, however, he was said to have sold out to baker Michael Crummy.[3]

In 1875 credit entries for Maidment resume with the statement that he was "doing bus[iness] in his wife's name," a point repeated by examiners the following year ("everything is in his wife's name"). Credit reports under *her* name begin in 1874 (when she would have been 54 years old), with the note that she had "retaken their old prem[ises]" and left her daughter to run a store in Saratoga, also in Mrs. Maidment's name. By 1876 Harriet's entries explain that Edward had entered "an inebriate asylum on a/c[count] of his habits," while she was described as "a v[er]y indus[trious] well meaning woman of v[er]y fair capac[ity]" who was "d[oin]g v[er]y g[oo]d busi[ness] tho[ugh] not making much more than expenses wh[ich] are large"—including a store rent of $1,500 a year.[4] (However, the census of 1880 lists Edward at home, and as a "baker," while Harriet is identified, like so many other businesswomen, as simply keeping house.) From the available sources, it remains difficult to know at what point Mrs. Maidment really "began" her business career, and at what point Mr. Maidment should no longer be considered the proprietor of the concern, but there is no doubt that Harriet Maidment ran this business—as confirmed by Hamlin's memoir.

Hamlin's unique description reflects the richness of the shopping experience for an upper-class child of the late nineteenth century. Unfortunately, we have yet to find anything similar from the thousands of middle- and working-class customers of businesses operated by Albany's female proprietors. Most microbusinesses were undoubtedly less prosperous than this bakery, patronized by the elite of the city. Compare Hamlin's mouthwatering description of the Maidment shop to comments from the credit records on the grocery of Mrs. John Delehanty; according to reports of 1871, hers was a "low miserable place" whose "st[oc]k & fixtures would not bring 5$."[5]

Yet, even without further literary evidence about Albany's mid-nineteenth-century female proprietors, by using material from the R.G. Dun & Co. credit records we can draw conclusions that go far beyond those supported by evidence from city directories and the manuscript census. While these sources provide data that allow us to catalog the trades practiced by mid-nineteenth-century proprietresses in Albany and to analyze their demographic profiles, they tell us little about how and why women entered and conducted their businesses. Reports compiled by the R.G. Dun & Co. credit investigators, however, supported by data from the city directories and census, permit one to build up an outline of each woman's business career and to widen our discussion. These credit entries provide an exceptionally rich, detailed, and varied picture of female enterprise in the mid-nineteenth century. Through them one can learn—or extrapolate—women's motivations for entering business, the size and longevity of their concerns, the amount of their capital investment, as well as variations in types of female proprietorship and in the extent of women's involvement in business ventures. Analysis of aggregate patterns coupled with individual examples drawn from these reports permits us to probe women's business careers in Albany and to uncover the diverse opportunities open to female proprietors within the seemingly limited scope of endeavors in which most women engaged.

For purposes of this discussion, we must attempt to interpret the monetary sums expended by female proprietors, invested in their businesses, and the amount of their profits and overall worth. Estimates relating the value of money from the mid-nineteenth century to its value today vary widely. For the period covered by this study of businesswomen in Albany, the differential between mid-nineteenth-century monetary value and that of today ranges from approximately 20 times to more than 500 times, depending on the method of calculation.[6]

Not very useful! Considering which of these measures might prove most appropriate for this study, I created a ratio based on women's wages. For example, a common wage for women in mid-nineteenth-century Albany was about $3 a week, while the current minimum wage in New York State is $7.15 an hour, or $286 a week, slated to rise to $290 per week in 2009. Rounding this figure up to $300 a week, dollar values from the mid-nineteenth century can easily be translated multiplying by a factor of 100. Using this calculation, investing only $100 in a woman's business would have been risking the equivalent of $10,000 in today's dollars. Using the same ratio, a business worth $5,000 in the 1860s would compare to an enterprise worth $500,000 today; those exceptional female-run ventures worth from $20,000 to $100,000 would compare to businesses worth $2 million to $10 million. An alternate, and somewhat less dramatic, computation would be based on the late-nineteenth-century "living wage" of $9 a week, compared to the late twentieth-century's $9 an hour—or, a factor of 40. Using this ratio, an investment of $50 in the nineteenth century would equal about $2,000 in today's dollars, while $100 would equal $4,000; $1,000 would equal $40,000; $5,000 would equal $200,000; and $100,000 would equal $4 million.

Motivations

Because no personal papers from Albany's businesswomen appear to have survived, it might be assumed that we are ill-equipped to make statements about their motivations. Yet by analyzing these women's career patterns and the choices they made—for instance, choices to enter, remain in, or leave business—one can draw conclusions about their attitudes and values. Each of the over two thousand women who entered business in mid-nineteenth-century Albany chose a rather visible career that required interaction with the public (including strangers), negotiation with suppliers (usually male), the pursuit of profits, and—in the case of the vast majority of these women—the introduction of the marketplace into the home. Such characteristics challenge our understanding of mid-nineteenth-century notions of respectable femininity.

For most women in Albany, as for most men, the reason for entering business was clearly "to make money." Although businesswomen were rarely pathetic victims of fate, most needed to make a living and many undoubtedly hoped to do better. Their enterprises might be dictated by the necessity of self-support or family survival, by the hope of supplementing the wages of other family members, or by the desire to amass enough capital to invest in real estate or even retire to the country. For instance, milliner Mary Harris, who was said to "own a farm in the country" with her husband (a coach painter) in 1856, by 1857 had "moved out of town."[7] In some cases businesswomen clearly gained personal satisfaction from running a successful venture, acting with ambition and energy to triumph in the marketplace. In others a small business provided an occupation and an identity. At times mothers opened or kept up a concern in order to build or maintain a viable trade for their children—at others, children backed their widowed mothers in enterprises that provided a modest income. Nor were such motivations necessarily mutually exclusive. The decision to enter and remain in business probably resulted from a multitude of intersecting financial, professional, personal, and familial goals.

To begin at the most basic economic level, in the case of lone single women or widows supporting their families, a key motive was clearly survival. For instance, according to the census of 1880 dressmaker Kate Bragen was an unmarried woman boarding with nonrelatives—one assumes, then, that she must have been responsible for her own support. Necessity was clearly also a factor for widowed milliner Charlotte Armington, who entered business around 1848. This mother of a "lar[ge]" and "expensive" family, according to the credit reports, was burdened in particular with "two v[er]y hard boys to care for" who gave her "a great deal of trouble." Armington, however, did manage to support "her family out of her bus[iness]" and to bring up her difficult sons; still, she never accumulated more than "a little p[ro]p[ert]y" in mortgaged real estate, and kept working until her death at the age of 59 in 1877.[8]

Even married women with employed husbands might need their business profits to keep the family afloat. Joanna Nolan, for instance, did a very small fancy goods business said not to "pay anything over a living, if it does that," according to the credit reports of 1881. On the other hand, Nolan's earnings probably served to supplement the wages of her husband, John, who worked as a laborer.[9] Seckel Mendel and his wife also provide a good example. Mrs. Mendel ran the millinery and glove business listed in her husband's name while he worked as a peddler. In 1871 their credit report stated that they made "a living between them."

An underlying, unspoken assumption in the question "why did mid-nineteenth-century women enter business?" is the suspicion that they would have undertaken such an unfeminine step only if they were forced into trade by bad fortune. Were the majority of Albany's female proprietors destitute widows, impoverished spinster daughters, or neglected and abandoned wives—the victims of men who left them to fend for themselves with few resources? Were they the daughters, wives, mothers, and sisters of irresponsible and worthless men? This description does fit some of Albany's female business owners. Husbands identified as problems by the credit reports were most often characterized as either drunk or lazy. For instance, Hibbard Todd, a drover (a man who drove cattle or sheep to market) married to a milliner, was described in 1855 as "a shiftless husband who is principally supported by her." While Mrs. Todd was called "honest and indus[trious]," as well as "enterprising," "smart," and "v[er]y attent[ive]," Hibbard was characterized as "lazy" and "a poor cuss."[10] Another female entrepreneur married to an unreliable spouse was Jane Regan, the owner-operator of a commercial laundry. In 1880 Regan was considered a better credit risk than her husband John, who was said to be "somewhat given to drink." While Jane was described as "the Boss of the establishment," the R.G. Dun & Co. credit examiners concluded of John that "it would be better that his wife should endorse for him."[11] Other businesswomen were married to invalids or to men who had themselves been entrepreneurial failures. For instance, in 1868 Sarah Clinker was described as a "very industrious" dealer in fancy dry goods with a "husband in bad health" whom she supported (along with their three young daughters).[12] In 1879 Mrs. William Barringer became the proprietor of an enterprise that sold dress patterns, after her husband—a commission merchant who had previously done a trade of $75,000 per year—went out of business.[13] However, in Albany the proportion of women with "problem" husbands—invalids, drunks, lunatics, and what one might call "lazy bums"—appears to be only 8% of the number of married women located in the R.G. Dun & Co. credit records.[14] (This matches the small proportion of husbands identified as unemployed or disabled in the 1880 manuscript census, as reported in the previous chapter.)

The vast majority of wives described by the credit entries do not seem to have been forced into trade because of the failure of indolent, drunken, incapacitated, or bankrupt men to provide for their dependents. Rather, the husbands of female proprietors were often businessmen, artisans, or wage earners. For example, in the 1860s Mrs. Edward Jacques attended to her dry goods business in a small store connected to her husband's boot and shoe shop; both left business at the end of the decade, owners of a farm and an estate of approximately $20,000.[15] Many husbands of Albany businesswomen were also self-employed skilled craftsmen such as carpenters, shoemakers, chairmakers, and umbrella makers. For instance, Eliza Brate was a millinery proprietor between 1860 and 1874; during the same period, her husband Nicholas was a carpenter. In the 1870s Mrs. William Keay, a fancy goods dealer, shared a store with her husband, a paperhanger.[16] Other husbands worked at physical jobs, as laborers, teamsters, and carters. Numerous husbands also held regular salaried employment as bookkeepers, clerks, customs officials, hotel managers, firemen, and policemen, while their wives conducted business on their own. For instance, George Gale was employed as a salaried clerk while his wife Josephine "entirely managed" their ornamental hair business, worth approximately $5,000 in the 1870s.[17]

For women in mid-nineteenth-century Albany, marriage did not necessarily mean the end of a business career. In one striking case, Mary E. Hickey was a fancy goods dealer in her own right both before and after her marriage to grocer James W. Gillen in 1868, and operated her independent venture for over 55 years.[18] Nor did remarriage necessarily spell the end of a successful enterprise for widows. Mrs. John Carlton, for example, managed a grocery and saloon during her first marriage, after the death of her husband ("a very likely man" who left her property worth $4,000 or $5,000 in 1868), and again after her second marriage, to Pat Scully, in 1879.

Although many widowed businesswomen were left without substantial "means," few were entirely destitute. Indeed, most had to have some capital at their disposal in order to enter a business enterprise at all, and in many cases widows inherited their husbands' "entire" estates. Such estates might amount to a mere $1,000 (or less) in real estate and personal property, but they could range far higher. At the lower end of the scale, Mary Conroy inherited "by will the entire estate" of her husband Charles in 1878, including his saloon: "the prem[ise]s worth $3[000]—ho[use] & lot $3[000]—m[or]tg[ag]e $8[00]."[19] Receiving substantially more was Magdalene Hoffman, who inherited "all" that her husband Philip, a grocer, had left in 1878, estimated to be worth in the $10,000 range.[20] Four years later, the brewing business of Jacob Kirchner & Co., "est[imate]d worth

$40[000] or $50[000] independent of the Real Estate," was left entirely to his widow, Doretha.[21] What is notable in all three of these cases is that the widows did not unload the property or merely transfer ownership to male relatives (although Kirchner was assisted by her sons, and Hoffman lived with a son—a bookkeeper—old enough to run the business). Instead, all three women—two of whom could clearly have afforded to step out of the marketplace—continued to do business in their own names for years. Indeed, both Hoffman and Kirchner carried on their enterprises for more than a decade.

As for single women, although a few appear to have had no other means of survival than their own business enterprise and no discernible family support network, most were neither isolated individuals nor the sole providers for impoverished families. First, many single women either lived with, or received assistance from, relatives. Some were the daughters of successful entrepreneurs, artisans, or blue-collar workers. For instance, milliner Kate Bateman's father and brother were pavers, and according to the censuses of 1860 and 1870 she lived at home with sisters employed as a seamstress, a dressmaker, and a bookkeeper. When Bateman entered business in 1876, credit reporters noted that "her mother sold a house for $3m[3000] and no doubt helps her along."[22] Even if single businesswomen were operating without the support of their fathers—many of whom were deceased or otherwise absent—they were often the sisters of employed siblings, including brothers. Thus Mary Ann Duffy, the proprietor of a fancy goods establishment from 1830 to 1870, lived with her brother Edward, a physician and "at one time surgeon of police."[23]

Even those few businesswomen who were separated and divorced seem to have entered the marketplace with a specific skill or family backing— again, they were not simply victims of hard times with nowhere else to turn. For example, from 1869 through 1879 Margaret Heck (also identified as Margaret Schaffler), a divorcee, carried on a small business manufacturing cigars and selling tobacco. Though she had "not much means," she was able to parlay her previous experience and skills (her former husband was also a cigar and tobacco dealer) and her business acumen (she was called a "hardworking good bus[iness] woman" by credit examiners in 1875) into a venture that provided her with a living at least.[24]

What part did ambition play in the decision of women to enter the marketplace? Like many businessmen of the same period, some of Albany's female proprietors were working women who had made a conscious decision to move from employment to entrepreneurship, carefully saving funds from their earnings in order to strike out in business for themselves. Maggie Robb was a milliner who had been employed by a fancy dry goods shop for "quite a no. of y[ea]rs" before opening her own "small" store in 1867.

By 1874 Robb was said to be "d[oin]g ab[ou]t the best bus[iness] in the city"; a year later credit reports noted that she was "making a nice profit every year." By 1884, the year her credit entries end, her business was estimated worth up to $8,000—approximately eight times the capital she had started with 17 years earlier.[25]

Sharp businesswomen saw private enterprise as a moneymaking option and as a means to exercise their considerable business talents. Mrs. A. Hunt, the proprietor of a "snug" shoe business for more than 20 years (1851–73), was described as attending "to her bus[iness] from early morning till late at night." While the credit examiners characterized Mrs. Hunt as "the man of the concern," as well as "sharp as a thistle" and "good as wheat," her second husband was dismissed as a "Mr. Nobody." By the time the elderly Mrs. Hunt passed the business along to her son (or son-in-law; the records are unclear) in the early 1870s, her worth was estimated at $20,000 to $25,000, and she had moved out of the city.[26]

Some women, particularly female artisans such as dressmakers and milliners, appear to have entered business as an outlet for their skills and creativity—that is, their financial circumstances do not indicate a pressing need for employment; nor did they manage to generate large profits from their enterprises. For instance, three sisters, the "beloved" milliner siblings of successful steamboat captain Isaac Newton, carried on a small custom business for decades, from 1830 until about 1867. By 1859 the credit records noted that the surviving sister was "not d[oin]g much bus[iness]" but was "doing bus[iness] merely for occupation."[27]

Size, Worth, and Longevity of Women's Businesses

Despite women's prevalence in a variety of trades over these decades, there were only a handful of truly wealthy and prominent businesswomen in Albany, and no female tycoons. The stories of most female entrepreneurs tend to be "limited" success stories. Even the most profitable of their concerns never built up enterprises or personal estates worth more than $150,000, and many of their ventures were estimated as worth little or nothing by credit examiners. At the high end of the spectrum, the dry goods, cloths & cassimere business of Pohly & Company, owned by the widowed Hannah Pohly, employed a "working capital" of $85,000 and was doing a business of approximately $225,000 per year in 1881; the company was estimated to be worth $150,000 in 1883.[28] At the low end of the scale, dozens of tiny grocers, saloonkeepers, fancy goods dealers, variety store owners, and dressmakers were judged essentially "worthless"—an economic, rather than a moral, judgment—as in the case of Mrs. David Jackson, who ran a grocery and saloon described as a "one horse 'dive'" with "a few empty barrels, two or three bottles & a counter" in 1876.[29] Most typical were businesses that (at some point in their existence) were valued from a few hundred dollars to $1,000. For instance, the millinery establishment of Maggie Grimmons was estimated to be worth amounts fluctuating up and down from $600 to $1,000 in the sixteen years between 1866 and 1882.[30]

The size of women's endeavors can also be judged by the number of employees they supported and the types of services they advertised. On the basis of sporadic references, it appears that most female proprietors employed relatively few, if any, workers outside the family. At the modest end of the scale, Mrs. C. F. Carter, a fancy goods dealer, was reported to employ only "2 girls to do m[a]ch[ine] stitching" in 1871.[31] More unusual was Sarah Devlin, who was said to "have quite a shirt trade," giving "out work to some 10 or 12 girls" in 1875.[32] The largest workforce described in the credit ledgers under the name of a female entrepreneur was that of milliner Mary Harris, who was described as doing "the best bus[iness] here in her line" in 1850, and as keeping "20 or 30 women employ[e]d."[33] According to the Census of Manufactures of 1860, however, it seems clear that businesses owned (or co-owned) by women employed relatively few workers; only 12 of the enterprises belonging to female proprietors were listed (and one assumes these were the largest manufacturing concerns): 1 plumbing company, 1 trimmings business, 1 hair jeweler, 2 confectioners, and 7 milliners. Ridgeway & Co., plumbers, employed the most workers (12 men); the remaining businesses paid from 8 to 1 employees, with an average workforce of 4 individuals, mostly women.[34]

What of the longevity of women's enterprises? The mean length between the starting and ending date of female proprietors in Albany active between 1875 and 1885 (identified in the 1880 census and at least one other source) was more than 11 years, and the median length of such business activity was 7 years.[35] Only 15% left business within a year, and two-thirds remained active in business for more than 4 years. Statistically, as many of these female proprietors were active for more than 19 years (some 20%) as left business within 2 years. Most impressive, 10% of businesswomen were still in business *25 years* after they first began.

There was clearly a wide range in the longevity of business ventures in mid-nineteenth-century Albany. Numerous female-run enterprises visited by credit examiners lasted for only a year or two, such as the grocery operated by Ellen Berrigan in 1877. With "small means & prospects indiff[eren]t," it was reported "out" of business in August of 1878.[36] Some female proprietors went in and out of business in a matter of months. In

April 1852, for instance, the first credit entry for Mrs. C. Rafferty stated that she was "reputed" to be worth $4,000 or $5,000, but her business venture ended in failure only three months later in July.[37] In the case of Mrs. Margaret Hunter, the Fancy Goods business established in March of 1871 with a cash outlay of $1,200 had failed by October of the same year.[38]

The operations of other businesswomen, however, spanned decades, some careers stretching into twenty, thirty, forty, or even fifty years. Milliners appear to have had particularly long-lasting ventures; Mary Roberts, for instance, was listed as a milliner in the city directory of 1830, and in the R.G. Dun & Co. credit records from 1840 until 1883, meriting twice-yearly entries twice at the height of her popularity from the late 1840s through the early 1860s. Described as "one of our best & most fashionable milliners" in 1842, she was called "one of the princip[al] milliners in town" in 1854, and the "leading milliner of the place" ten years later. However, according to the last entry under her name in the 1880s, when she would have been about 70 years old: "She is a person quite advanced in years . . . & does only a sm[al]l business."[39]

Sources of Capital and Credit

It appears that women tapped a wide array of sources for start-up cash to fund their enterprises. Even the smallest required some minimal outlay, since inexperienced women were rarely judged good risks for credit unless they had substantial "means" (for instance, real estate holdings). Yet money had to be found—a female peddler needed goods to hawk on the street, as did a small shopkeeper selling from behind a counter out of her rented rooms. Stock worth $50 to $100 might be seen as "poor" by the R.G. Dun & Co. credit examiners (though worth considerably more in today's dollars, as previously discussed), but some stock had to be purchased, and some type of fixtures—if only a modest sales counter—installed. Larger and more ambitious enterprises required the rental of a storefront, the outfitting of an elegant salon (in the case of fashionable milliners), or even newly constructed buildings (as in the case of dry goods dealers or hotel keepers). In addition, for all but the smallest ventures, employees had to be paid a minimal wage, or at least supported with room and board (in the case of apprentices and relatives).

R.G. Dun & Co. credit records indicate that most women raised the funds to start new businesses by using personal savings, inherited cash, loans from relatives, or money from insurance policies. In Albany, the source of savings most often mentioned by credit examiners seems to have been women's previous earnings. For example, when Madame J. DeBlock opened a dressmaking establishment in 1875, it was said that she had previously been in the "employ of a N[ew] Y[ork] house" and was "known to have several [hundred] dollars in [the] savings b[an]k."[40] Two other sources of cash for starting—or continuing—a business came from inheritance and loans. Thus, when Hattie Reno and her partner Miss Alida Tandy set up a millinery shop in 1879, credit reports noted that Tandy had "inherited $1[000] from her mother a few mo[nth]s ago & is using 7[00] in the bus[iness]," while Reno ("said to be assisted by her sister") contributed the same amount.[41] Insurance policies were also an important source of cash for businesswomen in Albany. In 1875, for instance, Mary Dinkel established a bakery with some $2,000 worth of life insurance paid to her after her husband's death.[42] Even money won through the courts could be used to fund business endeavors—thus Catherine Bernhardt set up a millinery business in 1859 based on "a j[u]dg[men]t" from "one of the Eastern RR C[ompanie]s for $4[000] for killing her husband."[43] Many women also borrowed from relatives, or received outright gifts of cash for the purpose of "setting them up" in trade (more examples appear in the following chapter on family networks).

In addition to using cash directly to establish their businesses, most women had to be able obtain credit for their purchases, at least from local suppliers. Generally, credit investigators recommended a limited credit in cases where women were known to "be worth" some money in terms of savings, real estate, or personal property. However, despite the warnings of credit evaluators, most of Albany's businesswomen appear to have been able to supplement their personal investments with at least "a small line" of credit from "one or two" local wholesale supply houses in order to stock their concerns. Even a modest grocery and saloon, such as that of Margaret Delancy, estimated in 1878 to be "worth 00" and to merit only "COD" sales, was acknowledged by the same credit examiner during the following year to have received "a small line of cr[edit] on usual time" from "one house here," and to have made payments that were "reasonably prompt."[44] For many of Albany's businesswomen, such local trust seems to have been all that was needed to assure at least a minimal level of business survival. Delancy's small enterprise, for instance, was evaluated in the credit records for four years, and listed in the city directories for eleven.

Variations in Proprietorship

The words "business proprietor" suggest an individual with sole responsibility and authority to act on behalf of an enterprise. In the case of

Albany's mid-nineteenth-century businesswomen, however, proprietorship can be a slippery concept to apply, as has been discussed in the previous chapter. There were certainly individual women who ran their businesses alone—spinsters and widows for whom there is no hint of confusion regarding their legal authority and personal responsibility to run their ventures as "femme sole" traders. For instance, there was no ambiguity for a single milliner such as Matilda Cornock, who did a "small custom and retail bus[iness]" from 1868 until she "sold out" in 1872.[45] Even married women in Albany were able to pursue their own independent business careers. For instance, in 1867 credit records noted of Eliza A. Anthony, a dealer in children's clothing and the wife of a machinist, that "'Mrs. A.' manages her own affairs & pays her own bills."[46] In the 1870s, when the widowed baker Elizabeth Herzog married dry goods dealer Joseph Belser, she carried on the bakery business "in her own name & independent of that of her husband," according to credit reports.[47] Interestingly, Herzog even lived separately from Belser and his children while, with her own children, she operated the business she had inherited from her first husband.[48]

But in many other cases, the R.G. Dun & Co. credit records reveal a wide range of legal and financial responsibility for women associated with capitalist enterprises. Businesswomen in mid-nineteenth-century Albany acted in partnerships, both legal and informal, as legal principals in endeavors managed by male relatives, and as investors. Although the role of women in each of these situations differed, it is important to recognize and acknowledge such variations in order to appreciate the complexity of female involvement in the marketplace during this period. I argue that Albany businesswomen included not only women who owned and operated businesses in their own names but also those identified by credit records as running, or actively assisting in, businesses officially listed under the names of male relatives.

In cases of partnerships, obviously, the proprietorship of an endeavor was shared, as was legal responsibility for its operation and debts. Mary and Ellen Hartnett were sisters of "good char[acter] and hab[it]s" who opened a combined millinery and dressmaking business in 1860; in 1866 credit records praised them as "g[oo]d steady industrious girls doing a good bus[iness]," and they continued operations into the 1870s.[49] Outside the typically female realm of fashion, Mrs. John Henry and her daughter ran a saloon "between" them in 1881. Even unrelated women joined in partnerships, as in the case of milliners Maggie Manifold and Johanna Murray, known to the trade as Manifold & Murray, who joined forces in 1880 and continued as partners until 1886.

Brothers and sisters, or husbands and wives, also became legal partners. In 1882 John M. Briggs & Co. opened a shop featuring gentlemen's furnishing goods; the "company" was Sarah D. Briggs, his wife, who brought about $2,000 "of her own means" to the concern, while her husband furnished $4,000 and "a good knowledge of the bus[iness]."[50] That same year Catharine Bleecker, variously described as the sister or wife of Thomas S. Bleecker by the credit examiners, entered into a partnership with Thomas to sell wholesale liquors. She was said to have invested $4,000 in the venture and to be worth approximately $10,000.[51]

One exceptional businesswoman even became the partner of a man to whom she was not apparently related. The widowed Rosa Orthelier was a "smart" entrepreneur who had been a forewoman at a large fancy goods store before her marriage to peddler Daniel Orthelier. During his lifetime she was described as the manager of their dry goods shop, and at the time of his death credit examiners reported, "wife manages the bus[iness] well. She is intelligent &c. Think the bus[iness] will prosper in her hands." Soon after Daniel's death in 1874, Rosa formed a partnership with jeweler Ferdinand Neuman "under the style of Orthelier & Newman." Together they shared a store that specialized in millinery and jewelry, each of the proprietors being worth about $8,000 individually. Their arrangement was dissolved, however, after little more than a year, with each returning to his or her previous independent ventures.[52]

In Albany women also became the legal "principals" in business, while their male relatives acted as their agents—generally in the cases where male relatives had previously failed and could not legally operate in their own names (approximately 6% of businesswomen had husbands or other male relatives who were said to be acting as their agents, according to credit reports).[53] Indeed, over the decades women in Albany acted as business principals for fathers, husbands, brothers, sons, and sons-in-law. Thus in 1874 Fanny Loveday, married to a man of "no ability or means" who had previously failed in business twice, served as the legal owner of the confectionery and candy shop where he was "doing bus[iness]" in her name.[54] A decade later, in the 1880s, the Thompson Chemical Company was officially owned by Helen Thompson but "carried on under the management of her husband," Ashley, "a bankrupt" who, credit reports warned, "does not hold anything in his own name."[55]

Overall, it is evident that female microentrepreneurs in mid-nineteenth-century Albany employed a range of business strategies in terms of raising capital and establishing proprietorships, and indeed that many women who were active in the marketplace did not necessarily fit the simple concept of "proprietor" at all. A study of the credit reports for Albany reveals many fascinating variations in the characteristics and experiences of individual female entrepreneurs, which will be analyzed at length in following chapters.

Conclusion

The range of women's experiences in the mid-nineteenth-century Albany marketplace was quite diverse. Businesswomen could be single, married, widowed, separated, or divorced. Their trades might be associated with the female sphere, such as dressmaking and millinery, or they might own the controlling interest in a far more "masculine" type of business, such as a livery stable or brewery. They might be operating tiny groceries out of the front rooms of their dwellings, or they could be supervising stores or factories with separate, official business premises. Their customers might be made up primarily of neighbors and acquaintances, or they might advertise in city directories that their services were available "throughout the state" (as in the case of plumbing entrepreneur Julia Ridgway, whose career will be discussed in chapter 7). Women's enterprises might last for a season or two, or as long as fifty years. Although most engaged in only one line of work, some branched out into other businesses—as with Caroline A. Sill, who operated both a gentlemen's furnishing goods store and a commercial laundry. If such variety existed within their ranks, is it possible to draw any further conclusions about this population and their businesses as a group?

First, women did not enter the competitive realm of business only when "forced" to do so. Proprietorship was a choice taken by specific individual women for particular reasons—financial, personal, familial—at particular points in their lives. Or, as Edith Sparks has concluded of San Francisco's female proprietors:

> The majority of businesswomen . . . [were] motivated by personal as well as economic factors. Neither paupers nor independently wealthy, they chose proprietorship both because it earned them income to support their families, help buy a house, or pay for their own monthly expenses, and because it utilized their skills, engaged their interest, and fit their schedules and budgets. More importantly, they turned to small business ownership because it enabled them to make money without abandoning their family obligations.[56]

Although the patterns of their participation varied by class, race, nativity and region, and over time, it is evident that many women of diverse backgrounds made the choice for proprietorship, and that over the century tens of thousands of individual women braved the perils of an erratic capitalist economy by going into private enterprise.

There does, however, appear to have been a "glass ceiling" above which female-owned and -managed businesses in Albany never rose. This is particularly clear in the case of millinery establishments. While women built up their businesses slowly, year by year, to perhaps the $10,000 range, a few men beginning with the same capital were able to transform their millinery enterprises into large wholesale houses or jobbers by the 1880s, businesses worth up to $150,000. In terms of other types of commercial and manufacturing endeavors, it is clear that the most successful businessmen in Albany—men such as the hardware magnate, railroad investor, and bank president Erastus Corning—were able to become millionaires in the same period in which the wealthiest businesswomen very rarely earned personal fortunes approaching $100,000 (and all of these women were widows carrying on a family business started earlier in their husbands' names).

Most women who succeeded in "big" business required capital from men—generally fathers, husbands, or lovers—to launch their ventures. Wives who assisted in family enterprises continued to bear primary responsibility for housekeeping, child-rearing, and entertaining—tasks that necessarily limited their ability to concentrate fully on business matters. While it was common for women to establish home-based shops and to take part in family concerns, it was quite unusual for them to set up incorporated firms outside the home, to travel extensively for business, or to engage in long-distance commerce. Overall, most nineteenth-century American businesswomen were self-employed free agents hoping to earn a livelihood or to supplement their family income—not venture capitalists.

Still, in a period when most wage work available to women offered options that were severely restricted and poorly paid, the cash income generated by female business enterprises made a significant contribution to their own survival and the welfare of their families. Although female microentrepreneurs may have faced prejudices based on sexual stereotypes, as well as significant legal challenges, and while most encountered problems raising capital and securing credit, they also found ingenious ways to circumvent these difficulties and to forge ahead with business careers. Whether they were elite entrepreneurial leaders, active contributors to family enterprises, or minicapitalists struggling to use small business as a means of self-employment, women made a significant contribution to the burgeoning economy of the United States and (as will be discussed in the following chapter) formed a vital link in local business networks.

CHAPTER FOUR

●

Micronetworks and the
Family Business Economy

The enduring presence of women in family firms argues against the prevailing history, which emphasizes individual male self-interest and success, the importance of male inheritance of businesses across generations, and the understanding of finance and capital accumulation as a man's world.

Apparently, the business world within which men and women worked was less heroic and more familial than hitherto imagined.

—Pamela Sharpe (2001)[1]

JOHN JACOB ASTOR IS A FIGURE of mythic proportions in the history of American business, and one of perhaps half a dozen businessmen (including Andrew Carnegie, John D. Rockefeller, J. P. Morgan, Henry Ford, and now Bill Gates) whose place is enshrined in the narrative of U.S. history as well. His wife, Sarah Todd Astor, is not well known in American, business, or women's history. Yet as an example of how our conventional models of business activity and achievement need to be modified, we might briefly consider the intriguing story of her contribution to the Astor business empire, presented almost thirty years ago in the first history of businesswomen in the United States, Caroline Bird's *Enterprising Women*. According to Bird, Sarah Todd and her mother were running a boarding house (a typically female business), when a young German immigrant, John Jacob Astor, arrived almost penniless in New York City. After Todd married Astor (her former boarder) in 1785, he was able to leave his job as a clerk for a fur-trading concern; with the money from her dowry, they opened a small shop selling imported musical instruments and furs. Since John Jacob was often away purchasing furs, the running of the shop was frequently left to Sarah, who also gave birth to eight children and raised them in the rooms above the store. Sarah assisted in the difficult work of processing furs, and became an expert in assessing their quality. Finally, Sarah advised her husband to invest the family profits in New York City real estate and took advantage of her family connections to arrange deals—a move that, even more than the China trade, eventually provided the basis of Astor's fortune. Once that fortune was established, Sarah asked to be paid for her "consulting" work evaluating furs for trade with Asia, and was indeed paid $500 an hour by the company for her expertise—money she used for charitable purposes.[2]

The wealth of John Jacob Astor, America's first millionaire, is legendary. As a "self-made man" of the early republic, Astor follows in the footsteps of Benjamin Franklin (whose wife, Deborah, was also closely involved in his business affairs) and foreshadows the Horatio Alger model of the post–Civil War period.[3] In the history of American business, Astor is conceptualized as an icon, a hero—an individual.[4] Consider the difference between the history recounted by Bird, summarized above, and the narrative of John Steele Gordon in *The Reader's Companion to American History,* which makes no mention of Sarah Todd Astor at all—no mention of their marriage, her family connections, the role of her dowry in establishing their business, or her subsequent management, expertise, and advice.[5] Yet once one begins to look at the businesswoman in this picture, the Astor business clearly appears as a family business, and John Jacob's brilliant entrepreneurship as part of a "team" effort, at least during its formative years.

Although a few businesswomen in Albany—single women and widows without children—may in fact have pursued entrepreneurship as individuals, most female proprietors were enmeshed in family relationships and responsibilities. Rather than echoing the model of the self-made man as an independent economic actor (a model that, in any case, has been overdrawn), these women acted within networks that both supported and constrained them.[6]

Patterns of interdependence dominated the careers—and lives—of mid-nineteenth-century businesswomen in the city of Albany. The vast majority of these female proprietors were not isolated, independent, individualistic entrepreneurs fighting a lonely battle in the cutthroat marketplace of nineteenth-century commerce and industry. They were instead members of multiple intersecting, interactive, and interdependent networks—networks made up of family, friends, neighbors, suppliers, creditors, and customers. Such networks provided labor, managerial expertise, capital investment, collateral, commercial space, credit and loans, personal endorsements, goods and supplies, and ultimately profits—yet some networks also operated in ways that constrained businesswomen's options by limiting credit, refusing support, draining financial resources, or blackening business reputations. Contacts, particularly between family and friends, were vital to female microentrepreneurs, just as these businesswomen were vital to local economic networks. Evidence from mid-nineteenth-century Albany reveals an economy in which men and women often interacted, and the most basic categories of analysis—including proprietorship itself—once again appear far more fluid than anticipated.

An interesting case of dual male-female family management and ownership can be seen in the story of the theatrical Trimble family. John Montague Trimble was a noted theater architect who managed Albany's Academy of Music in the early 1860s but suffered from ill health. According to Henry Pitt Phelps's *Players of A Century: A Record Of The Albany Stage* (first published in 1880), the Academy opened in 1863 under the "nominal management of J. M. Trimble, Jr." Unfortunately, the "Young Trimble was then only 18 years old, and hardly fitted for the responsible position in which he found himself . . . and was continued there only one season." After his son's departure, the elder Trimble, though virtually blind, once again took over management. An attempt to sell the theater was unsuccessful. He was assisted until his death by his daughter, who in 1867 assumed the entire operation of the theatre as "sole lessee and proprietor." As Phelps tells the tale, during her father's infirmity Miss A. G. Trimble had "been his constant attendant in the box office, and aided him all that she could, even to counting the house." As death approached, Trimble asked his daughter to "undertake the management when he was gone." Though only 24, and "reluctant to assume such responsibility," she eventually agreed. Described as an "enterprising and plucky little manager," Miss Trimble carried on for five months, until the theatre burned and the season abruptly ended. Nevertheless, the shortened season had netted some $8,000, and the young woman was soon engaged to one Lucien Barnes, who proceeded to build the Trimble Opera House—named for her father.[7] Mrs. M. A. Trimble, Miss Trimble's mother and the owner of the Olympic Theatre in New York City, backed Barnes (now her son-in-law) in erecting and operating the new theatre. When his attempt ended in failure two-and-a-half years later, he owed her approximately $26,000.[8]

The "enterprising and plucky" Miss Trimble appears as a businesswoman in none of the usual sources, and we would not know of her existence without Phelps's history. Yet the joint management of a father-and-son enterprise, followed by a father-and-daughter operation, followed by the sole proprietorship of a daughter for one season, followed by the marriage of that daughter to another theatrical manager, Lucien Barnes, and his construction of a new theater funded by her mother (the widow of the original J. M. Trimble), reveals the type of mixed family proprietorship and management common to many of Albany's smaller enterprises.

Unfortunately, the major sources used for this study (city directories, the manuscript census, and credit reports) do not allow us to fully investigate and chart the complexity of family and business networks. Rather, they provide a glimpse into a variety of situations in which one can see fragments of networks in operation, enabling us to speculate on the scope and impact of such connections. Many of what one might call credit report "snap-shots" disclose overlapping networks, areas where webs connecting business associates and family members, friends and lenders, or credit examiners and suppliers appear as interwoven. As revealed by the credit reports of R.G. Dun & Co., women's microentrepreneurial networks in the city of Albany were wide-ranging and complex. Familial, business, neighborhood, and community networks both supported and limited businesswomen.

Just as we must challenge the standard definitions of terms such as "success" and "entrepreneurship" as applicable to nineteenth-century businesswomen in the United States, it is necessary to tweak the definition of "network" in order to make it useful for most female proprietors in this period. It was only the rarest American businesswoman who was directly connected to national or international networks of materials, labor, or finance. The networks of Albany's female microentrepreneurs were local and personal, creating interdependence between individuals. The complexity of this interdependence contrasts both with the Victorian stereotype of female dependence and the nineteenth-century model of the independent, individualist businessman. Yet these micronetworks made it possible for female proprietors to function on a day-to-day basis, contributing to the support of their families, providing goods and services to their customers, and operating as a vital link of supply (to workers and their families) and demand (from wholesalers) in the local business economy of an industrializing city.

Most businesswomen in mid-nineteenth-century Albany established modest, home-based businesses that began and remained small. Women who were dressmakers and milliners tended to set up "independent" concerns or partnerships with female relatives or associates. Dry and fancy goods dealers, grocers, saloon- and hotel keepers, bakers and confectioners, however, were often involved in family enterprises that included male relatives. Women who appear as owners of unusual types of concerns (such as undertaking, pharmaceutical manufacturing, blacksmith shops, or furniture dealerships) were usually either legal principals for their previously bankrupt husband-managers, or the widows of men who had established and run these businesses before their deaths. Above all, the majority of these female proprietors were firmly ensconced within social networks of family, friends, and neighbors who assisted their business endeavors in a wide variety of ways, while operating within local business networks that sometimes supported—and sometimes restricted—their success.

The Family as a Supportive Network

The most important supportive network for microentrepreneurs in nineteenth-century Albany was clearly the extended family (including spouses, parents, siblings, children, aunts, uncles, nephews, nieces, cousins, and in-laws). Businesswomen in mid-nineteenth-century Albany enjoyed the assistance of family members as co-proprietors, paid and unpaid workers, and domestic helps, as well as sources of start-up capital, loans, commercial space, and other types of financial and moral backing. Many families worked together, either in the same family business, or side-by-side, in complementary ventures. Research on Albany's businesswomen has uncovered multiple female-female partnerships of sisters, or mother and daughters, in such trades as dressmaking or millinery. However, the R.G. Dun & Co. credit records also reveal a far more complex picture, with mothers and sons, fathers and daughters, husbands and wives, brothers and sisters, even aunts and in-laws forming familial networks that sustained female proprietors in a wide variety of ways. In some cases these relatives were partners, in others backers, in others founders who passed a business on or followers who took over a business. There is some overlap here as well, since in some cases women-owned businesses interacted with several relatives for different reasons.

Numerous relatives are cited by credit examiners as the partners, employees, and supporters of female-owned or -operated enterprises, while census records confirm that most businesswomen lived in households with several relatives. A statistical analysis of individual businesswomen located in the 1880 manuscript census showed that their household size ranged from one to thirteen individuals, with an average household size of four. In the most basic day-to-day operation of a home-based business—running a boarding house or a small store, for instance—family members were on the scene and contributed to the family enterprise with their labor, expertise, and a myriad of domestic services required for the maintenance of nineteenth-century households. Let us start, then, by exploring the range of ways in which relatives assisted female proprietors.

An obvious form of networking is the formation of a partnership, legal or informal. For female microentrepreneurs, partnerships shared the work, and the risk, while increasing a business's capital and connections. In Albany, female relatives typically joined each other as partners in the needlework trades. For example, milliners Hannah and Jane Singer, called "industrious women and worthy of credit," lived and worked together from approximately 1870 to 1880.[9] Mothers and daughters became partners as well. In 1871 Frederica Meroth and her daughter Christine entered the millinery and fancy goods business; although the mother's moral character was suspect because—as the credit examiners put it—she "don't live with her husband," the daughter was considered "a very nice respectable hardwork[in]g girl," and their fledgling enterprise received a little credit "on her a/c[count]."[10] In other cases the ownership of a concern was passed from mother to daughter, as when the "widow Lady" Sarah Devilin—described as "very indus[trious] & econ[omica]l in her hab[it]s"—saw her business in ladies' underwear closed by the sheriff in 1877 (after some twelve years of operation) but reopened almost immediately "in the name of her married daughter Mrs. W. Wood."

Outside the realm of needlework and female fashion, mothers and daughters in Albany also joined in running groceries and saloons, selling boots and shoes, and operating bakeries or small retail stores. However, in these cases it was far less likely that the family would set up an official partnership under both names. Often the daughter's name does not come to light until her mother's death, when the credit entry states that a previously unnamed daughter not only inherits the business but is well qualified to carry it on. As noted in chapter 1, when Mary Roseboom inherited the fancy goods business of her mother Mary McAllister in 1883, the credit examiners noted that "she has had management of the bus[iness] for sometime & understands it well."[11]

Yet it was actually more common for businesswomen to engage in enterprises with male relatives—husbands, brothers, fathers, and sons—in both official and unofficial partnerships. For instance, the name of Ellen Owen never appears in city directories as an entrepreneur, yet credit records refer to the dry goods business she and her husband operated from 1868 to 1879 as "Mrs. E. Owen & Edward Owen." According to their entries, Ellen was "a smart bus[iness] woman that helps him consid[erably]" and "a careful manager."[12] In fact, the credit entries abound with examples of women independently operating commercial concerns that legally belonged to their husbands, fathers, or brothers. For example, in 1869 credit examiners noted that in the case of a small grocery and saloon owned by one George Dell, his wife Anna "manages the bus[iness] in his absence," while her husband worked "by the day."[13] In the similar case of Mrs. William Colvin, a fancy goods dealer from 1868 to 1883, credit reports revealed that "bus[iness] is the 'husbands' but 'wife' attends to it."[14]

Or consider the family of Michael O'Sullivan, a "smart active man." Beginning their careers as teachers in the 1850s, his wife and daughters ran his Catholic bookstore while he became a boat inspector, a captain in the 63rd Regiment during the Civil War, and later a clerk in the secretary of state's office. His daughter Eliza continued in the book business (which she and her mother inherited) after his death in 1874, finally becoming the legal proprietor. Carrying on in her parents' entrepreneurial footsteps,

Eliza O'Sullivan remained in this line for more than twenty years, despite the fact that she married one Charles McAuley in 1883, owned real estate, and was estimated to be "safely worth $4,000."[15]

Another common situation found a husband and wife, or father and daughter, working side by side. One couple with complementary business interests were Mr. and Mrs. Theodore Yaumans—she was a hairdresser, he a jeweler, and together they manufactured the elaborate hair pieces and hair jewelry (rings, broaches) so popular in the late Victorian period. Credit reports describe them as "comfortably off," and worth $5,000 each.[16] Although such wives might not have enjoyed any legal status as proprietors while these husbands were alive, they often became the "sole" inheritors of their spouse's estates and were able to carry on business without interruption. Widows of bakers and confectioners in Albany, for instance, frequently took over business operations on their husbands' deaths and continued to run their concerns for years. Thus Grace Anderson kept up the bakery started by her husband, Charles, from his death in 1844 until 1857, while Elizabeth Crummy, widow of the baker Michael, began to do business in her own name after his death in 1875 and continued to do so at least through 1891.

Evidence from the R.G. Dun & Co. credit ledgers also reveals a surprisingly strong connection between business-minded mothers and their sons. While young sons provided reliable labor as clerks and errand boys, mothers trained them in business methods and prepared them to take over business management—and proprietorship—later in life. As boys became men, they often managed in their mothers' names before inheriting the business. Three women even used "& Son" in the names of their firms: Mrs. James Blake & Son were saw manufacturers from 1859 to 1861, Mrs. E. Owens & Son opened a confectionery in 1878 (after which son George took over sole proprietorship), and Barbara Singer & Son operated a grocery (she alone from 1874 to 1879, his name added then.)

The occupations of bookkeeper and store clerk appear regularly among the sons of female proprietors, suggesting that young men were often "brought up" in business techniques, even if they did not move into their mother's enterprises. It appears that small businesses served as a training ground for commercial careers and a means of passing on business acumen. Mrs. Alida Hendrickson, praised in her own right as "much respected" and making "something over" a living in her dry goods business for 15 years, was described in 1862 as having "3 enterprising sons, 2 in store with her."[17] Twenty years later, they were running a real estate venture.

It is difficult to judge, in many of these cases, who was helping whom. In the case of mothers and sons in business together, for example, was the son "assisting" the mother, or was she assisting him by setting up or continuing a business until he was of legal age or otherwise ready to "take over" the concern? Was the mother's business an inheritance for the son, or simply a training ground for any business career? Let us consider two stories from the boot and shoe trade in the 1870s and '80s. In 1875 Mary Hansen was the proprietress of a "Catholic" bookstore she had inherited from her husband, while her son John, aged 16, worked as an "errand boy"—possibly hers, though perhaps for wages outside the family in order to bring in needed cash.[18] By 1879 credit records note that her son was "assisting her in the purchase of stock & c.," and by 1883 the ledgers note, "in the matter of correspondence the son assists his mother & looks after her affairs more or less," although (according to the census) John was working in a shoe factory at the time.[19] In 1877 Rosalie Blatner opened a boot and shoe business in partnership with her nephew, A. B. Nye, who had "no experience" in the business, though a "young man of g[oo]d rep[u]t[atio]n." The wealthy Mrs. Blatner (her estimated worth was a whopping $100,000) was not only partnering with her nephew but planning "for the benefit of her son a minor (17)," to whom she planned to transfer her share when he came of age. Indeed, in 1881 the original partnership was dissolved as Mrs. Blatner withdrew, while it was reported that "her son Meyer H. B. takes her place & the firm name is continued," each partner now putting up half of the start-up capital of $15,000. By the time Rosalie Blatner died in 1883, both her nephew and her son appear to have been well established in a "good" business.[20] Sons-in-law also played an important role in this web of family-business relationships, marrying into a family business.

It was far more common, however, for mothers to be active in their son's business, or sons in the mother's, without an official joint proprietorship. For instance, in 1844 the widowed Ruth Waterman was carrying on her dry goods business at "the old stand" started by her husband Jeremiah, now "aided by her son." By 1849 the concern had been transferred to the name of her son Edgar, but she was still said to be both "interested" and "responsible"; in 1850 the credit entry judged them to be "alike in int[erest]"—that is, investment—in the enterprise.[21]

A different kind of female-male business management can be seen in the case of milliner Mary Roberts and her husband, Asa. In the 1840s credit reporters wrote scathingly of Asa as "a poor lazy husband whom she supports," though Mary herself was called "one of our best and most fashionable milliners." In the 1850s credit reports continued to complain that Mary was supporting "a good for 00 husband," adding that he was "said to be a lawyer" but characterizing him instead as "a sort of pimp supported by his wife." As decade followed decade, credit examiners stressed that Asa ("an extravagant fellow") was supported by his wife's business. However, the back of one of Mary Roberts's bills from April 1840, addressed to Mrs. Erastus Corning, wife of the prominent citizen and entrepreneur, notes that payment was received by "A. C. Roberts." Might Asa have been acting as his wife's business manager while she designed and made hats, and supervised the shop? (On the other hand, most of the bills were signed by Mary herself, so perhaps the credit investigators were correct about Asa's "shiftless" ways.)[22]

Paid and unpaid helpers obviously provided a vital support system for all but the smallest female microentrepreneurs, and many businesswomen in Albany appear to have employed their own relatives. Credit entries on milliners and fancy goods dealers often mention daughters as assistants, though it is impossible to determine whether they were paid. In the case of Melia Epstein, a widowed millinery who failed in 1883, the credit report noted, "Her failure is said to have been brought about by the extravagant habits of her son, who has had the charge of her books & financial matters." Not only was her son acting as the business's bookkeeper but it was reported that Epstein owed $350 to her daughter Ida, "claimed to be the amt due her for services & c.," suggesting that Ida, too, had been working for her mother.[23]

Daughters assisted female proprietors in equally important, if officially unrecorded, ways. Statistical analysis of the 1880 census reveals a large proportion of businesswomen's first and second daughters who were neither attending school nor engaged in wage work. This female labor pool—comprising more than half of eldest daughters, and more than a third of second daughters, or more than 200 individual women for the 623 proprietors located—provided their mothers with an important source of labor for work in a home-based business and assistance with other household work. The fact that these young women were not recorded as employed or occupied by census enumerators can be considered "natural" in light of the underreporting of female occupations in city directories and of female business activities in the census itself. Since 90% of daughters were unmarried, most would not have had children of their own to care for and would have been free to assist their mothers with both business and household work. Whether they would have been paid for such labor or simply "supported" by the family cannot be determined from the sources used for this study.

Similarly, the officially unemployed adult sisters and mothers of single business owners may also have formed a labor pool of female workers who were available to assist in home-based business or, alternately, to provide businesswomen support on the domestic front by cooking, cleaning, shopping, and doing laundry, errands, and all the necessary tasks to support the family businesswoman and any wage earners within the household. In fact, single businesswomen lived in slightly larger households than average for all female proprietors in 1880, with a mean household size of 4.9 individuals. In these households, 70% lived with at least one female relative. For instance, of the 140 single female proprietors identified in the 1880 manuscript census, 42% lived with their mothers. With a mean age of 54, many of these mothers would have been capable of assisting their daughters with commercial or domestic chores; according to the census, only 6% of these mothers were employed. Although none of these female relatives were counted as being in business by the census or city directories, and it is impossible to quantify their contributions, they were undoubtedly important supports to each family enterprise.

The Family Business Economy

In many cases, a jointly operated business appears to have engaged the entire family, but it was actually more common to families in Albany to mix a home-based business with wage earning by some family members. Given evidence from the credit ledgers, manuscript census, and city directories, I would suggest that the concept of a nineteenth-century "family wage economy," famously described by Joan Scott and Louise Tilly, needs to be broadened to include a "family business economy" as well.[24] In some families, two businesses operated at once (often in the same location) to support the group. In other Albany families—especially immigrant families who had come from Ireland or Germany—the family business and family wage economies worked to complement each other, with some members engaging in wage work while others ran the home-based business—even switching off from time to time. Much as Carole Turbin has described the ways in which wage earners in Troy were able to balance the family economy by diversifying occupations, family business endeavors provided a safety net of support for family wage workers, and vice versa.[25] Or, as Sarah Deutsch noted in her study of Boston, "The slim phrase 'family economy' stands for more than cooperative housekeeping by multiple earners. It stands for continual shifting of roles between men, women, and children or earner, caretaker, and housekeeper and a continual jockeying for resources."[26]

Thus, millinery proprietors lived with sisters or daughters who were wage-earning needleworkers, and retail dealers with husbands or sons who were artisans or salaried government clerks. For instance, Mary Miller operated "her husband's" grocery store in 1871 while he worked as a cutter, and Mrs. Joseph Young attended to the family variety store (legally in her husband's name) from 1877 to 1882, while he worked "at his trade" as a cooper.[27] Children were clearly a vital part of these family ventures. In the mid-1870s the fancy goods and millinery shop owned by Peter Hecker (who worked at "the RR depot") was managed by his wife, "help'd by daughters who are smart girls."[28]

In addition to providing partners and workers, relatives sometimes shared or directly provided businesswomen with commercial premises. From 1857 to 1883, Elizabeth Bingham ran a fancy goods store in the same space where her husband worked "at his bench" as a boot- and shoe maker.[29] In 1868 Fannie Mendel opened a fancy goods and millinery shop in the "same store as her father's jewelry" establishment (in this case, her father also provided the capital and stock for his daughter's venture).[30] Likewise, the location of a dry goods store operated by widow Margaret Kempf in the 1870s was owned by her father, who was said to have "helped her" establish the shop.[31]

Financial Assistance

As we have discussed, loans, inheritance, or backing by family members provided many of Albany's businesswomen with start-up funds and a creditworthy reputation; women borrowed from relatives or received outright gifts of cash for the purpose of "setting them up" in trade. For instance, the widowed Minnie Redstone continued the family dry goods store after the death of her husband Isaac in 1865 by using "some means" provided by "a brother in the west," while a cousin, Mr. Mann, of the large dry goods store Mann Waldman & Co., did "all the buying for her."[32] Similarly, Mrs. Myer A. Lind, a fancy goods dealer separated from her husband, was assisted by her brother. According to a credit report of 1881, "Owing to troubles between herself & her husband she has put her bus[iness] into the hands of her brother Sol. Levy of Amsterdam where he is engaged in the D[ry] G[oods] bus[iness]. He virtually owns the establishment, but Mrs. Lind has the care of it and her earnings are accounted her own." It seems that Mrs. Lind's family assisted her—not with money, but with the necessary help to maintain her own business and make an independent living for herself.[33] In the 1870s the fancy goods and shoe shop of Mrs. Patrick Kieley was "started by her sister Mrs. Catherine Deering who bo[ugh]t the stock wor[th] ab[ou]t $8[00] to be paid for out of the proceeds of the sales."[34] In 1882 credit examiners noted that the fancy goods dealer Mrs. James Fisher had been left a widow with "no prop[ert]y" by the death of her husband (a butcher) the previous winter but "the relatives" had "raised an am[oun]t of 4 or 5[00] $ wh[ich] they gave Mrs. Fisher for the purpose of setting her up in bus[iness]."[35]

Some women entered business by directly inheriting a going concern as well as the profits it had generated. For instance, in 1878 Harriet Minch inherited "the greater part of her mothers estate," estimated to be worth $8,000 to $10,000, including her retail grocery store—the business and building.[36] At times, businesswomen simply took over enterprises built up by their relatives; in a second case from 1878, Miss Delia Devereux assumed proprietorship of the grocery and fancy goods business of her brother Thomas, who, according to credit reports "retires on a[c]c[ount] of ill health."[37]

Gaining credit in Albany often depended on a woman's financial worth—whether she had assets enough to be able to pay her debts if her business failed. Such assets were often inherited from relatives. The widowed and remarried Eliza C. Carey began a hotel in 1876 backed by property she had "acquired thro[ugh] her former husband," and later inherited money from an aunt, enabling her to invest in more real estate and to be estimated "safely worth $10,000 & good for eng[agemen]ts."[38] Women in business also depended on the "backing" of relatives (that is, their guarantee) in order to obtain goods on credit. In the 1870s the grocery operated by Mrs. Sarah Grattan was backed by her brother George Martin, a builder, who also owned the house where she lived and worked.[39] In 1882 the widow Mary A. Hawe, proprietor of a cooperage, was said to be "backed up by her daughter Mrs. H. Weatherhead who holds a mortg[ag]e on the establ[ishment]."[40]

Although most support for women's microbusiness came from relatives, Albany's businesswomen also formed linkages with friends, neighbors, and former co-workers. In some cases, a woman without "means" would enter into a partnership with another woman (a friend or relative) who provided all of their business funds. For example, in 1873 two widows—Margaret Callahan and Mary Dorney—opened a small business described as a grocery and cigar shop. According to the credit investigator, Callahan had "all the means" (she was called "an honest saving woman wor[th] $2[000]"), while Dorney had "no means" but was also judged "honest."[41] Friends also assisted businesswomen who had failed. For example, Mark Cole ("sexton of the 1st Baptist church" and a "very worthy man") and his wife ("a careful manager" and a "smart woman") failed in 1874, after about ten years in a combined business in which he manufactured linen collars while she ran a fancy goods and millinery store. After noting that Mrs. Cole "cant pay her debts," the credit examiners added, "some of her friends will help her." In fact, the Coles reopened their store a few months later.[42]

Customers, Suppliers, and Creditors

Customers clearly provided one of the most vital supportive networks for women running small businesses. For instance, when Maggie Manifold opened her millinery "parlor" in 1878, her customers were said to be among the "upper ten" of Albany. Despite the fact that her worth was estimated at a mere $1,000 to $1,200, because she enjoyed such a fashionable trade and appeared to be making "good profits," it was reported that "her cr[edit] is good at home for anything she calls for." After she took on partner Johanna Murray in 1880, credit examiners reported that they were "both practical milliners & have a large acquaintance." Here, social and business networks appear to have blurred, just as the respectability of customers seems to have affected the creditworthiness of the enterprise. Even Mary Chapman, said to be "doing a small bus[iness] with an old class of customers of the cheaper kind" in her dry goods store in 1859, probably depended on a network of said "cheap" customers to spread the word about her wares.[43]

Finally, as discussed in the last chapter, most businesswomen in Albany needed at least a little credit from suppliers to carry on their concerns, however small. Again, although credit examiners regularly advised "no credit" or C.O.D. terms, their reports indicate that local suppliers tended to trust female proprietors with whom they had established relationships. For example, the credit report for widowed grocer Catherine Burns advised that she "sh[oul]d pay cash" in June of 1868, but noted that she was a "slow pay" the following December, indicating that she had received goods on credit from at least one source.[44] Even Annie Dunn, a dressmaker described as a "dead beat" in 1869, was said to get "a little credit here" in 1870.[45] There does not appear to have been much change in this practice as the decades progressed; in 1878 the credit entry for Mrs. Pierce Fleming, a grocer, read, "Good for 00/COD," yet the report for 1882 noted, "she is given a few dollars wor[th] of goods at a time on credit but is slow in payments."[46]

Limiting Networks

So far we have conceptualized networks of family and friends as positive forces, supporting businesswomen in their endeavors. But these social networks could also become factors limiting women's entrepreneurial success. Mothers running home-based businesses with children to care for, or with dependent parents, were surely limited in their ability to concentrate on their work. An elderly parent might be a help or a hindrance in conducting business, as might be a teenage child. We have little evidence of such difficulties, though they can easily be imagined. The credit records are more useful in detailing problems with partners, employees, customers, competitors, creditors, and of course the credit examiners themselves.

While partnerships did assist businesswomen, most partnerships dissolved within a few years. Almost all of the official partnerships between women listed in the credit records—whether between sisters, mother and daughter, or unrelated women, were eventually dissolved. We do not know whether these women "failed to agree" or parted ways for other reasons, but the term "dissolved" may represent a long and acrimonious struggle over the control and direction of even a tiny microventure. Problems with employees noted by credit examiners ranged from being "not so attent[ive] as they ought to be" in the case of liquor dealer Jane Davey in the mid-1870s, to being actively dishonest in the case of Phoebe Earl, a fancy goods and millinery dealer in the late 1860s.[47]

Even customers created problems. Thus, although dressmakers Anna Keenan and her sister Mary Frame enjoyed "the cream of their trade" in Albany, these high-class customers were described in the credit records as "very slow pay" in 1875, leaving the sisters "often pushed for funds." The wrong kind of customer might be a block to one's reputation. For instance, it was said of dressmaker Eliza Jones that "her class of customers are chiefly among those known as 'unfortunate'"—not a good recommendation for a trade that depended on a fashionable clientele.[48]

Although testimonials from family, acquaintances, former employers, and the business community at large sometimes supported female ventures, bad reports had the opposite effect. While "the opinion of the trade" could (and did) add a positive value to some women's endeavors, negative word-of-mouth could make it difficult—if not impossible—for her to conduct business. Numerous credit entries record what was "said to be" true of a female microentrepreneur's character, financial worth, or credit-worthiness. Thus Mrs. Fanton Lawlor, a provisions dealer, was reported to own "p[ro]p[ert]y said to be mortg[age]d" in 1860, while in 1876 Catherine Sill, a dealer in gentlemen's furnishings, was "said to be very slow" in her payments.[49] Similarly, the credit examiners reported on the general judgment of "the trade" toward individuals and their businesses, as when they recorded of Catherine Paulus, a notions dealer, in 1880 that "the trade dont care to trust her over small bills of $15 to $20," or in 1882 that "some of the trade do not entertain friendly feelings toward the family" of widow Anna Beck and her son Joseph, dealers in boots and shoes, because of her dead husband's past "bad" failure.[50] For Jane Davey, the liquor dealer with less-than-attentive employees described earlier, "the opinion of the trade that she is running behind" resulted in the judgment that "considerable caution sh[oul]d be used in crediting," followed by a series of judgments and failure. It is impossible to know in which cases credit reports simply warned against an inevitable failure, and in which the inability of female microentrepreneurs to obtain ready credit may actually have hastened the failure that credit examiners feared.

The R.G. Dun & Co. records are most useful, of course, in demonstrating the ways in which the information network composed of credit reporters and the business community it served limited microentrepreneurial options by sharing information that often led to recommending only a small credit, or advising against credit at all. The most striking subtext in credit assessments for Albany's microentrepreneurs is the refrain that they should ask for no credit "away from home"—that is, they should be limited to local suppliers. Such a recommendation kept businesswomen tied to the home market, which might not be as cheap as buying "abroad," particularly in New York City. Yet suppliers "outside" the local market would logically be more dependent on credit evaluations than those who knew businesswomen personally or by local reputation. Thus the R.G. Dun credit reporters could influence not only whether a woman obtained credit but also where and with whom she could order her goods.

Women's Contribution to Business Networks

Clearly, Albany's businesswomen depended on familial, friendly, community, and business networks to support their enterprises in a wide variety of ways. But Albany's business community also depended on women who entered the marketplace in a wide variety of roles, as revealed in many of the previous examples. Women in Albany served as legal principals for male relatives who had previously declared bankruptcy, invested in male- and female-owned business, trained their sons and daughters for commercial careers, bequeathed their ongoing enterprises to relatives, left estates to relatives who used the money to start new businesses, provided essential goods and services to their customers, patronized local suppliers, and—of course—gave the R.G. Dun & Credit examiners hundreds of businesses to report on.

To add just a few brief examples to those provided in earlier chapters: Elizabeth Lathrop became the sole legal proprietress of a wagon and carriage company in 1880, acting as the principal for her husband Ralph, who managed the concern and had a "power of att[orne]y from her to transact all matters."[51] That same year Bertha Michaels entered a partnership in a pharmaceutical goods firm on behalf of her husband, a chemist but "a bankrupt."[52] In 1872 Caroline McGinnis formed a partnership with her brother Herman Muller in the hay and straw business, employing a joint capital of about $15,000.[53] In 1877 Elizabeth Anderson purchased $2,000 worth of stock for a drugstore to be run by her son, John, while Lydia Hodges of Cambridge, Massachusetts (herself a boarding-house keeper), invested the same amount in the drug business her son-in-law George Ferguson opened in Albany in 1881.[54]

At the same time that female proprietors contributed their legal identities and fortunes to a myriad of business ventures, however, women also had a negative impact on creditors and suppliers who were cheated out of their payments by bankruptcies and various shady dealings. The word "tricky" appears far less often in the credit records for Albany's businesswomen than the almost ubiquitous descriptors such as "respectable," "attentive," and "hardworking," but there were women who cheated their suppliers and creditors either deliberately or because of difficulties beyond their control. (Such shifty businesswomen are discussed in more detail in chapter 8.)

As can be seen in many of these examples, the family and the business community outside it often acted as rival networks. On the most obvious level, small businesses were in competition with each other. But beyond this arena of business-to-business competition, the credit records reveal another wide area of conflict—the conflict between the family's desire to protect its assets and maximize its profits set against the desire of the business community (and its representatives, the credit examiners) to protect the interests of suppliers and creditors while still profiting from the custom of these small family firms. Proprietary arrangements could become frustratingly complex for creditors, as in the clothing business of Rosalie Levison and her husband Lewis (or Louis). According to the credit investigators, Lewis Levison conducted business "first in his own name, then in his wife's, father's, and other members of his family" so that, the report complained, "the ownership of the concern changes with the moon."[55] As the proprietorship of a concern passed from husband to wife and vice versa, creditors and credit examiners became both confused and suspicious—as is evident in the 1882 entry for grocer Mary (Mrs. Daniel) Cox: "The bus[iness] was formerly carried on in the name of her husband but she claims to be proprietress of the concern now & that she is buying in her own name."[56]

The question of legal restrictions is a complex and interesting one.[57] Although New York State passed a series of Married Women's Property Rights Acts beginning in 1848, the exact meaning and application of these laws is unclear. Norma Basch, in her 1982 study of women, property, and law in nineteenth-century New York State, argued that although such laws were passed, "Conflict permeated the public discussions, ambiguity clouded the intent of the Legislature, and conservatism suffused the interpretations of the courts. Large remnants of the wife's former inferior status survived the legislative assaults of the nineteenth century."

In particular, Basch cited cases such as that of Caroline Switzer, a married boarding-house keeper in the 1850s who offered a chattel mortgage on her furniture in exchange for a loan; when the loan was not repaid, and her creditor foreclosed, Switzer's carpenter-husband claimed that his wife had no legal right to sign this, or any, mortgage. The courts agreed with Mr. Switzer, casting doubt on the reality of a wife's legal independence and ability to conduct business. According to Basch, "women's legal status with respect to the boardinghouses they ran were a common source of litigation in this period," and "such enterprises as boardinghouses and farms, businesses frequently operated in the family's place of residence and closely related to women's customary domestic duties, were often construed as belonging to the husband."[58]

Evidence from the credit records shows that although the right of married women to conduct business in their own names and to sign for loans was questioned, and such circumstances made the credit examiners uneasy, these women often did so anyway. Basch's own example makes clear that Caroline Switzer "leased houses in her own name, placed a brass nameplate reading 'Mrs. A. Switzer' on each door, contracted independently with the boarders, cooked and cleaned for them with the help of her daughter Harriet, and collected the rents." That is, like married female proprietors in Albany, Switzer acted independently until hounded by a creditor. Only then did her husband interfere, and, as Basch also points out, "From the Switzers' point of view, the technicalities of ownership were irrelevant. Undoubtedly they used both their incomes to support their family and were eager to defeat the creditor by any available means."[59]

Thus, instead of proving that women could not engage in business because of legal restrictions, Basch's example actually proves that women and their families flouted such restrictions until they could be turned to their own advantage.

Conclusion

To return briefly to the case of Sarah Todd and John Jacob Astor, historical accuracy does not demand that Sarah Todd Astor's biography appear next to her husband's in standard reference works (though perhaps she could be mentioned as part of his life story). The point here is really not that Sarah Astor was an "exceptional" woman, as suggested by Bird's approach, but that she was one of numerous American businesswomen who worked alongside their husbands. And, to look at the other side of the business couple equation, I would argue that John Jacob Astor was also engaged in a family business that precluded his concern with individual upward mobility alone. Surely he also felt the responsibilities of wife and children as he was attempting to make a fortune. In fact, looking at the Astors' story in comparison to evidence on nineteenth-century female proprietors in Albany, I would argue that it was the formative years of the Astors' business—the years of joint management—from which we can learn the most, because they were more typical of the period.

Multiple interacting, intersecting familial, community, and business networks were a fact of life for Albany's female microentrepreneurs. Their business enterprises were hardly the product of a sole individual's ambition and effort. Instead, family, friends, neighbors, and business associates—who were also partners, employees, creditors, suppliers, and customers—provided both supportive and limiting factors for women's business endeavors. As we begin to place women into the story of American business, then, let us not duplicate the old-fashioned (if seductive) narrative of the self-made man with that of the self-made female entrepreneur—in her case risking not only her energy and fortune but her reputation as well. Let us understand that the vast majority of nineteenth-century businesswomen in the United States (and elsewhere in the world) were microentrepreneurs supported by their families, friends, neighbors, and business community. Rather than exceptional, path-breaking feminists, they were mostly workers who struggled to make a living for themselves and their dependents, or to at least contribute their share to a family economy that often mixed business with wage work. Although their numbers were smaller than those of male proprietors, their contribution cannot be fully appreciated by looking only at women who were sole proprietors. Instead, by looking inside home-based family businesses we begin to see the role of microentrepreneurship in women's lives.

We can also see that the contributions of women to hundreds of microentrepreneurial endeavors provided necessary goods and services to the growing urban population of a city such as Albany, New York. Enterprising microentrepreneurs served as a link in the chain between large suppliers and local customers. Certainly wholesale businesses in Albany, especially those selling dry goods and millinery supplies, depended on the business of a myriad of small, female-run shops to support them. Female proprietors and their family concerns were granted small lines of credit precisely because suppliers depended on their business.

Finally, while mid-nineteenth-century middle-class mothers provided their children with an education and respectable moral values, these working mothers provided practical experience, working capital, and ongoing business enterprises for their children, male and female. They generated cash for family needs while remaining at home and supervising domestic responsibilities. In this complex web of interactions, female proprietors were not relegated to a "female economy" or business "at the service of women" but formed links in chains that bound men and women, the young and the old, family and acquaintances, individuals of different national, ethnic, and religious backgrounds, into a network of shifting alliances where people struggled over money and power as expressed through business enterprise. In that sense, all the women described in this chapter were indeed "enterprising women."

CHAPTER FIVE

●

Business or Labor?

Blurred Boundaries in the Careers of Self-Employed Craftswomen

But the ebb and flow of this great sea of toiling humanity wipes out all dividing lines, and each class so shades into the next that formal division becomes impossible.

—Helen Campbell, 1886[1]

IN 1886, THE JOURNALIST-INVESTIGATOR Helen Campbell published a series of articles on working women in *The New York Tribune*—a series that subsequently gained fame when reprinted under the title *Prisoners of Poverty*. Campbell's focus was the dreadful plight of female wage earners in New York City, and she located the roots of their exploitation in both the unscrupulous practices of business owners and the demand of their customers for bargain prices. Although most of her profit-driven villains were male, Campbell did not spare those business*women* she discovered cheating their employees. Indeed, her female entrepreneurs—such as Madame M——, "one of the best-known fashionable dressmakers"— evince no trace of feminine pity as they literally drive their unpaid workers to death's door.

Following the typical literary conventions of the period, Campbell sketched a detailed portrait of one of Madame M's victims as a New England milliner and dressmaker "bitten by a desire to see larger life," who became beaten down by illness and unemployment in the big city. Finding a place with the "smooth-tongued" Madame, the skirt-hand Mary M—— (described by Campbell as a "small, pale, dogged-looking little woman") soon discovers that her employer pays only in dribs and drabs for constant overtime. But the final straw for Mary comes when another hand, nineteen-year-old Jenny, is left without enough money to replace her worn-out shoes or to purchase warm underwear, thus catches "quick consumption," and dies. The older Mary M—— then turns against the hard-hearted Madame, going so far as to camp out on her doorstep and warn away prospective employees.

The outlines of this story are immediately recognizable, as are the characters. In moving from the countryside to the city in search of excitement (not a livelihood, one notes), the simple Mary M—— exposes herself to all the evil inherent in the cutthroat competition of the modern marketplace and the world of fashion. There is no confusion between the owner and the workers, the exploiter and the exploited. While the wily Madame rakes in a minimum of $50.00 for each outfit, the girls who have fallen into her snare freeze and starve, wither, and die. When they complain and turn to the law, Madame manages to slip through its clutches and is even observed—by the irate Campbell—bribing a policeman to harass the hapless Mary M—— and drive her away from the door of this fashionable establishment.[2]

But let us consider another story, "May Flowers" written just a year later by Louisa May Alcott.[3] (Coincidentally, in this short story about a Boston girls' club established for "mental improvement," *Prisoners of Poverty* is the first book selected for reading aloud.) One of several subplots in Alcott's fictional tale follows a wealthy young girl who accidentally discovers the plight of a businesswoman running a small fancy goods store in a run-down Boston neighborhood. Here again, a former milliner from the New England countryside—in this case, "a tall, thin, washed-out looking woman" who looks "blue and rather sour"—has come from Vermont to the city. Circumstances have also forced Almiry Miller into an unpleasant situation—running a tiny store so that she can look after her ailing mother, who lies in the back room.

In this case, however, the outline of the story is less stereotyped, and the roles of business and labor are not so distinct. The former milliner and her mother have come to the city not for glamour but because their father and husband has died and the farm has been sold. Forced to take up shopkeeping by necessity, not through ambition, the craftswoman misses her original trade and takes great pleasure in mending or trimming bonnets when she has the chance. The exploited employees of the enterprise are the owners themselves, and the profits they manage to earn prove barely enough to maintain the household, pay the doctors' bills, and stock the little shop with goods.

The contrast between these two stories illustrates the gap that still exists between our rather rigid conceptual classifications of "business" and "labor" and the evidence uncovered in research on female proprietors in mid-nineteenth-century Albany. Campbell's investigative account reflects a theoretical framework in which business and labor are seen as oppositional and mutually exclusive categories, while Alcott's fictional, though moralistic, tale reflects an understanding that in small, female-run concerns, the owner may well be a self-exploited worker herself. Because labor historians have often relied on the reports of reformers, from Matthew Carey in the 1830s through Helen Campbell in the 1880s, Victorian working women have often been portrayed as victims, while their employers have been seen as rapacious exploiters. The oversimplified picture sketched by nineteenth-century investigators is not surprising—they were crusaders, much like the temperance advocates of the same period, and it would not have been in their interest to explore or report on areas of complexity and nuance in the lives of women workers or business owners. Yet by reading their accounts as "factual" rather than "constructed," twentieth-century historians risk treating propaganda as objective evidence. This is not to suggest that nineteenth-century working women did not work in exploitative and inhumane conditions—many, if not most, did (as did male workers of the same period).

As Christine Stansell has written, "Like other philanthropic constructions, the sentimental seamstress, solitary, pallid and timid, embodied bourgeois aspirations and prejudices, but there can be no doubt she also represented, however distortedly, real situations."[4] Still, although needlewomen were often used as the very symbol of oppressed Victorian female workers, the stories of actual needlewomen in Albany rarely fit the suffering worker/swindling owner stereotype presented by reformers such as Campbell.

Consider, for instance, the case of Mrs. Clegg, a milliner who (according to the R.G. Dun & Co. credit report of 1877) "Pays $15 a month rent for store & apartment. Helped in shop by 2 daughters & employed hand. D[oin]g plenty of work. Cons[idere]d indust[rious]."[5] As in Alcott's fictional account, the owner and her family were also "workers" in the concern. In addition, whereas proprietors of dressmaking and millinery businesses have often been imagined as the rapacious "Madames" of Campbell's exposé, only a handful of the hundreds of fashion entrepreneurs in Albany ever assumed that sophisticated French title. (Here my evidence appears to contrast with that discovered by Wendy Gamber in her study of milliners and dressmakers in Boston; she found that the "adoption of the sobriquet" Madame was "near universal" in both fact and fiction.)[6] Far more typical for Albany were Irish dressmakers Mary A. Murphy and Annie M. Dunn, each described as "living from hand to mouth" in the credit reports of 1870.[7] In fact, Dunn and Murphy were identified in city directory listings simply as "Annie M." and "Mary A.," without even the polite "Miss" or "Mrs."—much less Madame—before their names.

Although the histories of business and labor have developed into separate subdisciplines, their narratives are clearly interrelated, and the boundaries between the two have often been far less distinct than contemporary historical categories suggest. In the nineteenth century many businesswomen were self-employed craftswomen (such as dressmakers, milliners, confectioners, and makers of hair jewelry or wax flowers) rather than capitalist entrepreneurs entering the marketplace in order to risk their fortunes. Like the artisans of the preindustrial era, these women (1) ran both workshops and stores within their own dwelling places, (2) trained apprentices and sometimes lived in extended households with their employees, (3) hired or worked alongside family members, and (4) mixed domestic tasks with commercial activities throughout the day. Indeed, although the mid-nineteenth century was undoubtedly a period of rapid technological growth for the United States, resulting in a "new" economic structure for the nation, research on Albany suggests that historians should not ignore continuity as an important force in urban economies.

As we have seen, needleworkers made up a large segment of Albany's mid-nineteenth-century businesswomen, generally about one-third of all female proprietors as reported in city directories, or one-fourth as reported in the census and credit ledgers. Within the needleworking trades, milliners dominated in the early years and dressmakers later in this period. Another 5% to 6% of female proprietors in Albany who might be described as self-employed artisans (that is, craftswomen) included confectioners, the designers of hair "work" or hair jewelry, and makers of wax flowers. For example, when credit examiners noted that Madame Helen Baker had opened a "Hair Goods & C." establishment (which they also described as a barber shop) in 1879, they described her employees as "lady artists."[8] Other craftswomen who were evaluated for credit by R.G. Dun included "a very clever artist," portrait and landscape painter Miss E. A. Rockwell in 1869; and Abbie S. Scott, who opened a decorative art gallery where she gave lessons in art and fancy needlework in 1882.[9] In addition, women who ran fancy goods shops also made some of their wares (such as trimmings, artificial flowers, decorative purses, and pincushions), as in the store of "Almiry Miller" described by Alcott. For example, the city directory of 1849/50 carried an advertisement for Madame Paepke's Worsted and Fancy Repository, with "Embroidery and Fancy Work done to Order."[10]

Conceptual Challenges

The first conceptual question arising in the study of craftswomen who were also proprietors is simply who in this category should be included as "businesswomen." Within the mass of self-employed, home-based working women, is it really possible to make a clear distinction between small businesses (generally assessed in positive terms by both contemporary observers and later historians) and homework or the sweated trades, with their notorious connotations of victimization? That is, how can one distinguish a dressmaker-entrepreneur running a small shop from what one might think of as a "freelance" dressmaker going out by the day to her patrons' homes, from the independent dressmaker who brought her work back home and sewed far into the night?

Is it really possible to distinguish between a milliner operating a store and one who did only what was described as "custom work" at home—and to what extent do such distinctions matter? Cases from the R.G. Dun & Co. credit ledgers illuminate this difficulty. According to these reports, it was only the exceptional female dressmaking entrepreneur who, like Campbell's Madame M—— or Albany's Madame J. DeBlock, did a "large bus[iness]," enjoyed "the very cream of the trade," and received "high prices for her work."[11] Far more usual were those dressmakers and milliners who were said to be "doing quite a light business," with "very small means," making "nothing over a living," and who should pay their suppliers "COD." Thus, Anna Andrews's first credit entries in the late 1850s note that she "has a small st[oc]k in a front room of a dwelling" and call her a "private milliner" who "buys goods only to make up"—that is, she worked on consignment rather than offering a large selection of goods for retail sale.[12]

In the following decade, milliner and dressmaker Isabella Bussey was said to have a "nice little store" in 1867, but by 1869 she had "no store." Instead, the examiners reported in staccato phrases, she "does work by the job. Has a machine. Makes about a living. no credit." Four years later, examiners considered her of "no ac[count] whatever" and complained that she was "constantly changing style [that is, the ownership of the concern] between herself & husband."[13] So, was Bussey "in" business—or not—and what year represents the "real" end of her business venture? Another Albany milliner, Miss M. B. Crandell, was described as having "small stock" in 1871, but by 1872 was reported to have "no store now" and to be "virtually out of business"— doing only "a little work at home."[14] Since credit reports on Crandell's business continued to be entered for the next two years, how should one evaluate her claim to proprietorship?

Like other historians of businesswomen, I have chosen to consider self-employment as a small business venture, and I myself have generally related my analysis to business rather than labor history, although (again, like most scholars of women's business history) I entered the field because of an interest in working women. Yet enterprises run by craftswomen in mid-nineteenth-century Albany might also be understood as a variation on the type of household self-exploitation that has been postulated for home-based industries by historians of protoindustrialization.[15] In many cases it appears that these home-based artisanal businesses employed several family members toiling in both the shops at the fronts of their dwellings and the backroom living quarters that must have doubled as workrooms. To turn once again to literary evidence, the crippled mother of the milliner-turned-fancy-goods-dealer in Alcott's "May Flowers" was constantly "busy with her 'pin-balls and knittin' work'" while she sat in bed in the room behind the store.[16] Another vignette in the same short story tells of a shopgirl who, kept home with a lame knee, takes in "jet and bead work" and "buttons to cover."[17] Similarly, one can visualize the Albany milliner Mrs. Clegg and her daughters hard at work in their "apartment" after a busy day at the shop, trimming hats for the morrow.

A few of the largest and most prominent of Albany's milliners did live with several of their employees. Evidence is provided by the manuscript census, which shows mature milliners—not just apprentices—living with premiere milliners Olive Blanchard and Mary Roberts. In 1850 Roberts and her family lived in the same household with women aged 12, 24, and 26; although no occupations for females are indicated in the 1850 federal census, information on Roberts's trade and status in the R.G. Dun & Co. credit ledgers strongly suggests that these women were one millinery apprentice and two mature milliners in her employ. In 1860 Blanchard's household included four milliners aged 18, 19, 20, and 22. All were identified as milliners—not apprentices—in the census.[18] But in Albany it was far more common for millinery proprietresses to have their milliner sisters and daughters living and working with them at the same address. For instance, in 1859 Catharine Bernhardt was described as employing her daughters Mary and Julia "as clerks" in her business, which was identified variously as millinery, millinery goods, and fancy goods at different points in her career, while millinery proprietor Matilda Cornock lived with her younger sister Caroline (also a milliner) according to the census of 1870.[19] In cases where milliners' daughters or sisters were not assisting them, millinery employees might live within the household or nearby. The previously mentioned Anna Andrews—who appears to have had no daughters—was by 1870 living with a young milliner, Kate Late, as one of her household, and in the same building with Ella Christy, a milliner's apprentice.[20] Although we have no conclusive evidence, it seems extremely likely that these women were Andrews's employees.

Interestingly, from time to time credit examiners referred specifically to individual craftswomen in their role as "workers." Thus, dressmakers Mrs. E. Cochrane and Elizabeth LaGrange were each described as a "good worker," while one Miss Lewis was called a "hard working girl," and Miss E. Smith was said to do the "work of some of the first families."[21] When milliner Maggie Robb opened her own shop in 1867, she was reported to have "all the work she can attend to"; since milliner Kate Bateman had "no store" in 1881, credit examiners explained that "all her work is done at home."[22] Similarly, in 1859 credit examiners called dry goods dealer Alida Hendrickson a "v[er]y Indus[trious] worthy woman" who "does her own work & has always supported her family."[23] In 1871 portrait and landscape artist Emily Rockwell was said to get "good prices for her work."[24] Again, it is evident that for small businesswomen in mid-nineteenth-century Albany, the roles of owner and laborer overlapped.

Workplace, Marketplace, Homeplace

The integration of workplace, marketplace, homeplace, and community in the lives of mid-nineteenth-century craftswomen has been confirmed by Melinda Talbot, in her analysis of the daybook of Mary Anne Warriner, a milliner in Rhode Island. Covering the years from 1834 to 1841, the daybook reveals that Warriner, widowed in 1817 when her son was only three years old, "knew most of her customers and was involved in their lives not only as the maker of baby bonnets and grave clothes, but as a neighbor, fellow churchgoer, and friend."[25] Like many of the craftswomen of Albany described in this chapter, Warriner supported herself and her son, lived with her widowed mother, and employed her nieces as assistants. She made enough money to invest in bank stocks, and even loaned capital to her brother. Interestingly, Warriner did not always work for cash but sometimes bartered, exchanged goods, and extended or received credit. At her death she left significant legacies to her nieces, particularly "The sum of One hundred dollars," which she directed that her niece Abby use to purchase "a Silver cake basket or any other piece of the same value" and to have it engraved with their names and the date and year of her death.

Literary sources also confirm that milliners and dressmakers who owned small shops worked as well as supervised—and that they integrated domestic chores into their workdays. For instance, milliner Alvira Slimmens, the "heroine" of a serialized novelette in *Godey's Ladies Magazine,* was described as cooking, dispensing her own quince jelly, and raising chickens, as well as bleaching bonnets, trimming hats, and selling ribbons. In addition, she took part in community activities such as the Missionary Club, quilting bees, and tea parties, and attended Lyceum lectures.[26] Such a mix of occupations captures the imagination—the blending of small business with domestic chores, self-improvement, and leisure activities. Evidence from nineteenth-century women's fiction also suggests intriguing mixes of shopkeeping and artisanry, as with milliners who sold candy as well as hats and trimmings, while fancy goods shops offered both mass-produced items and goods handcrafted by the proprietress. For instance, Fanny Fern's novel *Rose Clark* (published in 1856) describes "some gawky boys . . . eyeing the tin soldiers and peppermint candy" in the window of her Aunt Dolly's millinery shop.[27]

Perhaps the most fascinating aspect of this subject is the realization that whereas "women" and "the marketplace" have often been held up as oppositional categories in nineteenth-century women's history, for Albany's small craftswomen the workplace, marketplace, and homeplace were identical—just as they had been for the artisans of the early modern period. While, as we have seen, many of these women had male and female relatives (husbands, brothers, fathers, sons, sisters, and daughters) who went out to work for wages, they themselves brought the commercial arena home, into the very center of family life. Cooking, housekeeping, and even tending children had to be juggled with fashioning products for sale and serving customers.

In addition, it appears that the lines between diversion, employment, and commerce were also blurred in those nineteenth-century feminine trades that employed skills often performed (if not mastered) by amateur as well as professional craftswomen. Thus, a genteel woman fallen on hard times might take orders for painted china among her acquaintances, while a professional dressmaker would lend out a special bridal gown to friends without charge, or a former milliner could continue to trim hats on a part-time basis for extra cash. To provide anecdotal evidence from a slightly later period, Jennie Brown Spence remembered that her mother "sold ready made hats" and "made hats" as part of the family novelty store business in Meeker, Colorado, beginning around 1903, adding this detail: "One time she was uptown and sold the hat that she had made right off her head to a certain lady."[28]

Class Distinctions

An underlying assumption of much business and labor history is that businesspeople and laborers belonged to different, distinct classes with opposing interests. Among Albany's craftswomen, however, one finds strong familial connections between the business and laboring "classes." For example, while Jane Allen was "doing well" as a milliner in the 1840s, her husband Lucius was described simply as a "laborer."[29] Nor was Lucius Allen an aberration—although some milliners and dressmakers were married to business and professional men, others were married to men who were working-class. Needlework proprietors active from 1875 to 1885 included those whose spouses were laborers, carpenters, sign painters, shoemakers, teamsters, drovers, porters, stove mounters, moulders, carvers, patternmakers, and machinists.

According to the 1880 census, fathers of dressmakers also included blacksmiths and wheelwrights as well as a carman, a baggageman, and a stonecutter. Brothers of dressmakers were employed in laboring occupations as mill hands, factory workers, masons, moulders, boatmen, and workers in lumberyards and planing mills; sisters included servants, factory workers, and women who took in washing, as well as needleworkers and teachers. Male relatives in the households of confectioners included a laborer, a currier, a ship's carpenter, a truckman, a lamplighter, and a butcher's apprentice. Only the sons and daughters of dressmakers appear to have been engaged in mainly middle-class pursuits as white-collar workers, such as store clerks and schoolteachers. Unless one imagines that husbands and wives, parents and children, brothers and sisters were somehow of different classes, one needs an understanding of class more fluid than that posited by an oppositional business/labor dichotomy.

Conclusion

Let us return, briefly, to another literary contrast, this time from the work of Edith Wharton. Literary critics and feminists have acclaimed *The House of Mirth* as one of Wharton's greatest novels and one which has achieved the ultimate distinction by being made into a Hollywood movie. Lily Bart, the heroine of the story, becomes a tragic figure because—despite her beauty, taste, and breeding—she cannot find a place for herself in turn-of-the-century New York society without either marrying for money or accepting the support of a married man—compromises she cannot force herself to make. As one step in a long decline that ends in her death, Bart becomes a millinery apprentice in a fashionable establishment. Although she has the ability to trim her own hats "beautifully," Lily fails in the workroom of "Mme. Regina." Wharton's "Madame" is not the heartless exploiter pictured by Campbell in *Prisoners of Poverty,* and her twenty workers suffer from "the unwholesomeness of hot air and sedentary toil rather than with any actual signs of want"; they are "fairly well-clothed and well-paid, but the youngest among them was as dull and colorless as the middle-aged." Yet under the strict oversight of a "tall forewoman, a pinched perpendicular figure," Lily Bart is never allowed to move beyond basic stitching to attempt the more artistic trimming and designing of hats.[30]

Once again, this image of a crowded, unhealthy workroom with long hours of labor under the direction of a forewoman and, more distantly, the proprietress "Mme Regina" herself, matches our assumptions about the place of "business" and "labor" in the endeavors of female proprietors. Less familiar is Wharton's novelette "Bunner Sisters," also set in New York City, but in the 1870s, in a very different location, and among another class of female proprietors. The sisters of the title operate "a very small shop, in a shabby basement, in a side-street," where they rent the basement floor of a "private dwelling," using the front room as a store and the room in back as their living quarters. At the beginning of the story, the spinster sisters are "proud of the neatness of their shop and content with its humble prosperity. . . . [I]t enabled them to pay their rent and keep themselves out of debt; and it was long since their hopes had soared higher."[31] Like most of the businesswomen in Albany, the fictional Bunner sisters—Ann Eliza and Evelina—own an establishment where they themselves supply the labor as well as the capital. Their clean showroom offers both modest hand-made goods and cheap manufactured items: "artificial flowers, bands of scalloped flannel, wire hat-frames, and jars of home-made preserves."[32] In the evenings, after the shop is closed, they do "pinking" (cutting bands of trimming material into scallops), make the artificial flowers, trim hats, or even "take in" machine sewing for extra money—all in the same room where they cook, eat, and sleep. Thus, their workday, domestic chores, and leisure blend in much the same way as their work and home space. And, despite their status as business owners, they work much the same hours as seamstresses in the sweated trades or immigrant lace makers—that is, almost all of their waking hours. (In this, however, they are little different from other working-class women whose domestic chores dominated their lives; my own grandmother described working in the silk mill full-time as a teenager in Paterson, New Jersey, in the 1910s, then coming home and assisting her own grandmother in baking, sewing, and mending.)

Evidence on Albany suggests that the situation of two struggling sisters depicted in Wharton's less famous tale, "Bunner Sisters," was more common than that of the elegant and extensive millinery establishment described in *House of Mirth,* just as Alcott's glimpse of a mother-and-daughter fancy goods shop in "May Flowers" was more typical than the fashionable but exploitative dressmaking business highlighted in *Prisoners of Poverty.* Most millinery and dressmaking shops were small concerns where owners and workers were one-in-the-same, or where owners and workers were closely related.

To conclude, trying to force the rich multiplicity of businesswomen's experiences into the rigid categories of business and labor presents the historian of businesswomen with a frustrating struggle. Moving beyond the arbitrary distinctions taken for granted by such classifications, an analysis of self-employed craftswomen presents an opportunity to develop a more complex view of nineteenth-century economic interactions, interactions far more diverse than can be understood by dichotomous terms such as "capital" and "labor," or "home" and "marketplace." Indeed, understanding women in business also requires a reconceptualization of women's—and men's?—labor history away from the apparent distinctions between domestic labor, "wage work," and "business," and an ability to see far more fluid boundaries on a continuum encompassing these categories, as well as movements back and forth. Such a multifaceted view, reflecting human life-as-lived rather than rigid academic classifications, can begin to provide a richer and more accurate picture of nineteenth-century economic, social, and cultural networks, regardless of the gender of those whose lives were immersed within them.

CHAPTER SIX

"A Small but Safe Business"

Gendering Success for Nineteenth-Century Female Proprietors[1]

> Sempstresses, we know from the rates paid to them, and the accounts of tra-
> vellers, cannot make enough to support themselves; but shopkeepers can.
> —Virginia Penny, 1863[2]

> "If women," said a gentleman to me, "find themselves capable of conduct-
> ing mercantile affairs, and have the capital, they can succeed. Men cannot
> prevent them, and will not."
> —Virginia Penny, 1869[3]

IN 1859 *GODEY'S LADY'S BOOK* carried a serialized novelette titled, "Miss Slimmens' Window." The heroine (or, rather, antiheroine) of the tale—a small-town milliner who makes and sells bonnets with the help of two young female apprentices—is presented by the anonymous author as a ludicrous and pathetic creature: a vain, silly, selfish type of woman who apes cultured airs and graces while spending her days in idle gossip and romantic fantasies. The six-part story was written almost entirely in the form of a monologue spoken by Miss Slimmens herself, revealing through constant chatter her foolish little concerns, her absurd self-absorption, and her self-deceptions in the matter of love, for which she is constantly search-ing. No longer young, Miss Slimmens has resorted to bleaching and trim-ming "herself, as well as her bonnets," yet even her professional talents in this area are never adequate to the task of making her palatable to a suitor. By the end of the narrative, the perpetually deluded milliner has lost a talented apprentice (who elopes with a young man Miss Slimmens fancied for herself), lost her savings (to a confidence artist who had prom-ised to marry her), and even lost much of her business (to a rival milliner who establishes a more up-to-date shop). Throughout the entire novelette, Alvira Slimmens is presented as a failure—both as a "true" woman and as an entrepreneur.[4]

Through the comic character and tale of Alvira Slimmens, we can glimpse some of the presuppositions and prejudices of a mid-nineteenth-century middle-class author and her female audience toward business-women. To begin with, Miss Slimmens appears as an isolated figure, one of a mere handful of working women in the small community of Pennyville (a fictional town located near Lowell, Massachusetts). Second, she is an unwilling spinster, a female predator on the lookout for any man to "res-cue" her from the grind of commerce. Third, she is involved in the fashion trades and has taken on many of the characteristics associated with female fashion by nineteenth-century moralists—particularly vanity, frivolity, and deception. Fourth, she attempts to exploit her young charges, though they in turn manipulate her and play on her weaknesses. (In a memorable scene, they hide her false teeth so that she cannot attend a romantic assignation.) Fifth, she constantly attempts to trick, cheat, and thwart her own custom-ers—by using expensive materials they had paid for to trim her own bon-nets, for instance, or by regularly refusing to finish an eagerly awaited hat out of laziness, or just for spite. And, finally, when she fails in business it appears to have been entirely her own fault. Throughout the story Miss Slimmens exhibits no commercial interest or acumen, and she forfeits any sympathy for her plight by her own foolish chatter and absurd actions. Alvira Slimmens presents no success story.

What of a "real" Alvira Slimmens? Shall we conceptualize her through the eyes of the educated, middle-class writer for *Godey's Lady's Book,* or per-haps through the lens of Horatio Alger–type success stories?[5] As we have seen, in the city of Albany, New York, between 1830 and 1885, hundreds of businesswomen carried on their trades for decades, only to eventually go "out" of business—much like the fictional Alvira Slimmens. How shall we understand nineteenth-century businesswomen—as victims of circum-stance or as entrepreneurial exceptions? Or shall we count the very attempt to run a business as some kind of "success"? Ultimately, should we admit that, at least in comparison with their male contemporaries, these female proprietors were generally failures?

We might begin by challenging the literary caricature of a "Miss Slim-mens." Let us compare the "Alvira Slimmens" type to an actual Albany milliner of the same period—Mary Hogeboom.[6] Like Slimmens, Hoge-boom was in business for many years, from 1852 to 1872. In contrast to Alvira Slimmens, however, Mary Hogeboom had been a married woman, later a widow bringing up two sons (born in 1848 and 1850). The real Hogeboom was unlike the fictional Slimmens in another impor-tant respect—whereas Slimmens was portrayed as idle and frivolous, Hoge-boom was described by the R.G. Dun & Co. credit examiners as "honest and upright," "atten[tive] to business," and "v[er]y industrious." Nevertheless, the same credit reporters consistently judged her enterprise to be "small."[7]

Faced with credit records alone, one would imagine that Mary Hogeboom was just scraping by. However, according to the 1860 census of manufactures, she employed an average of five female hands with a payroll of $60 per month, and used hundreds of dollars worth of materials (velvet, ribbons, and other articles) in the production of approximately 1,000 hats and caps in that year, worth a total of about $3,700. This is the same year during which the sole credit entry next to Mrs. Hogeboom's name is "small affair." Thus one must assume that what constituted a small affair for R.G. Dun's credit examiners may well have been a significantly larger affair than the fictional business of Alvira Slimmens, or indeed than our common stereotype of a female-owned small business. Yet looking at her enterprise from the point of view of R.G. Dun & Co. and Albany's male business community, Mary Hogeboom's millinery shop was indeed a modest venture, with capital of only about $1,000.[8]

To consider another case, let us review the career of Wilhelmina Jenkins, who succeeded her father as the proprietress of a modest watch and jewelry shop in 1866. Eight years later, credit examiners dismissed her store as a "small bus[iness] principally repairing," with a "poor class of goods," and characterized Miss Jenkins as "honest but not suited for such a bus[iness]," judging that she "cant possibly make much headway." Two years later her credit report concluded that the concern "ab[ou]t drags along."[9] Yet in 1877, eleven years after inheriting the family business, Wilhelmina advertised herself in the Albany City Directory as "W. Jenkins, Dealer in Watches, Clocks, Jewelry, Silver Plated Ware, and spectacles of all descriptions." Her advertisement continued by highlighting expertise in "Engraving, Hair work and repairing, of all kinds, by skilled workmen. Particular attention paid to the Repairing of French and Swiss Clocks."[10] It appears that Wilhelmina Jenkins's own view of her business enterprise was not accurately reflected by the negative tone conveyed in the credit records. In terms of creditworthiness, Miss Jenkins's shop was not a success. Yet, as suggested by the length of time it operated and the goods and services mentioned in her advertisement, the small business clearly supported its owner, employed others, and provided useful merchandise to the community. What is the meaning and significance of the discrepancy between what the credit evaluators sent by R.G. Dun thought a "good" business should be and what Wilhelmina Jenkins's business actually was?

For more than a decade, feminist scholars have challenged the hegemony of "male" models in a variety of fields, such as biography and literary criticism.[11] Rejecting an individualistic, independent, goal-oriented, linear pattern as the sole archetype for a successful human life or literary hero or heroine, scholars search for models that will be more inclusive of female experience. To theorize about what business enterprises may have meant to the mid-nineteenth-century women who pursued them (in Albany and elsewhere), I would like to appropriate some of the ideas explored by anthropologist Mary Catherine Bateson in her 1989 group biography *Composing a Life*. In this provocative study of five women, Bateson argues that conventional paradigms of achievement have become "overfocused on the stubborn struggle toward a single goal." According to Bateson, "Much biography of exceptional people is built around the image of a quest, a journey through a timeless landscape . . . in which it is essential to resist the transitory contentment of attractive way stations and side roads, in which obstacles are overcome because the goal is visible on the horizon."

In contrast, Bateson suggests that feminists should re-model the image of a successful life, exploring "the creative potential of interrupted and conflicted lives," "lives in which commitments are continually refocused and redefined." Instead of envisioning life as a "monolithic" sculpture, she proposes that we recognize that there may be equal value in lives that resemble collages, patchwork quilts, or creative jazz "improvisations." According to Bateson, even today, among intelligent, educated, motivated women, lives tend to be "subordinate," "contingent," and "discontinuous."[12] If this is true of our own era of relative opportunity for women, how much more so must it have been the case one hundred and fifty years ago, when women's lives were far more bound by the limitations of biology, patriarchy, and tradition.

In order to understand the role of women in business history, and business in women's history, it is necessary to propose new, female paradigms for business success and entrepreneurship in mid-nineteenth-century American cities. Such models may also prove useful for studying other small businesses, particularly those operated by individuals from ethnic and racial minorities. As revealed by research on Albany, most female-owned and -operated enterprises differed dramatically from the standard "male" model of nineteenth-century business success. An essential challenge of any project on mid-nineteenth-century businesswomen is to problematize the basic concepts and definitions of business and labor history and to break through the gendered assumptions that underlie terms used to describe both business and labor for the mid-nineteenth-century period.

When embarking on women's business history, one is tempted to focus on those businesswomen who enjoyed the most "success" within traditional definitions of the term. We are attracted to stories that highlight business expansion, upward mobility, the gradual accumulation of capital and property, and in particular those unusual women who illustrated what one might call "Horati*a* Alger" tales of achievement and rising prosperity.[13] This approach permits the inclusion of a few notable women but lacks gender as a category of analysis. It also ignores the experiences of the majority of mid-nineteenth-century businesswomen. For example, Albany's mid-century female shopkeepers could not have begun their careers as homeless vagabonds, like the quintessential Alger hero Ragged Dick—a young girl living on the street as Dick does would surely have been prey to exploitation and sexual violence. Nor were Albany's working girls quickly able to rise from rags to respectability through a simple decision to become frugal, sober, better-educated, well-motivated white-collar employees—most were already respectable young ladies living with working-class families, frugal and hardworking by necessity. Indeed, a close reading of *Ragged Dick* and other Horatio Alger novels reveals the gendered construction of business identity in the mid-nineteenth century. Successful middle-class men consistently assist Alger's heroes because these young men remind male entrepreneurs of themselves—through strong links of gender, race, and ethnicity superseding class. A careful reading of such Alger classics as *Ragged Dick* suggests that mentoring—as much as luck and pluck—was an essential ingredient in the Alger success formula.[14]

Nor could many of Albany's adolescent female workers find opportunities to move up an existing chain of command to positions of prestige and authority in management, as did the young Andrew Carnegie, before venturing into their own grand entrepreneurial ventures. Although some young women did manage to save enough money from their salaries to invest in their own businesses, such nest eggs never approached the fortune Carnegie built through his speculation in the Pennsylvania Railroad. Instead, the most striking theme in the business lives of the majority of women who entered the industrial and commercial arena of mid-nineteenth-century Albany was their dependence on enterprises that began and remained small, in the eyes of both the nineteenth-century male-dominated business community and of subsequent historians.

Relative Success

In attempting to categorize the "success" of female proprietors for this period, one might develop a hierarchy of levels ranging from "worthless" to "best" based on the R.G. Dun & Co. credit reports. At the bottom would be those concerns examiners dismissed as not worth mentioning, too small to be of account, and essentially worth nothing. For example, in 1876 fancy goods dealer Matilda Hart was described as "worth 00 and vy slow pay," with the additional note that she was given no "cr[edit] where she is known," while Fanny Loveday's candy shop was called "wor 00 whatever."[15] One step up would be those businesses whose owner-operators were described as "not making over a living," such as notions dealer Catherine Paulus in 1880, or "making only a living," as with proprietress Catherine Laitz, the owner of a news depot in the late 1870s.[16] This subsistence plateau was common for women in Albany who ran small businesses, and most female-owned businesses—even endeavors lasting for decades—seemed to remain at this level year after year.

A more positive marker for credit evaluations was the use of the term "snug" to identify those enterprises reporters judged to be profitable, even if on a minor scale. Thus, Mrs. James Hayes's fancy goods store was described as small, but she was said to enjoy a "snug little trade" in 1868, while the business in ladies' furnishing goods run by Anna Davis was called "a snug little bus[iness]" in which she was thought to be "m[a]k[in]g a little money" in 1879.[17] Still, even a "snug" enterprise might be netting little in terms of profits, at least according to credit evaluations. For example, variety dealer Marion Weidman had a "sm[all] store and stock" but was also characterized as "good for wants"; she was said to be "doing a snug bus[iness]" in 1872 and "doing a small but safe business" six years later in 1878. Nevertheless, in 1880 Weidman's business was judged to be "limited" and "not making over expenses."[18]

Businesses that did better than merely providing "a living" for their proprietresses were described as "doing well" and "making money"—that is, a profit. Harriet Lowenthal, for example, who dealt in knit underwear in the 1870s and '80s, was described as "d[oin]g well," "good beyond question," "making money annually," and worth approximately $20,000 by 1879.[19] Similarly, milliner Ella Lyons and her husband Moses, a dry goods dealer, were said to be "doing well" in 1874 and worth $20,000 by 1876.[20] Such praise was relatively rare in credit entries on businesswomen, applying to less than 5% of Albany's female proprietors—and then, not consistently over the years. Thus fancy goods dealer Sarah W. McGuigan was commended in the 1860s and '70s for her "nice snug bus[iness]," "m[a]k[in]g" money," "d[oin]g v[er]y well & making something besides a living," "d[oin]g a good bus[iness] & saving something," and "steadily accumulating." However, by 1880 she was said to be "d[oin]g a small living bus[iness] only," and in 1882 she sold out "at auction"—though she had no trouble paying "all" her debts "in full."[21]

Finally, a few business endeavors run by women were said to do a "large" business or to be "the best" in their line in the entire city. For instance, the corsetware rooms owned by Mrs. M. Cook in the 1850s were said to be "d[oin]g a l[ar]g[e] bus[iness] making money."[22] Similarly, the concern operated by Clara Martineau and her husband Frank in the 1860s and '70s (identified variously as a business in "laces &c.," fancy goods, then hosiery and gloves) merited many positive assessments from credit reporters, despite the fact that Mrs. Martineau started with more "impudence" than capital. In 1864 they were said to "do good retail business," in 1866 they were described as "a first rate trade," in 1869 "a lar[ge] bus[iness] in gloves the largest in the city" and to be "mak[in]g money," in 1873 to enjoy "a splendid trade" and to be "adding to means," in 1874 to "do the best bus[iness] in the city" and to be "adding to means rapidly," in 1875 to be "making money" and worth about $20,000, and in 1876 to be "mak[in]g a nice profit" on a patent glove powder. That Clara Martineau was a major factor in the success of this business (which operated two stores) is illustrated not only by comments such as "his wife manages the bus[iness] in his absence" (1868) and "she is the bus[iness] man smart 1st rate saleswoman & understands the bus[iness]" (1869) but also by the fact that their business's reputation suffered after she became ill and died in the 1880s. According to credit examiners, Martineau's financial affairs had been managed by "his wife," and while she was sick bills were left unpaid and Martineau himself fell into "immoral habits"; in 1882 they stated that "the bus[iness] suffers from the loss of his late wife's attention."[23]

Yet remarkable proprietresses such as Martineau were clearly in the minority among businesswomen assessed for credit in Albany. The single most notable, almost universal characteristic of women's businesses in Albany between 1840 and 1885 is that they were small businesses located in the businesswoman's own place of residence (whether rented, mortgaged, or owned outright). The terms "small business," "small means," "small stock," "small affair," and "small concern" pepper the entries in the R.G. Dun & Co. credit records describing Albany's businesswomen during this period, along with "small store," "small capital," "small trade," and "small place." In fact, the term "small" appears in 59% of female proprietors' credit records, appearing even under the names of women who were deemed worthy of credit—the recommendation for which was also often "small." For example, 70% of milliners located in the credit records had entries including the word "small" at some point in their careers. Of these, 42% were described as "small business," 25% as having "small means," 17% as "small affairs," 16% as having "small stock," 13% as "small concerns," 10% as "small stores"—and 23% were said to have or deserve only "small credit."[24] Businesswomen in trades outside millinery were somewhat less likely to be judged "small"; about 55% of other female proprietors identified in the credit ledgers had the word "small" included in their entries. Of these, 45% were described as having small businesses; 12% as having small means; 9% as operating small "affairs," "concerns," or "establishments"; 4% as having a small "store," "place," or "stand"; and 4% as offering a small "stock." In addition, 6% were recommended for only a small "credit"; 9% were said to be good for small "amounts," "sums," or "bills"; and 5% were said to be doing well in a small "way."[25]

Further, of the credit entries that did not include the term "small," many incorporated even less encouraging descriptors such as "C.O.D.," "worthless," "worth nothing" (or the quaint "worth 00"), "no means," and "no credit"—suggesting that most of those not labeled as small were actually minuscule, rather than "large," concerns. Of the entries on milliners that did not include the word "small," 25% included the word "nothing" or "00," and 12% the term "no means." Of the remaining listings, many included references to small business couched in slightly different terms (such as "doing little business" or "not doing a large business"), and several had listings of a single line only, or simply the comment "out of business." In fact, only five female millinery proprietors listed in the R.G. Dun & Co. credit ledgers had businesses that were never judged "small" in any way. Interestingly, these were not the five most successful female milliners by other measures reported in the Dun records themselves (such as monetary value, share of trade, or class of customers). As for other types of businesses listed in the R.G. Dun & Co. ledgers, eliminating variations on terms such as "small," "little," "C.O.D.," "no means," "worth nothing," "no credit," and "should pay cash," one is left with only about 10% of the total number—that is, 90% of businesswomen who were not milliners were described by one or more of those terms at some point in their careers.

Even women praised by credit examiners were often characterized in a minimalist fashion, as with milliner Maggie Kappes, who was said to have "done well in a small way" in 1879, or dry goods dealer Mary Mann, whose business was "thought to be paying well in a small way" in 1883.[26] And, in comparison to contemporary male-owned and -operated ventures in Albany worth tens or hundreds of thousands of dollars, the businesses of most female proprietors were indeed relatively small. The average businesswoman invested little capital in her enterprise, and her entire business was rarely estimated to be worth more than a few thousand dollars. Only about 57% of female-run businesses located in the credit records include specific estimates of monetary worth. Of these, the largest number (40%) were estimated to be worth somewhere in the thousands of dollars (m$ in the shorthand of the reports), about one-third received estimates ranging from hundreds to thousands of dollars, and about one-quarter were estimated to be worth only in the hundreds of dollars (c$).

The difficulty here is not only in the accuracy of the characterization "small" (since, as we have seen, credit entries tend to be somewhat inconsistent in the valuation of the "worth" of women's enterprises) but even more in our interpretation and evaluation of the term. If we automatically equate large with good, and small with "bad"—or at least "minor"—then we will naturally see most businesses run by Albany's mid-nineteenth-century female proprietors as peripheral and unimportant. The key is turning our focus from "business" to "women"—and asking what role these businesses played in the lives of the women involved. A new definition of "success" as the term might be applied to mid-nineteenth-century American businesswomen considers a female-owned or -operated business to have been successful whenever it provided opportunity as good as or better than was available in the existing female labor market at that time. When applying this yardstick—comparing female business opportunities to other opportunities for nineteenth-century working women rather than to the possibilities open to businessmen—commercial potentials for women appear in a new light. Relevant aspects of this comparison include all aspects of business "employment": financial support of oneself and one's family; control over the workplace; a chance to practice one's craft, skill, or trade; opportunities for supervision (of oneself and others); the possibility of relative independence; a potential for advancement; the opportunity to turn industry, initiative, and a business sense into profit; and the ability to profit from the value of one's own labor—by spending, saving, or investing. Here we will consider a *range* of definitions of success, paralleling the range in size, scope, and purpose of women's business ventures; these new paradigms of female "success" will be based on the needs, desires, and motivations of individual women rather than on a single, universal, abstract formula.

A good example of a proprietress successful in terms of self-support and economic survival who did enter the credit ledgers is Mrs. Julia Donn, who in 1858 was left a widow at the age of 28, with no estate and a boy of 4. Beginning her millinery business in a "sm[all] estab[lishment] in an out of the way place," she had by 1860 joined forces with Isabella Crew, a single corsetmaker, sharing both her home and her shop with Crew and her sister Sarah (who presumably kept house for the rest). The "very worthy and prudent" Donn and the "hon[est] & industrious" Crew never made "m[u]ch above a living," despite more than twenty years in business; at the time their credit records end, in 1881, they each appear to have been "worth" less than $1,000.[27] Still, Donn had supported herself, arranged an informal partnership, provided commodities and services, and raised her son to a productive adulthood as a bookbinder, while Crew had done the same while supporting her sister, and both women continued to be listed in city directories until the late 1890s.[28]

Businesswomen such as Julia Donn and Isabella Crew failed to amass handsome profits or to build up their businesses significantly. Yet in light of the difficulties facing these women—limited capital and credit, for instance, as well as lively competition—it is remarkable how many (40%) managed to survive in business for ten years or more. Although small shops often did not impress credit evaluators as good risks, the ability of such female-run businesses to support their proprietors over a period of years in itself seems to confound the stereotypical picture of the nineteenth-century working woman for whom work was only a temporary stopgap or emergency measure.

Economic Support and Survival

To begin with the most basic definition of business "success"—providing financial support for oneself and one's dependents—a female-owned or -operated enterprise should be judged successful whenever it provided monetary support during whatever period of time was deemed necessary or desirable to the businesswoman herself. Using such a definition, it becomes irrelevant whether a business lasted two or twenty years. We ask, rather, Did it last as long as it was needed to support the individual, and did it provide financial remuneration as good as or better than was available in the local job market? Did it protect a woman from depending on the support of her relations, or from applying for charity, or from falling into abject poverty? A failed business, then, would be one that could not, or did not continue to, provide support during the period considered necessary or desirable by the woman herself, so that she was forced into unsatisfactory wage work, or onto the support of relatives or charity, or into poverty.

Using this definition, hundreds of Albany's mid-nineteenth-century businesses should be judged "successful" for the women who owned and operated them. Indeed, the rather dismissive credit evaluation—"makes only a living"—takes on a far more positive implication when one considers how difficult it was for women wage earners to make "a living" at all in the nineteenth century. The inadequate wages offered to women workers in the United States have been extensively documented by both nineteenth-century reformers and modern women's historians. In Albany, although salaries for exceptional working women ranged up to $10 or even $20 a week (for saleswomen in large stores), in 1860 (near the mid-point of this study) the average wage for a working woman appears to have been closer to $3.50 per week, or about $175 a year if she worked consistently.

According to credit records, highly paid saleswomen included Joanna Murray, who was making $20 per week at Whitney's, Albany's largest department store, in 1880; more usual was the salary of $7 per week paid to saleswomen at the fancy goods shop of Charles and Martha Torrey in 1872. In contrast, the Federal Census of Manufactures for 1860 reported millinery and trimmings businesses with female hands whose earnings averaged from $2.50 to $5.00 per week. For example, the millinery business of Hannah Singer employed five female hands at $60 a month, milliner Mary E. Wood employed two female hands at $20 a month, and the trimmings business of John and Sarah Denmead employed five female hands at $50 a month.[29]

Similarly, investigator Virginia Penny reported in 1863 that average wages for "a girl, at most mechanical employments" was $3 for sixty hours of work per week, the equivalent of five cents an hour. Indeed, according to Penny, "One clothier in Albany, New York, pays $3 a week to his hands working eleven hours a day." Seamstresses might make as little as two cents an hour, saleswomen ranged from as little as $3 to as much as $8 per week, and relatively well-paid office jobs, such as bookkeeping, also provided about $8 per week.[30] Skilled female workers, such as women who ironed collars in Troy (Albany's sister city across the Hudson River), made a maximum of $14 per week in 1869, according to Carole Turbin's extensive study. Although this was "almost twice [the wage] of the average working woman and nearly as much as some working men," it would have taken such a highly paid, experienced woman worker more than half a year to earn several hundred dollars, even if she had been able to save all of her wages.[31]

Obviously, businesswomen did not pay themselves standard "wages," and it is difficult to determine exactly what level of survival is suggested by credit entries such as "makes only a living." Yet, at the very least, a woman who could afford to rent her premises, stock her shop, and remain in business for a period of several years was able to provide herself with the necessities of life. Clearly, most businesswomen in Albany mustered financial resources in excess of what the majority of working women could depend on. Perhaps the best examples of such businesswomen were those who never even made it into Albany's credit reports, or merited only a single line, yet were listed in the city business directories year after year. For example, milliner Abigail Adams received only this brief notice in the credit ledgers—"small means cr[edit] not of the best"—yet when she was evaluated in 1876 she had been in business for 16 years.[32] Despite the limited capital and visibility suggested by their lack of attention from credit reporters, somehow such women managed to stay afloat.

As we have seen in previous chapters, small business provided a livelihood for single women, widows with and without children, and married women whose husbands could not (or would not) work. For example, Sarah Cannon—a single woman—carried on a "v[er]y sm[all" dressmaking business from 1868 to 1876, despite the fact that she had "no capital to speak of" and that R.G. Dun & Co. credit reports almost always recommended that she be sold goods "cash" or "COD."[33] Widowed mothers especially found opportunity through self-employment in the commercial world. In 1860, at the lower end of the spectrum, Catherine Powers, an Irish immigrant with a "personal estate" worth only $150, supported herself and her daughter Mary by operating a grog shop.[34] Illiterate Irish-born grocer Alice Cassidy also supported herself and three children aged six, three, and one; their total family worth was estimated at $250. All of these women needed their businesses to survive.

A small business could provide a woman with economic security during marital problems, even divorce; it could also protect women against the vagaries of a drunken, abusive, lazy, or disabled spouse. Once again, the question of how best to interpret such stories of survival and security can be raised and reexamined. That is, one might argue these women *had* to run businesses because their husbands' salaries were inadequate, or the men themselves were "no good"—thus insinuating that business was not a "genuine" or "free" choice by Albany's women (and that all men who entered business were somehow free of similar economic or familial constraints). However, one might propose instead that businesswomen with unsatisfactory spouses were able to overcome financial and personal obstacles that most mid-nineteenth-century women would have lacked the resources to face. Thus, when William Daley was carted off to the lunatic asylum "sev[era]l times" in the 1870s, his wife did not have to appeal to the kindness of relatives, the charity of strangers, or the compassion of the poor commissioners—she continued to run her grocery.[35] Similarly, after George Schwarzman shot himself in 1875, his widow was able to carry on "a living bus[iness]" by operating the saloon formerly run in his name, while Johanna Barrett continued to make "a fair living" after her husband Richard disappeared mysteriously in the winter of 1876.[36]

A Relatively Long Career

Simply providing support for several years would mark a business as successful for the female proprietor, since we know that typical lengths of employment for female workers in mid-nineteenth-century America were relatively short. Let us consider, for example, the fact that a significant proportion of businesses operated by women lasted no longer than a few years: 30% of Albany's female proprietors identified in the 1880 census remained in business only three years or less. Even more than the relatively modest scale of female-owned ventures, this quality of "going in-and-out quickly" seems to have caused scholars to dismiss the impact of business on women, and vice versa.[37] But why must the limited length of most female business endeavors be interpreted as reflecting "failure"? Many aspects of life are transitory—is an occupation meaningless because it proves temporary? Shall we discount the commercial *experiences* of women who did not create long-lasting firms?

A typical example of a short-lived business is the millinery shop of Mary T. Carroll, listed in a series of Albany City Directories from 1860 to 1864. Her store was not large or important enough ever to merit the attention of credit examiners; indeed, her total property was only worth about $40 in 1860, according to census records. The Irish-born Carroll lived in a household with an older woman, also Irish-born (probably her mother), and two young daughters. Neighbors included several young milliners who were not in business for themselves, quite possibly her employees.[38] Mary Carroll is exactly the type of minor dealer who has been seen as of little account—not only by nineteenth-century credit examiners but also by business historians, and more recently by historians of women as well. Yet surely her small business was integral to her life, and to the lives of her family and employees, for the four years during which it operated.

Instead of contrasting the length of operation of small businesses operated by women to firms created by the most successful businessmen, it is illuminating to use the experiences of other nineteenth-century working women as the point of comparison. When "self-employed" small businesswomen are compared to female wage workers during the same period, an establishment operating for 2 or 3 years seems far less of a failure. For instance, in his extensive research on the most common nineteenth-century female occupations, Thomas Dublin has determined that the mean length of employment for women in the Lowell mills was 2.7 years; for shoe workers in Lynn, Massachusetts, 3.8 years; for servants in Boston, 4.8 years; and for needleworkers in that same city, 5.9 years.[39] In comparison,

Wendy Gamber found that the average millinery establishment in Boston lasted about 6 years, and the figures from Albany (reported in chapter 3) suggest even longer mean (11 years) and median (7 years) lengths for women's business endeavors in all fields.[40] To assume that the only "successful" model is a job, or business, spanning several decades is to ignore the reality of nineteenth-century women's lives. In fact, when seen in comparison to the longevity of female employments as a whole, proprietorship appears as a relatively stable and long-lasting career for mid-nineteenth-century women.

Control over the Workplace

In terms of control of the workplace (hours, working conditions, location, supervision), business concerns provided a better situation for their owners than the rather grim options open to most women workers in the mid-nineteenth century. Indeed, small business provided not only a respite in necessity but also a positive opportunity for many women. In this period, employment choices were extremely limited for both mature women and mothers of young children; most wage work available for females was poorly paid, and working conditions were demanding and often oppressive. Outwork as sweated labor represented the most common choice by desperate mothers and elderly widows, who (according to newspaper exposés) worked extremely long hours—up to 18 hours per day. According to Helen Campbell, whose *Prisoners of Poverty* first appeared as a series for the Sunday *New York Tribune* in the 1880s, women who sewed at home might work 10, 12, 14, or 16 hours a day. Her description of two German immigrants, mother and daughter, is typical: "It is early that we begin,—seven maybe—and all day we shall sew and sew. . . . It is fourteen hours efery day—yes, many time sixteen [hours]—we work and work. Then we fall on the bed and sleep, and when we wake again it is work always." Examples presented by Christine Stansell (also based on the writings of nineteenth-century reformers) suggest that seamstresses worked from "sunrise to nine or ten at night" in the 1830s, and by the 1850s might work up to 18-hour days.[41]

In contrast, using capital investments as small as $50 ($5,000 today), women in Albany were able to set themselves up in business. Thus they could reap the profits of their own labor, control their work environment and conditions, supervise other workers, and employ themselves for a period of time (dependent on market conditions). Above all, small businesses were convenient workplaces since they were usually located in the same building where women and their families lived, often in the front room of a flat.

Because of this common arrangement, operating a modest-sized business was one of the few jobs available to the mother of small children. Confirming and fleshing out the evidence provided by statistics on business and motherhood reported earlier, the reconstructed biographies of a number of Albany's businesswomen reveal that children were raised—even born—during the same years their enterprises were flourishing. For instance, Irish-born Sarah Neville gave birth to three children and brought them up while she and her husband operated a canal grocery stand in the 1840s.[42] Caroline Keeler, who ran a millinery establishment from 1850 through 1868, raised four children, three of whom were born after she started in business; her husband worked on the railroad, quite possibly at some distance from home.[43]

Albany's businesswomen were also able to make the choice to continue working into their later years. Elsie Dickerman, a "nice old lady" according to credit examiners, was still running her drugstore—"a sm[all] bus[iness] in an out of the way place"—at the age of 60. Although she owned property, was worth several thousand dollars, and could count on assistance from a prominent son, the widowed Dickerman remained in business from before 1859 till 1871.[44]

Satisfaction and Skill

One of the most positive opportunities provided to the female owner-operators of small business ventures in Albany—at least in terms of mid-nineteenth-century restrictions on female activity—was as an avenue for competence. When credit examiners praised businesswomen such as Ellen Owen as doing a "nice snug bus[iness]" in the family's dry goods concern, or commented that Mrs. Kate Henry got "good prices" as a dealer in human hair, when they noted that Mrs. Mary Roseboom understood her fancy goods business "well," or that milliner Olive Blanchard was a "first class workwoman," they reflected more than the satisfactory credit standing of their subjects.[45] If individuals as sparing of praise as the R.G. Dun credit examiners found positive attributes beyond hard work and respectability, one can assume that these women were noteworthy within the business community where they operated daily. Indeed, while dry goods merchant and former peddler David Orthelier was described as "no bus[iness] man," his wife Rosalia was praised for her competence seven years before his death in 1874; that year, a credit examiner noted that while the nominal head of the concern was "very sick & may not recover," his wife was capable and "intelligent," concluding with the remark "think the bus[iness] will prosper in her hands."[46]

Business careers were also unusual in providing for women "ladders" of opportunity on which the "aspiring" could "rise."[47] (In this period it was hardly possible for women to climb the ladder of success through such typically male venues as white-collar office work). Millinery, for example, provided a craft system (beginning with apprenticeship, moving on to "making," then "trimming," then "designing" and supervising) that might lead to business ownership.[48] Miss Maggie Robb, who entered business for herself in 1867, was one of the few single women to enter the ranks of Albany's more successful milliners by ascending this ladder. Having previously been employed in the dry goods and millinery establishment of Ann Smyth, by 1870 Robb was "doing a nice little bus[iness]"; three years later she was described as "doing a good bus[iness]" with a "fair assorted stock of goods" and estimated to be worth $3,000 to $4,000 clear. The next year, 1874, she was worth $1,000 more and thought to be doing "ab[ou]t the the best business in the city." Again in 1875 she was described as "making $ every year," and finally earned the accolade of "smart woman, do[ing] a good bus[iness] and making a nice profit every year."[49]

Opportunity and Profit

In terms of financial rewards, it appears that (at least in Albany) small businesses provided women with a unique means of generating profits. For instance, although Lucretia Blessing's confectionery and toy shop was considered a "sm[all] concern," with "very light stock" by credit examiners, who speculated that she was "barely making a living" in 1870, Miss Blessing did manage to support herself through her business from 1869 until at least 1885. By that time, she had paid off an $800 chattel mortgage against her stock and her estimated worth had increased to about $1,500. By definition that $1,500 represents the profit Blessing was able to make over and above whatever her living and business expenses may have been. In a period when $15 a week would have been considered an excellent salary for a woman worker, $1,500 clearly represents a generous financial cushion.[50]

Many female proprietors earned enough to invest in real estate, and numerous credit entries speak of houses, lots, residences, and places of business owned by businesswomen—though often mortgaged for much of their worth. Rather typical would be the case of Anna Beck, a widowed dealer in boots and shoes. According to the credit records of 1882, Beck owned both her "bus[iness] prem[ise]s worth $6,5[00], but mortgaged for $2,5[00], and additional property worth $1,500, mortgaged for $500."[51] The most remarkable real estate empire was that of grocer Jane Kieley, who remained in business from 1877 to 1888; she owned eleven houses, which were "rented at good paying rates" according to the credit ledgers. Thus Kieley was in two lines of trade—as both a grocer and a landlord. Her worth during this period was estimated at between $20,000 and $25,000.[52]

For some businesswomen, profits were employed not only in savings, business expansion, or investment in real estate, but also for personal pleasure—much to the dismay of credit reporters. For example, although Mrs. Olive Blanchard ran the "most fashionable bus[iness] in Albany" in the millinery line throughout the 1850s and '60s, getting "high prices" for her goods, her entrepreneurship never extended to any significant commercial expansion of her shop. Instead, according to the R.G. Dun & Co. credit report of 1871, "she & family live high & save 00$." Yet the profits from *her* business allowed the Blanchards to continue their "gay" lifestyle (the "slack and lazy" James W. Blanchard had previously failed "several times" as a wig maker and had even left Albany to fight as a captain in the Civil War). Despite the concerns of creditors, who often did not trust either Olive or J. W. to pay their bills, the couple was able to make a "show of extravagance" as well as purchase real estate from the profits of her enterprise.[53]

Obstacles, Limitations, and Failures

If success, defined in relation to a nineteenth-century woman's prospects, was possible or even common among Albany's female proprietors, what obstacles and limitations did such businesswomen face? At what rate did they fail to succeed, and what caused their failures? First, as we have seen, more than half of female proprietors operated within a segmented business sphere that paralleled the segmented labor market of women workers. Much as the concentration of women workers in the needlework trades kept down wages, so the concentration of businesswomen in the enterprises of dressmaking, millinery, fancy goods, and other clothing-related trades increased competition and—one assumes—must have decreased prices and profits. The difficulty faced by small, capital-poor businesswomen in rising above a stable level of subsistence documented earlier in this chapter can

also be seen in the almost painfully slow progress of even relatively successful female proprietors as they attempted to increase their personal and
business "worth." As will be detailed in the following chapter on female
entrepreneurship, male proprietors—including those in the fashion fields
dominated by women—were able to build up their businesses, profits, and
total worth far more quickly and dramatically.

Perhaps the most obvious difficulty faced by female proprietors in
Albany was their inability to obtain ready credit. The common assumption
of credit reporters was that tiny, female-run businesses (estimated between
$50 and $2,000) did not deserve, and should not ask for, credit—at least
not "away from home." Albany's female crockery dealers, dressmakers,
confectioners, and saloonkeepers were clearly considered reliable credit
risks by local suppliers but were most often judged "unworthy" of credit
outside the area by the R.G. Dun & Co. examiners. (Indeed, credit evaluations, a major source on which business historians must depend for
information about female-run businesses, tend by their very nature and
purpose to discount small business operations.) Despite these businesswomen's good qualities and best efforts—the adjectives "honest," "prudent," "industrious," "attentive," "hard working," "respectable," and
"worthy" appear repeatedly in the Dun credit reports—small businesses
generally remain relegated to a kind of "second-class" category of credit
"risks." The result of this evaluation was clearly to limit women's access to
credit outside of the local business community, making the modest size of
most enterprises owned and operated by women into a self-perpetuating
condition.

Success afforded by modest concerns, such as the variety of endeavors
described above, contrasts with female-headed businesses that can only be
described as failures. In developing a gender-dependent, liberal, and inclusive definition of business achievement, one runs the danger of hailing every
female attempt toward self-sufficiency, self-employment, and independence
as a "success." Yet there were failures among Albany's mid-nineteenth-
century female proprietors. Just as businessmen in this period succumbed
to the competition of the marketplace and the vagaries of economic cycles,
so businesswomen also failed—had judgments brought against them in
court, assigned their debts, attempted to settle with creditors, declared
bankruptcy, and ultimately went out of business, never to be heard from
again. The challenge is once again to develop a definition of "failure"
consonant with the business struggles of *women*. For the purposes of this
discussion, business failure for women in mid-nineteenth-century Albany
will be defined as an enterprise that failed to provide its proprietress with
even a modest living. That is, a female-owned business "failed" when it

could not support its proprietress, and when such failure caused it to be closed.

The most evident failures in mid-nineteenth-century Albany are businesses that lasted less than a year, as in the case of Rosa Cunningham's grocery, which had "already lost more money than she originally invested" a few months after it opened in 1879.[54] Clearly this enterprise had failed to provide Cunningham with a living, or an employment, and in fact had cost her probably hard-earned—if modest—savings in a relatively short period of time. As we have seen, about 10% of female proprietors remained in business for a year or less; it seems reasonable that these enterprises be counted as clear failures. Another type of undoubted failure would be the millinery, worsted, and fancy goods business of Mrs. Thomas Gough, which (according to credit ledgers) lost thousands of dollars for its proprietress, who parlayed an inherited estate of at least $5,000 into insolvency in the years between 1847 and 1853.[55]

Yet after categorizing ventures that either were extremely short-lived or squandered substantial capital as failures, one discovers that relatively few businesses run by women in Albany ended in formal "failure"—that is, default and bankruptcy—at least according to the credit records. Indeed, the word "fail" appears most often in the credit entries of those enterprises where a husband was doing business in the name of his wife because he had previously "failed" or "failed badly." In fact, of the mere 6% of entries on Albany businesswomen (outside of the millinery trade) containing the word "fail," 90% describe previous failures of husbands rather than a current failure of the wife's venture. Among female milliners, again, the entries of only 6% included the term "fail."

A typical example of an overt failure would be that of Louisa Guthinger, whose husband entered the furniture business in her name after he had previously "failed badly." (In their case, credit examiners' warnings appear to have been justified, since she was forced to make "a general assignment" of her debts in 1878, only two years after their first credit entry).[56] In contrast, the phrase "out of business" appeared in 46 out of 241 entries (about 20%) for milliners. Once again, one might argue that whether going out of business reflected a true business failure would depend on each individual proprietress's personal situation and goals. Although these are difficult to determine based on our limited sources, one can avoid automatically categorizing all "out of business" announcements as failures for the businesswomen themselves.

Some female proprietresses *were* clearly identified as failures in the credit ledgers, as when milliner Sara Bowes was described as "gone up" in 1872.[57] However, most business failures were naturally small, in proportion to the modest size of the businesses themselves. For example, when Lydia Mott's gentlemen's furnishing shop closed in 1847, the "Quakeress of g[oo]d reputation" was said to have "failed tho' not to a lar[ge] am[oun]t."[58] In an unusually thorough entry from 1881, Margaret Callahan, the proprietress of a grocery and cigar shop, was recorded as having assets of $1,048.47 and liabilities of $1,818.66, with a difference of $770.19.[59]

Only a few credit entries indicate reasons for business failure. These include Sarah Bowes, the failure of whose millinery establishment 1872 was attributed to buying "rather too many goods" and owing "more than she ought to."[60] The following year grocer Mrs. James Roberts was said to have "trusted out too much."[61] Margaret Callahan had also been "trusting out too much" and been unable to make collections of her accounts; in addition, it was thought that she had "too much money invested in her R[eal] E[state]." The itemization of her assets and liabilities noted that there was a discrepancy between both the "nominal" and "actual" value of her stock, and the "book" amount of her accounts and their "real value" in terms of probable payment.[62]

In some cases, businesswomen prospered for a number of years but eventually lost substantial funds through their endeavors. Still, even failure did not always mean the end of a woman's business career. For instance, the very credit entry of 1855 that reported the failure of fancy goods dealer Gitty Walker also noted that she "intends to go on," and Walker remained in business for at least four more years.[63] Milliner Sarah Bowes returned to her trade in her husband's name after having paid creditors only 17% of what she owed them in her 1872 failure.[64] According to credit reports, Mrs. John Delhanty went out of business in 1878, opened her grocery again in 1880, made assignment of her debts in 1881, and "resumed bus[iness]" and was "acting as an agent for her bro[ther]" the following year.[65]

Conclusion

Clearly, fashioning and applying a new, gendered, definition of success for businesswomen allows us to appreciate the myriad of ways in which business profits and proprietorship enhanced the lives of mid-nineteenth-century women in Albany, even when those individuals never attained unusual distinction or dramatic success. At the same time, this definition also permits us to categorize some business enterprises as failures for the women involved, their backers, and their creditors. However, the complex picture presented in this chapter cannot be reduced to a neatly ordered, linear, best-to-worst scale of success and failure. As we have seen, even success and failure were not mutually exclusive categories for Albany's female proprietors during this period. Female-run businesses might succeed for years only to fail in the end, or they might fail before succeeding. We expect and accept such ups and downs in the business careers of male entrepreneurs at this time of cutthroat capitalism—why deny female microentrepreneurs the same latitude?

At the end of the *Godey's Lady's Book* novelette "Miss Slimmens' Window," the protagonist's small millinery business ends in failure. Yet the following year Alvira Slimmens returns to the pages of *Godey's* in a new novelette and a new guise—as a boarding-house keeper. Once again, this antiheroine proves herself to be silly, stingy, and selfish; yet this time her endeavor survives. By the final installment, through marriage to a confidence man who is Slimmens's equal in false representations (extending in his case to false hair and even an artificial limb), she has even gained the assistance of his two daughters in her work.[66] This fictional conversion from self-sufficiency to minor failure to modest success mirrors the experience of Albany businesswomen as well, and reflects the complexities inherent in judging success—and failure—for mid-nineteenth-century female proprietors.

CHAPTER SEVEN

•

"Doing the Best Business
of Any Firm or Man in the Line"

Female Entrepreneurship
in Nineteenth-Century Albany

Women like Rebecca Lukens and Sarah Bowman often have been cited as exceptional. . . . However, the limited research on this period suggests that women such as Rebecca and Sarah, far from being the exceptional oddities of popular history, are firmly located on the spectrum of nineteenth-century businesswomen.

—Angel Kwolek-Folland, 1998[1]

IN 1858, IRISH-BORN BRIDGET MURPHY KENNEDY was left a widow with four young children (ranging in age from 7 to less than a year old) when her husband, Patrick Joseph, died of tuberculosis. At 37, Kennedy found work as a servant in Boston, depending on neighbors to watch her family. Later she became a saleswoman at a small "notions" store, which she then purchased and ran with the help of her three daughters and her son. She expanded her offerings from notions to groceries (probably including liquor) and variety goods; eventually she had made enough money to purchase the building where she worked and lived. Business profits enabled her to secure a parochial-school education for her son, P. J.—and to provide him with the capital to buy a tavern in the 1880s. With this tavern and other business enterprises, including investment in a hotel and a wholesale liquor business, Patrick Joseph Kennedy continued to build the family fortune, entered local politics, and created the foundation of the Kennedy dynasty for his son Joseph Patrick, the future American ambassador to Great Britain, and his grandsons, John Fitzgerald, Robert, and Ted Kennedy.[2]

The story of Bridget Kennedy's entrepreneurship echoes that of many women who built profitable businesses in Albany during the same period. Most strikingly, Kennedy was a middle-aged, widowed, immigrant mother who opened a small business associated with the female sphere of needlework and employed family members in the shop, which was located in the same building where they lived. Kennedy's small-scale entrepreneurship is demonstrated by her expansion into more profitable lines (groceries, variety goods, and probably liquor), and her ability to invest in real estate by purchasing her shop and dwelling place—much like the modest entrepreneurial efforts of Albany's female proprietors. The investment of hard-earned capital in her son's business certainly represented an entrepreneurial risk, and one that brought handsome familial rewards.

Bridget Kennedy and individuals like her, however, are hardly recognized as American entrepreneurs. Instead, particularly for the nineteenth century, a few prominent businesswomen tend to be featured in women's and business histories as exceptional individuals who attained remarkable success despite the odds against them. Virginia Drachman's *Enterprising Women* is the most recent example of this individualistic, celebratory approach, telling the story of women in business through a series of isolated biographies. Angel Kwolek-Folland's *Incorporating Women* presents a far broader view of businesswomen in the United States, more of a social and economic history, but she, too, describes a series of notable nineteenth-century businesswomen. To set a discussion of entrepreneurship for Albany's mid-nineteenth-century female proprietors in context, we will briefly consider the exceptional women identified by Drachman and Kwolek-Folland.

Both authors mention Rebecca Lukens, an iron manufacturer in Pennsylvania's Brandywine Valley from the 1820s through the 1840s; Elizabeth Keckley, the former slave who used the proceeds of a dressmaking business to buy her freedom in 1855; Lydia Pinkham, whose family began manufacturing her patent medicines in the 1870s; Ellen Demorest, who "built a fashion empire" through her magazines and by popularizing paper patterns during the Gilded Age; and her partner, Susan King, a real estate magnate with whom she started The Woman's Tea Company in 1872.

To this list Drachman adds biographies of Juana Briones, the Hispanic ranch owner who successfully held onto her business after the United States acquired California; Martha Coston, a manufacturer of pyrotechnic flares for naval use from the 1850s through the 1870s; Miriam Leslie, who legally changed her name to "Frank" in order to save her husband's publishing empire after his death in 1880; and financier Hetty Green, the so-called Witch of Wall Street, who made $100 million from her investments between 1865 and her death in 1916. Interestingly, none of these entrepreneurs are discussed by Kwolek-Folland.

Nineteenth-century female entrepreneurs mentioned by Kwolek-Folland (but not Drachman) include Madame Cecee McCarty of New Orleans, an African-American slave-owner, trader, and money-broker in the antebellum south; Julia Brown, a celebrity madam in New York City in the 1840s; Sarah Bowman, whose businesses provided food, laundering, and secondhand goods to the U.S. Army in Yuma, Arizona, in the 1850s; Laura Keene, a theatrical manager and theater owner from 1850s through the 1870s; and Madame Restell, who became a millionaire by providing abortions and birth control products until her suicide in 1878. (According to Andrea Tone's fascinating history of contraceptives in the United States, Restell was "the best known abortionist in nineteenth-century America"; wearing a "diamond-studded nightgown," she slit her throat on the eve of a trial engineered by Anthony Comstock.)[3]

From these sources alone it is clear that a few female entrepreneurs did succeed on a national scale, and in a variety of ventures. This list is hardly exhaustive, however, and it is unclear why some businesswomen are featured in both books, some in only one, and other notable nineteenth-century female entrepreneurs are ignored. For example, remarkable nineteenth-century businesswomen mentioned by Caroline Bird, the first historian of American women in business, include Margaret Haugherty, an Irish immigrant to New Orleans who made a small fortune selling milk, bread, and crackers before and after the Civil War, and Eliza Pointevent Holbrook Nicholson, who owned and managed the New Orleans *Picayune* from her first husband's death in 1876 through her remarriage, to the paper's business manager, until her own death in the 1890s.

This intriguing list of notable American businesswomen, active between 1830 and 1885, proves that there were certainly a few female entrepreneurs in the mid-nineteenth-century United States. Still, even Rebecca Lukens, one of the most remarkable and often cited of these women, was no Andrew Carnegie. Although she did manage her company, the business Lukens owned and operated is considered a relatively small enterprise by business historians. Like Lukens, most of these enterprising women were not millionaires, and few managed businesses that continued after their deaths. For example, Ellen Demorest's innovative paper pattern business was eventually eclipsed by Ebenezer Butterick's company, simply because Demorest and her husband had failed to patent their idea. Judged by the standard of male entrepreneurship, the most enterprising of these nineteenth-century women look rather second-rate. In addition, when seen in isolation the biographies of these individuals once again reinforce the impression that only rare women could become entrepreneurs—particularly since, through a process of selection, each monograph highlights only a few successful businesswomen for this period. Without community studies it is difficult to connect the stories of these remarkable enterprising women to the mass of female proprietors across the nation.

In addition to the reconsideration and reinterpretation of the term "success" presented in the previous chapter, historians of women in business are also redefining the concept of entrepreneurship, especially as it applies to American women of the mid-nineteenth century. This chapter proposes, develops, and illustrates such a revised definition, one that might fit the more "enterprising" women active in Albany between 1830 and 1885. The definition suggested here evolved gradually out of patterns recognized through research findings. Once again, the central proposition is that one ought to measure female entrepreneurship in terms of the commercial and industrial possibilities available to Albany's female population—not according to those supposedly universal paradigms of nineteenth-century entrepreneurship, which draw on models based on subjects who are exclusively male. Without a revised definition for entrepreneurship, the small scale of most women's business achievements precludes their consideration as entrepreneurial ventures in comparison to the most dramatic, innovative, capitalist enterprises of the century. However, using the term "entrepreneur" to describe any and all female proprietors seems to diminish the usefulness of this important descriptor as an analytical tool.

Defining Female Entrepreneurship

Most of the more than two thousand individual female proprietors operating in Albany between 1830 and 1885 were involved in modest endeavors that appear to have been strategies for economic survival and means of self-employment rather than business ventures inspired by an entrepreneurial spirit. Still, there were a number of women in mid-nineteenth-century Albany who—if they did not attain the eminence of local entrepreneurs such as Erastus Corning, a hardware mogul, railroad investor, and bank president—went beyond a strategy of simple survival and approached their business endeavors with more enterprise than the majority of their sisters-in-trade. These female proprietors demonstrated such characteristics as ambition, initiative, innovation, and, most important, *risk-taking* behaviors. According to Mansel G. Blackford and K. Austin Kerr, "Entrepreneurs . . . transform businesses in some important way. Entrepreneurs are innovators. They may observe and seize profitable opportunities, taking risks in doing so."[4] Female entrepreneurs, then, should be willing to take chances in order to increase their profits. Using specific examples drawn from the histories of Albany's businesswomen, it appears that for mid-nineteenth-century businesswomen, such risky behaviors included (but were not necessarily limited to) investing capital in a business venture, leaving salaried positions to enter business for themselves, expanding or diversifying their trades, upgrading or adding commercial locations, investing in improvements, enlarging their workforce and output, spending money on advertising, developing innovative sales and marketing techniques, and buying goods on credit, especially outside the local market.

Within the parameters of the definition proposed here, there is a sense in which even the most modest female-owned businesses were indeed "entrepreneurial." Consider the risks involved for women who set up their own ventures. One of the most evident and universal of these risks was the risk of capital—however small that investment may have been. Substantial risks were always taken when a woman invested everything she owned—all the little capital she could pull together—in her businesses, however small. With no financial cushion of savings or investment in real estate, such women chanced all they were worth on a few hundred dollars' worth of stock, in the belief that their investment in their own businesses would provide a greater profit than any alternate choice. A typical example would be widowed Babeth Doctor, a German-born fancy goods dealer who entered business in 1866 at the age of 42. According to credit reports, Doctor "about" made a living for herself and her four children with her "small store and stock." In 1868 it was estimated that "stock on hand $4 to $500 which is all her worth. Buys $50 worth at a time & pays for it." Clearly, a business loss or failure would have meant a substantial disaster to the entire Doctor family.[5]

Small businesses not only required some start-up money (since they were rarely judged creditworthy) but often continued to require most of a family's profits or savings. Thus, Anna Dell began a fancy goods business in 1868 (a "v[er]y sm[all] affair. would not cr[edit] the concern $10," noted the R.G. Dun & Co. evaluation), while her husband George worked "by the day." A few years later, George found employment as a cigar maker, while his wife opened a small grocery in his name. In 1883 Anna Dell was finally listed as the proprietor of the concern "in consequence of the illness of her husband." According to credit records, even after fifteen years of business, "they are not estimated worth to exceed 2 to $3[000] & that represents their investments in the bus[iness]."[6] Similarly, when widowed Abbie Lynch decided to continue in the family undertaking business in 1883, credit reporters concluded, "all she is worth is at the risk of the bus[iness]."[7] In some businesses, the capital invested by a businesswoman could be quite substantial. For instance, in 1858 Elizabeth Winne entered the grocery business with her son-in-law, Ferris D. Rosekrans, placing $10,000 of her own money "wholly at the risk of bus[iness]," as far as could be ascertained by the credit examiner.[8]

Even in cases where a small business did not require all of a woman's financial resources, it often drew on her major assets. Sources of capital risked on business included—as we have seen in chapter 3—government pensions, insurance policies, and inheritances, as well as loans from relatives and friends. Honora Devine's brother assisted her in 1874 after her husband, the proprietor of a hotel, died intestate, owing approximately $3,000. With a loan or gift of $3,000 that she put "down," Devine was able to purchase the premises with a mortgage of $10,000—a substantial risk. Luckily for Devine and her brother, by 1880 she was said to be "d[oin]g a better bus[iness] than when her husband was alive," and her business bore "a better reputation." By 1882 she had paid the original mortgage down to $5,000.[9] But the risks—of her brother's cash and goodwill, as well as her own time, energy, and good name—had been considerable.

One of the quintessential signs of male entrepreneurship in the nineteenth century was leaving paid employment in favor of starting one's own business. For women during this period, such a choice was relatively rare, and the nature of the choice was different. As I argued in the previous chapter, it appears that for many of the women who entered the mid-nineteenth-century Albany marketplace in business for themselves, such ventures represented their *best* chance of employment—for many milliners and dressmakers, for instance, self-employment provided the best monetary rewards and most satisfactory working conditions (especially if they were also the mothers of young children). But what of those women who had secured "good" jobs yet left them for the riskier venture of opening their own business? Although Albany's credit records abound with examples of male clerks who attempted to set up small businesses for themselves, women employees seem to have been far less likely to take this step—only about ten women in the entire population studied can be confidently said to have belonged to this group. Sacrificing a regular paycheck and risking their own savings, or convincing relatives to risk their capital on a female business venture, these women were exhibiting quintessentially entrepreneurial behavior. For example, in 1869 a Miss McDowell was reported to have left her former position of saleswoman at $10 per week (a rather princely sum by the standards of the time) because her employer refused her a raise. Though McDowell brought only a couple of hundred dollars into her firm (the millinery and dressmaking partnership of Ella and Mary Hartnett), this small sum undoubtedly representing her entire savings.[10] A few years later, in the mid-1870s, Kate Bateman left her position in the employ of John Markus (one of the largest and most prosperous millinery dealers in Albany) to start her own "custom" trade.[11] (In her case the risk seems to have paid off, since she was still listed as a millinery dealer in city directories twenty-five years later). The lure of being her own boss enticed Mary Frame to enter business twice: after a couple of years as the proprietor of a dressmaking establishment, in 1871 she became a fitter and saleswoman for Wm. Whitney's Dry Goods house at a "good salary," but after about a year of employment left Whitney's to form a new dressmaking partnership with her sister, Anna Keenan. The young women (described as "smart and indus[trious]" by credit reports, but also as having little financial ability) were said to "have the cream of the trade" in Albany; unfortunately, such elite customers often proved very slow in paying their bills. Had Miss Frame and her sister chosen steady employment at good salaries, they would *not* have risked the payment and credit headaches that consistently plagued their business over the next decade.[12] Johanna Murray was another employee of Wm. Whitney & Co. who decided to enter a business partnership instead; her salary in 1880 had been $20 a week, and the savings she was prepared to invest amounted to $3,000 or $4,000.[13] Even widows sometimes took the risk of entrepreneurship over paid employment: Minnie Robinson, a widow with a small child, left her place with John Myers (though she was "well spoken of" by that gentleman) in 1882 after three years to set up her own variety store with an initial investment of about $400.[14]

Having made their leap into the cutthroat nineteenth-century marketplace, businesswomen faced the same fierce competition as their male counterparts. For instance, in 1879 widow Theresa McKinley invested $2,000 (in cash) in stock for her shoe store, located in a neighborhood where competition for the boot and shoe trade was described as "lively" and "brisk."[15] In 1883 "competition from larger dealers" had reduced the estimated worth of the fancy goods and variety business of Mrs. Robert E. Morris's family (including her ailing husband and aspiring son-in-law) by several thousand dollars, although they had invested in the construction of a new and larger "brick store house" in 1876.[16]

Business expansion and diversification were typical entrepreneurial strategies employed by male business owners in mid-nineteenth-century Albany. However, expanding one's trade by adding locations was very rarely attempted by Albany's female proprietors, even those with the most prosperous enterprises. Female entrepreneurs were more likely to expand by moving to larger quarters, or to endeavor to improve their trade by moving to better neighborhoods. Credit examiners were quite sensitive to the location of a business, which might be condemned as attracting "a poor class" of customer, or praised as "a much better" place than formerly.

Business improvements were also noted by credit examiners, as in the case of Mrs. Alida L. Hendrickson, an American-born, entrepreneurial dry goods dealer. Hendrickson and her husband had commenced business by

1841, when she was 36 (the same year that the youngest of her four children was born). By the time credit records noted her existence in 1856, the widowed Hendrickson was said to be "d[oin]g v[er]y well"—in 1859 examiners noted that she "does her own work & has always supported her family." In 1860 Hendrickson had her small store "refitted." This may have been due to the influence of her "enterprising sons," two of whom were working with her in the store by 1862, when they were in their early twenties—but from whom had they learned such "enterprise" if not their mother?[17] In the early 1880s widow Doretha Kirchner also carried on and improved her business with the assistance of her sons, after her husband Jacob had left her his "entire prop[ert]y" consisting of a brewery and real estate estimated to be worth in the neighborhood of $50,000. Although in this case the sons Jacob and Augustus, described as "practical experienced men," took responsibility for managing the brewery, it was under her authority that brewing facilities were "improved" and production increased. The fact that her husband chose to leave this considerable estate to his wife rather than to his grown sons suggests that he himself trusted her entrepreneurial abilities.[18]

Though Albany's female entrepreneurs could not be said to have practiced the types of vertical or horizontal integration introduced into American big business during this period, they did manage to find avenues for modest growth through diversification of their products. For instance, Annie Brown's business combined several specialized lines: schoolbooks, stationery, confectionery, and toys, as advertised in city directories of the 1870s. Other businesswomen attempted to match less obvious trades, as when long-time confectioners Sarah Anderson and her sister Alida Mesick added a line of dress patterns. Some female entrepreneurs changed trades completely: from fancy goods or confectionery to groceries (as did Mary Miller in the 1870s). Although we have no evidence about these women's motivations, one assumes that a response to market forces was at work. It may be worth repeating here that small groceries usually sold liquor as well as food—possibly making them a more lucrative, if not more genteel, choice than shops selling ribbons or candy. But some entrepreneurs moved in the opposite direction, as when Margaret Winne (who was reported to have "lost money" in the grocery business) changed to fancy goods. Despite an estimate of her "bus[iness] cap[acit]y" as "below medium," Winne was able to obtain credit because she owned real estate and was worth several thousand dollars. In her case the fact that she chose to change trades, rather than to leave business altogether, suggests a desire for entrepreneurship, if not necessarily a talent in that direction.[19]

A component of the business expansion sought by most entrepreneurs is an increase in paid staff. As far as can be determined from existing records, very few businesses run by Albany's mid-nineteenth-century female entre-preneurs employed more than five individuals, and most depended on the labor of family members. Even concerns large enough to be listed in the census of manufactures (primarily milliners and confectioners) generally employed five or fewer "hands." Thus, proprietors such as Mary Harris, who kept twenty to thirty women employed in her prosperous millinery business (1850), or Sarah Devilin, who gave out work to ten or twelve girls in her ladies' underwear business (1875), appear relatively entre-preneurial in their willingness to risk the expense of a large payroll. Indeed, Devilin—a widow described as "very indus[trious] and econ[omica]l in her ha[bit]s"—saw her business "closed by Sheriff" in 1877, and was forced to reopen in the name of her married daughter.[20]

Advertising and self-promotion were not absolute requirements for suc-cessful commercial ventures in the mid-nineteenth century, and few women advertised their ventures in Albany's yearly city directories.[21] Because of the rarity of this type of self-promotion, I believe that such advertisements clearly mark businesswomen as entrepreneurs. Ads placed by women tended to be small, simple, and direct, without illustrations or elaborate descrip-tions. Yet some women took great care to promote their wares and skills, as did confectioner Grace Anderson. In the Albany city directory of 1844/45, the widowed Anderson described herself as an "Ornamental Confectioner" whose creations included "Pastry, Jellies, Charlotte Russe, Creams, &c., served up daily," as well as "Wedding Cakes, Ornamental And Plain, Orna-mental Pyramids, &c., & every requisite for parties."[22] Ten years later, in 1854, Anderson's advertisement described her "EATING ROOMS, Cake Bakery, &c. &c." as being located "Within one minute's walk of the dif-ferent Rail Road Depots" and offering "A large assortment of Cakes and Pastry. Oysters in every style. Together with a large assortment of Confec-tionery, Ice Creams & Soda Water, manufactured daily on the premises" (see figure 7.1).[23] Evidence provided by these advertisements also reveals that Grace Anderson employed the entrepreneurial strategy of changing her business with the times and responding to market demand, as she added oysters to her bakery and ice cream saloon. That Anderson's attitude was unusually entrepreneurial is confirmed by credit reports, which describe her as "enterprising," "v[er]y smart," "act[ive]," and "making money."[24]

Another self-promoter was Elizabeth McDuffie, who ran a dyeing and scouring establishment from 1855 through 1864, and again from 1880 through 1895. Born in Scotland, McDuffie carried on the business of her first husband (P. Leddy) while married to her second, a former police cap-tain turned stove and hardware dealer—indeed, they ran their establish-ments separately. She herself was praised by credit examiners as "d[oin]g a g[oo]d bus[iness] making money" in the late 1850s, and was said to

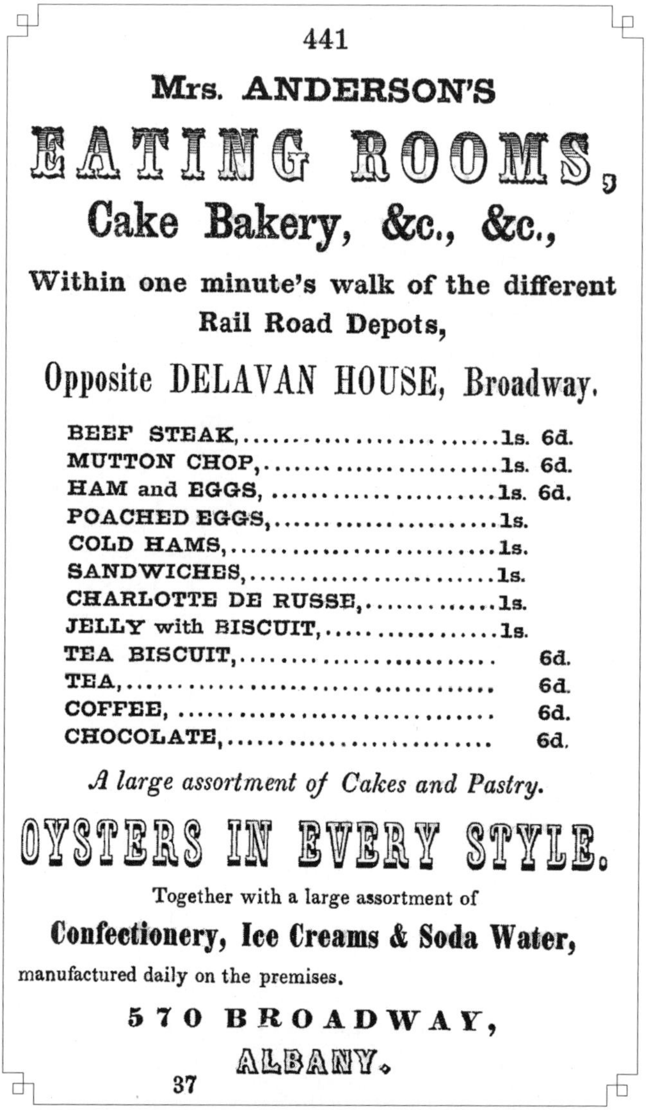

Mrs. ANDERSON'S

EATING ROOMS,

Cake Bakery, &c., &c.,

Within one minute's walk of the different Rail Road Depots,

Opposite DELAVAN HOUSE, Broadway.

BEEF STEAK,..........................1s. 6d.
MUTTON CHOP,.......................1s. 6d.
HAM and EGGS, ...1s. 6d.
POACHED EGGS,......................1s.
COLD HAMS,...........................1s.
SANDWICHES,.........................1s.
CHARLOTTE DE RUSSE,.............1s.
JELLY with BISCUIT,.................1s.
TEA BISCUIT,..........................   6d.
TEA,...................................   6d.
COFFEE, ...   6d.
CHOCOLATE,...........................   6d.

A large assortment of Cakes and Pastry.

OYSTERS IN EVERY STYLE.

Together with a large assortment of

Confectionery, Ice Creams & Soda Water,

manufactured daily on the premises.

5 7 0 BROADWAY,

ALBANY.

37

Figure 7.1
Advertisement for Grace Anderson, Confectioner, 1854.
Source: Munsell's Albany Directory and City Register for 1854 (Albany:
J. Munsell, 1854), p. 441. Courtesy of the M. E. Grenander Department
of Special Collections and Archives, University at Albany SUNY.

have "furnished" her second husband with the money to go into business for himself. Meanwhile, John McDuffie was criticized for knowing "nothing of the bus[iness]" he had entered and for not giving it proper attention—indeed, by 1863 he was said to be "of no a[ccount]," although she was estimated to be worth some $20,000 when she sold out the following year. Interestingly, the McDuffies were bringing up a young daughter at the same time, first mentioned in the credit report of 1858.[25]

More than a decade later Elizabeth McDuffie returned to Albany, having (according to the credit examiners) lost money in the lumber business in Sullivan County. Her advertisement in the city directory of 1880 presented her background, experience, and skills in impressive detail:

> ALWAYS DYEING & YET LIVING!
> MRS. JOHN McDUFFIE
> NEW DYEING AND SCOURING ESTABLISHMENT,
> 37 BEAVER STREET, Formerly of Norton Street.
> Mrs. McDuffie would respectfully inform her old and new patrons, that she has resumed her old business of Dyeing and Scouring in all its various branches. And she was the first one in 1855 in this city that applied STEAM to DYEING and FINISHING, therefore has made that business a SPECIALTY. Ladies' Silk Dresses Cleaned Entire without Ripping, also Lace Curtains, Shawls, Blankets, &c., cleaned in first-class style.
> PRINCIPAL OFFICE, 37 Beaver Street
> BRANCH OFFICE, No. 5 CLINTON AVENUE[26]

It would appear that such advertising did not overstate her expertise, since McDuffie remained in business at least until 1885, when she was about 69 years old. Thus, Elizabeth McDuffie was entrepreneurial in a variety of ways—she continued to operate independently in business after her remarriage, she lent money to her new husband to start him in his own venture, she changed lines from dyeing and scouring to lumber (relocating to do so and risking a capital of approximately $20,000), she opened a branch office when she returned to her original trade—and she advertised.

Innovative marketing techniques have also been cited as a classic aspect of entrepreneurship, and a few of Albany's businesswomen did break ground in this area. For instance, widow Jacobina Tietz (who transformed her husband's small business repairing pianofortes into a much larger concern after his death) developed a novel approach. According to the credit report of 1875, "she sells a great number of cheap class of pianos manufactured in New York. . . . Sales are principally on the installment plan & with people in mod[est] circ[umstance]s only." Such methods gained Mrs. Tietz praise as "a very shrewd businesswoman" by credit examiners in 1875.[27]

Despite the pleasure historians of women in business can derive from these tales of entrepreneurial success, it is important to recognize that the most entrepreneurial females were not necessarily more successful than those who continued to conduct small, safe businesses that provided "barely a living" year after year. An illustration is provided by the case of Clarissa Loomis, a milliner from 1840 to 1844; credit reports concluded that she "was amb[itious] of doing too much & therefore was unsafe."[28] Indeed, the risk-taking behavior associated with entrepreneurship might well have caused entrepreneurial females to fail more often than women who aspired to less spectacular results. The enterprise of Jacobina Tietz, for example, ended in direct competition with her own son, who opened his own store; complicated legal difficulties ultimately engulfed the rest of her family and appear to have driven her out of business.

Another self-promoting Albany entrepreneur was Mrs. S. S. Colt, who appeared briefly on the scene in the early 1870s and vanished almost as quickly. Previously, if briefly, the publisher of a newspaper in Manchester, New Hampshire (hopefully titled "Every Month," it lasted only from February through April 1867), Mrs. Colt appears to have arrived in Albany with big plans.[29] According to the credit records, Colt was an "energetic" woman who established a paper called "The Scientific Advertiser" with a small capital of about $1,500. Coming out every two weeks, the Advertiser was "distributed gratuitously the proceeds of the advertisements running the machine."[30] A description of the paper claimed that it owed its success to "its original literary character" and "its spicy editorial notices for advertisers, which are in themselves of interest to the public" (see figure 7.2) as well as "its method of placing from one-half to two-thirds reading matter on every page, thus rendering each page of equal value to advertisers." In addition to praising its style of writing and design, the ad went on to stress the paper's plans for distribution: "the publicity which is ensured-by keeping BOUND FILES in all prominent Places of Resort in and near the cities of its publication, and throughout the State."[31]

Mrs. Colt also advertised her "Scientific Advertiser" in the program of the Trimble Opera House (previously discussed as the theatre erected by Lucien Barnes, husband of the plucky former manageress Miss A.G. Trimble, with the support of Mrs. Trimble, his mother-in-law). The inside of one cover read:

IF YOU WANT TO SELL A FARM,
Want to Sell a House and Lot,
Want to Sell a Patent,
Want to Sell a Carriage,
Want to Sell Furniture,

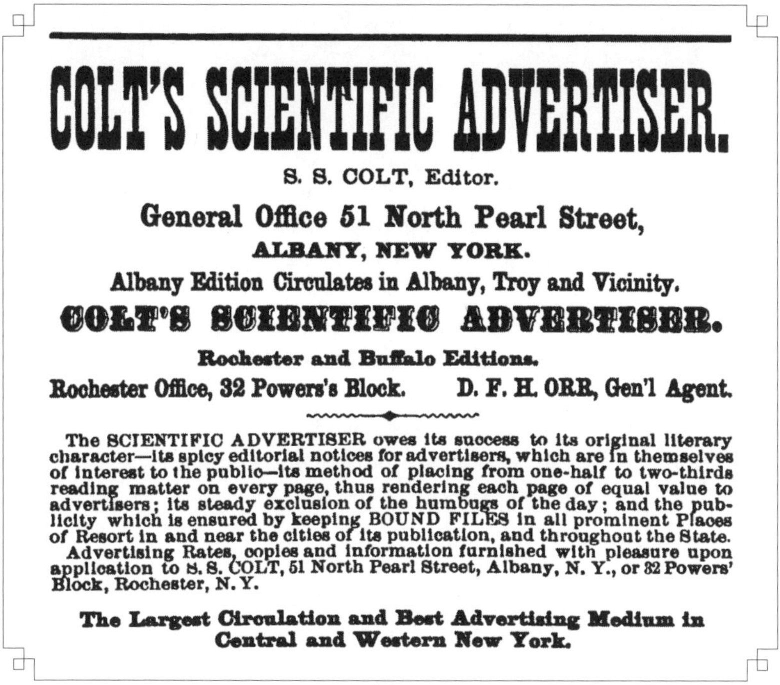

COLT'S SCIENTIFIC ADVERTISER.

S. S. COLT, Editor.

General Office 51 North Pearl Street,
ALBANY, NEW YORK.

Albany Edition Circulates in Albany, Troy and Vicinity.

COLT'S SCIENTIFIC ADVERTISER.

Rochester and Buffalo Editions.

Rochester Office, 32 Powers's Block.   D. F. H. ORR, Gen'l Agent.

The SCIENTIFIC ADVERTISER owes its success to its original literary character—its spicy editorial notices for advertisers, which are in themselves of interest to the public—its method of placing from one-half to two-thirds reading matter on every page, thus rendering each page of equal value to advertisers; its steady exclusion of the humbugs of the day; and the publicity which is ensured by keeping BOUND FILES in all prominent Places of Resort in and near the cities of its publication, and throughout the State.

Advertising Rates, copies and information furnished with pleasure upon application to S. S. COLT, 51 North Pearl Street, Albany, N. Y., or 32 Powers' Block, Rochester, N. Y.

The Largest Circulation and Best Advertising Medium in Central and Western New York.

Figure 7.2
Mrs. S. S. Colt's Scientific Advertiser, 1871.
Source: Inside front cover of *The tourist's guide through the Empire State: Embracing all cities, towns, and watering places, by Hudson River and New York Central Route . . .* (Albany: Mrs. S. S. Colt, 1871).

Want to Buy a House
Want to Sell Millinery & Fancy Goods,
Want to Sell Hats & Caps,
Want to Sell Boots and Shoes,
Want to Sell Roofing,
Want to Sell Groceries,
Want to Sell Dry Goods,
Want to Sell Jewelry,
Want to Sell Hardware,
Want to Sell or Buy ANYTHING,

You can make your wants known to
thousands of readers, by ADVERTISING
In COLT'S SCIENTIFIC ADVERTISER, offices,
51 NORTH PEARL STREET, ALBANY,
and No. 2 FIRST STREET, Troy[32]

The back cover of the same issue insisted:

IT WILL PAY YOU TO
ADVERTISE In
COLT'S SCIENTIFIC ADVERTISER,
The Cheapest and Best Medium for Reaching the Public
It is read in nearly every family in Albany and Troy and in all
The Towns in the vicinity of these Cities. TRY IT.

Soon after this ad appeared, Mrs. Colt advertised that she had become the publisher of the Opera House's programme itself, in the following terms:

NOTICE—The "Orchestra," the only authorized Programme for the Trimble Opera House, will be published on and after December 19, 1870, by the COLT PUBLISHING COMPANY, who will have charge of all the advertisements inserted therin.[33]

Sadly, Mrs. Colt disappears from the historical record (at least in Albany) after 1871. Her remaining accomplishment was the publication of *The tourist's guide through the Empire State: Embracing all cities, towns, and watering places, by Hudson River and New York Central Route . . .*, edited by herself. During her brief stay, however, she certainly "thought big," embracing a series of innovative techniques in her publications and their promotion, and indulging in what appear to have been somewhat grandiose claims. Although we have no idea what may have happened to her, or even whether her name (Mrs. S. S. Colt) was real or assumed, she certainly fits anyone's definition of a risk-taking and inventive entrepreneur.

Exceptional Entrepreneurs

The varieties of risk-taking behaviors described above encompass a wide range of business activities available even to relatively modest enterprises operated by Albany's female entrepreneurs. A few of the female proprietors in Albany, however, exhibited an evident ambition, significant innovation, or a scale of operation that set them apart from other businesswomen of the period. Choosing four examples, we will consider the entrepreneurship of Mary Leask, Julia Ridgway, Hannah Pohly, and Catharine Blake in some detail.

Mrs. Leask's first name never appears in city directories or credit records; her business manufacturing laces was officially listed under the name of her husband. Yet from the first entry next to John Leask's name in

1846, credit examiners noted, "keeps or rather his wife keeps a lace store." In 1847 the Leasks moved from a "tumble down tenement" to a "better store" with a larger selection of goods, for which it was speculated they must pay a high rent. Such a risky move suggests in itself an entrepreneurial drive, though at this point it would be difficult to attribute the move particularly to either husband or wife. Credit records do note, however, that although John Leask was a "first-rate business man when sober," he "sometimes goes on the spree most dreadfully & keeps at it for days." By 1850 John Leask had become more temperate and found a situation as a bookkeeper; Mrs. Leask continued "a fair business in the lace line." A year later her Scottish-born husband went to London, then in 1853 to Australia. Mrs. Leask, commended as a "very g[oo]d bus[iness] woman" by the credit reporters (a rare accolade), took this opportunity to expand "extensively," adding a millinery line to her store. At that time—1854—she was estimated to be holding stock worth $6,000 to $8,000 and selling goods for $10,000 to $12,000 a year. (Again, to set these amounts in context, an average wage for a female milliner in Albany in 1860 was about $3 a week).[34] In 1855 she sold her business to two former employees—her foreman and *his* wife, also an experienced worker—and left Albany—perhaps to join her husband in Australia? Whatever her history after leaving the city, Mrs. Leask's nine-year business biography in Albany clearly demonstrates the ambition, innovation, and expansion associated with entrepreneurship.[35]

The career of Julia Ridgway, a plumbing entrepreneur, illustrates how a businesswoman of exceptional drive and vision could move to the top, defying gender expectations by excelling in a trade strongly associated with the male sphere. Ridgway enjoyed a far longer career in Albany than Leask, and we know substantially more about her business history. Widowed in 1851, at the age of 26, English-born Ridgway regularly advertised her business—the New York State Plumbing Establishment, later Ridgway & Company, later Russ & Ridgway—in Albany's city directories, describing herself as "Proprietress" of the concern and "Licensed Plumber to the Albany Water Works."[36] Ridgway's early ads featured her own name in bold print (see figure 7.3) plus a line drawing of plumbing fixtures, including a bathtub and toilet (confounding our notions about Victorian propriety). According to credit records, Ridgway provided most of the capital for the company and kept the books, while she took on two partners who provided "the practical part of the concern." Thus, unlike even the most successful milliner or dressmaker, Ridgway was not an artisan carrying out her trade—she was clearly the owner-manager of a large enterprise. She was also the mother of a four-year-old daughter at the time she commenced business in her own name. By 1865 Ridgway was "doing

445

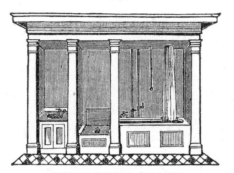

NEW YORK STATE
PLUMBING ESTABLISHMENT,
Nos. 115 & 117 State street, Albany.

The Subscriber, Proprietress and Licensed Plumber to the Albany Water Works, would respectfully inform her patrons and the public, that she still continues to carry on the Plumbing business in all its branches, as heretofore, by F. W. Ridgway, deceased.

This Establishment is one of the largest in the State, and is well known throughout the country as one of the leading establishments in the Plumbing business.

The following articles manufactured and constantly for sale at this Establishment: Hatters' Kettles, Iron, Copper and Brass Pumps, Bathing Apparatus, Water Closets, Kitchen Ranges, Copper Boilers, Stationary Fire Engines for Factories, Deep Well Pumps, Hydraulic Rams, Lead, Copper and Iron Pipes, Sheet Lead, Brass Cocks, Valves, Couplings, Leather Hose, and all other articles appertaining to the business.

The trade supplied with all or any of the above named articles at New York prices. Orders executed in any part of the United States by competent workmen.

Persons desiring the insertion of Water Pipes into their dwellings, will find it to their advantage to call and ascertain our prices, and examine the method of inserting the pipes, &c.

JULIA RIDGWAY.

Agent for Pierce's Kitchen Ranges, Chilson and Richardson's Metropolitan Hot Air and Cooking Range; also Stebbins' patent Compression Cocks, which will be supplied to the trade at the manufacturer's prices.

38

Figure 7.3
Advertisement for Julia Ridgway, 1854.
Source: Munsell's Albany Directory, and City Register, for 1854 (Albany:
J. Munsell, 78 State Street, 1854). Courtesy of the M. E. Grenander
Department of Special Collections and Archives, University at Albany,
SUNY.

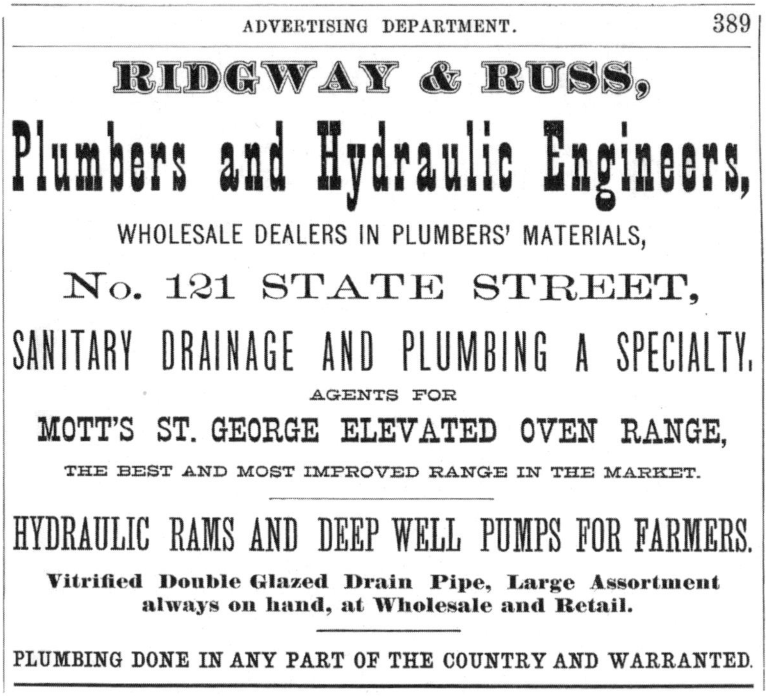

ADVERTISING DEPARTMENT. 389

RIDGWAY & RUSS,
Plumbers and Hydraulic Engineers,
WHOLESALE DEALERS IN PLUMBERS' MATERIALS,
No. 121 STATE STREET,
SANITARY DRAINAGE AND PLUMBING A SPECIALTY,
AGENTS FOR
MOTT'S ST. GEORGE ELEVATED OVEN RANGE,
THE BEST AND MOST IMPROVED RANGE IN THE MARKET.

HYDRAULIC RAMS AND DEEP WELL PUMPS FOR FARMERS.
Vitrified Double Glazed Drain Pipe, Large Assortment always on hand, at Wholesale and Retail.

PLUMBING DONE IN ANY PART OF THE COUNTRY AND WARRANTED.

Figure 7.4
Advertisement for Ridgway & Russ, 1878.
Source: The Albany Directory for the Year 1878, Containing a General Directory of the Citizens, A Business Directory, Record of the City Government, Its Institutions, &c., &c. (Albany: Sampson, Davenport, 1878). Courtesy of the M. E. Grenander Department of Special Collections and Archives, University at Albany, SUNY.

the best bus[iness] of any firm or man in the line in Albany undoubtedly making money," with a business worth estimated at $10,000—about three times the worth of the business her husband had left at his death. The "well managed" business continued to make money, providing Ridgway with funds to invest in real estate as well. Although one partner retired in 1871—surely providing a natural opportunity for her own retirement after twenty years in business—Ridgway chose instead to reorganize her partnership, continuing to oversee and "attend closely" to the business. By then the estimated worth of the firm had grown to $20,000.[37] An advertisement of the late 1870s (see figure 7.4) reads in part:

Ridgway & Russ, Plumbers and Hydraulic Engineers, Wholesale Dealers in Plumbers' Materials, Agents for Mott's St. George Elevated Oven Range . . . Hydraulic Rams and Deep Well Pumps for Farmers . . . Plumbing done in any part of the country and warranted.[38]

Clearly, twenty-five successful years in business had not diminished Julia Ridgway's ambition, self-promotion, appetite for expansion, or willingness to become involved in new ventures. About ten years later, in 1889, Ridgway & Russ had added a telephone number to their advertisement, as well as a line announcing "TELEPHONE COMMUNICATIONS to all parts of the city; and we are prepared to furnish a Plumber at any time during the Day or Night, or on Sunday."[39]

The credit examiner's description of Julia Ridgway as "doing the best business of any firm or man in the line" suggests the strong identification between masculinity and business enterprise during the nineteenth century itself. One might argue, in fact, that calling any businesswoman a "man" defined her as more entrepreneurial than her peers. Female proprietors in Albany who attained this accolade included not only Ridgway but milliner Olive Blanchard, described as "the best man of the two" compared to her husband, a wig dealer, in 1853; Mrs. A. Hunt, a shoe dealer called "the man of the concern" (in contradistinction to her second husband) in 1855; Sarah Denmead, "the principal bus[iness] man of the concern" for the family fancy goods business legally owned by her husband John in 1858; and Clara Martineau, of whom it was said in 1869 that her husband Frank, a glove dealer, had "the money the wife none but she is the bus[iness] man."[40]

The most powerful businesswoman in Albany, measured in terms of capital, was German-born Hannah Pohly, the widow of Nathan Pohly, a Jewish dry goods dealer who had been described by credit examiners as "a close cautious man" with an estate worth $75,000 to $100,000. On her husband's death in 1872, Hannah was 34 years old, with five children ranging in age from 2 to 14. The credit records noted that "the probabilities are that the widow will take a partner who underst[an]ds the trade & continue." Forming "Pohly & Co.," Hannah took her husband's former bookkeeper Joseph Friedman as a partner, lending him most of the capital for his share and offering "1/3 of the profits." Though the credit examiners feared that "there is not the same energy & keen judgm[en]t ab[ou]t the present conc[ern] as there was when 'P' was at its head," they were satisfied that the firm—with stock worth $40,000 to $50,000—was creditworthy. According to the credit ledgers, Pohly, unlike Ridgway, did not "interfere much with the bus[iness]," but by 1875 "Pohly & Co."—now described as jobbers in cloth (and described in city directories as dealers in "cloths and cassimeres")—maintained an "excellent standing." Two years later the credit records note that "Mrs. P." had $30,000 in investments outside the business plus a residence that she owned "free and clear." By 1879 the business of Pohly & Co., now described as wholesale clothiers, was estimated to be worth $125,000 "safely"; by 1881 Joseph Friedman was identified as Pohly's son-in-law, and the business—with a working capital of $85,000—was doing a trade of about $225,000 a year. In 1883 credit records note that the firm stood well "with the manufacturers & Jobbers of Cloths both in the home & foreign markets"; in the final entry of 1884, credit examiners added that "their capital has been increased from accumulations of profits," "that they are buying largely for cash," and that "they appear to be in easy circumstances." Easy indeed! Hannah Pohly's shrewd decision to invest in a junior partner and to stay in trade after her husband's death had been a wise business move, as well as a wise move for her family. Not only had Friedman become a son-in-law, but Pohly's own growing sons were left with a business to inherit.

A final example of an exceptional female entrepreneur is Catharine Blake. Unfortunately for our attempt to trace her business history, Mrs. Blake was neither widowed early in her marriage, like Pohly or Ridgway, nor separated from her husband like Leask. Thus her name does not appear in the business records until 1881, although her husband had been operating a hotel (presumably with, at the very least, her assistance) since 1868. In that year Adam Blake, described by R.G. Dun & Co. credit reports as "a gentleman of color," was set up in business by "subscription of citizens." Congress Hall, his hotel, was largely patronized by members of the New York State legislature. The hotel appears to have experienced a shaky beginning, with start-up debts to be paid, and a slack summer season when the legislature was out of session. Blake's stock speculations also had a negative impact on the business's cash flow and ability to meet its obligations. By 1878, however, the Blakes could afford to lease a newly constructed hotel, the Kenmore, at an annual rent of $6,000, and at one point they attempted to lease and run a summer hotel as well. It is hard to determine how much responsibility each party had for the running of these hotels, but like John Leask, Adam Blake was noted for "intemperate" habits and "indulging freely." Credit records indicate that Catharine Blake, after her husband's death, originally intended to dispose of the business, as long as she could do it "to advantage." An offer of $50,000, however, did not suit her, and under her sole management the concern prospered even more than it had before. According to an R.G. Dun & Co. entry of 1882: "She made money last year & there is every reason to believe she will have done equally well this year, provided she does not sell out. There is now being an effort made by C. E. Leland of the Delevan House [a rival hotel] to buy her out & some think he will succeed. She has been offered $50,000 for the bus[iness] & furn[iture] in the Hotel, but asks $75(000) and will prob[ably] get that or 00."[41] Presumably Catharine Blake was not satisfied with the offer she received, since she was listed as the proprietress of the Kenmore Hotel in city directories until 1887—some six years after her husband's death (see figure 7.5).

The stories of Leask, Ridgway, Pohly, and Blake stand out from the careers of most female proprietors in Albany not just because they were unusually successful but also because they conducted business in specific ways that set them apart from most other businesswomen. Most of Albany's microentrepreneurs did not attempt to expand their enterprises dramatically, as did Leask. No others supervised incorporated firms worth more than $100,000, as did Pohly, or refused offers of tens of thousands of dollars for their businesses because they felt the price was too low, as did Blake. Almost none entered fields strongly associated with male owners, took on male partners, or regularly advertised in city directories, like Ridgway. Most important, all four were unusual in the degree of risk they embraced, far more than the average Albany proprietress.

However, we must acknowledge that these women—along with Grace Anderson, Jacobina Tietz, and Elizabeth McDuffie, other remarkable Albany entrepreneurs—were able to risk more, and to innovate, because their enterprises had been founded by men—their husbands. For Albany, it seems that only businesses established under male names were able to gain the capital and credit to expand beyond the much more modest limit attained by women who had never been married, most of whom remained in the needlework trades.

These entrepreneurial wives and widows of Albany reflect a similar situation in the country as a whole. Rebecca Lukens followed in the footsteps of her father and husband; Ellen Demorest partnered with her husband William; Hetty Green inherited millions from her father and married a businessman (although she later divorced him). In the case of Lydia Pinkham, it was her sons who provided the entrepreneurial energy that made her a household name. In the nineteenth century, it was very rare for a single woman to amass a fortune or plunge into innovative entrepreneurship.

Male Entrepreneurship

Let us re-gender this discussion in a different way and bring men back into the picture, illustrating cases of "failure," "success," "enterprise," and "entrepreneurship" through male business ventures of this period in Albany. Using men who entered the millinery trade—a trade closely associated with women and made up of about 95% female owners—illuminating comparisons can be drawn between male and female concerns. This evidence demonstrates that although millinery provided a relatively good

Figure 7.5
The Kenmore Hotel, 1880s.
Source: Arthur James Weise, *The History of the City of Albany, New York, from the Discovery of the Great River in 1524, by Verrazzano, to the Present Time* (Albany: E. H. Bender, 1884), facing p. 464. Courtesy of the M. E. Grenander Department of Special Collections and Archives, University at Albany, SUNY.

opportunity for businesswomen in mid-nineteenth-century Albany, and although some male proprietors in the millinery trade failed dramatically while others made only modest successes of their ventures, it was possible for men to reach a pinnacle of entrepreneurial achievement far beyond that ever achieved by the most talented and enterprising women.

First, it is important to recognize that many men who opened businesses in mid-nineteenth-century Albany never achieved business "success" or displayed "entrepreneurship," either in the traditional senses of these labels, or in terms of the more "relative" definitions proposed here. That is, to be male did not necessarily ensure an individual of good credit, paying customers, or the capital required for significant expansion. For example, in February of 1848 milliner Lowell Gilmore entered a business partnership with bonnet bleacher Martin Cutler. By April their official association had been dissolved, and Gilmore was operating his own wholesale and retail bonnet store, going so far as to advertise his wares in the Albany City Directory of 1849. But by 1851 Gilmore had "fail[e]d all to pieces" and left business owing $2,500 to Cutler—his former partner and already a more prosperous wholesale dealer.[42]

Like most female milliners, some male dealers carried on small businesses that did little more than provide a livelihood for their families. English-born Joseph Walker arrived from New York City in 1850 to enter the commercial scene in Albany as a manufacturer of straw hats, shifting his line to millinery and fancy goods by 1860. His wife Elizabeth attended the store as well as their four children (who ranged in age from seven to a year old at the time their business opened). Credit entries noted that Walker owned no real estate and had "lim[ite]d" means, although he was characterized as "atten[tive]" and "indus[trious]," with "g[oo]d character and hab[it]s," as well as "hon[est]"—like so many women in small businesses. Similarly, his establishment was considered safe for only a "limited" amount of credit, and the R.G. Dun & Co. reports even announced him "out of business" in 1856, four years before his listings disappear from city directories.[43]

Martin Cutler, mentioned above, was one male dealer in women's hats who appears to have been quite enterprising. Beginning his business career as a bonnet bleacher in 1851, Cutler was immediately characterized by credit records as a "g[oo]d" businessman of "g[oo]d" character. His reputed worth was already $2,000 ("some say more") in 1852. By 1855 he was a bonnet manufacturer and wholesale and retail dealer worth up to $5,000. His evaluations rose steadily year by year; in 1859 his wholesale millinery business was described as the "principal one in this line." Employees included his brothers, who worked as clerks and salesmen. In 1863 he was said to be worth $8,000; by 1865, $10,000 to $12,000;

and by 1866, $12,000 to $15,000. Meanwhile, Cutler had purchased his store and the entire building. By 1870 his estimated worth had reached between $40,000 and $50,000, by 1874 it was up to $75,000, and in 1879 he still continued to do "the largest whol[esale] and retail trade" in the city. All this had been achieved by a relatively steady business growth under an individual whose character was described as "industrious," "prudent," "shrewd," and "upright in every respect."[44] One gets the sense of someone in the right place at the right time, a person prepared to take advantage of opportunities, but not necessarily one inclined to create opportunities where none previously existed. It is worth noting, however, that Cutler's steady character and timely entry into the wholesale millinery business were enough to bring him profits far in excess of what Albany's best and most fashionable female millinery establishments ever provided for their owners. Indeed, starting with a similar capital investment, Cutler managed to exceed even the most enterprising female milliners by a factor of about ten.

Possibilities for an entrepreneurial man who entered the millinery business are illustrated even more dramatically by the meteoric career of John Markus, a dealer in "French Millinery." Arriving in Albany as an outsider in 1871, Markus announced that he was from the "Cape of Good Hope," where he had spent fifteen years, five as a bank director. The last three years of his life, he claimed, had been passed in "England and the Continent" while "making arrangements for goods to be supplied him here," that is, imported to his new Albany millinery concern. Markus's extravagant claims included having paid $30,000 cash for his stock and being worth $50,000 personally. R.G. Dun & Co.'s initial credit report naturally bristled with suspicion, since "Little or nothing [is] known of him here."

A mere six months later, however, Markus's store was "doing well" with "a good class of customers"—in fact, the store was called "the best of its kind in the city." Despite continuing doubts on the part of credit examiners ("his antece[dents] are understood to be rather unfavorable" was noted more than a year after his opening), in 1873—a year of depression—they marveled that he "Keeps very fine & high priced stock & it is wonderful how he can command so much bus[iness] as he is known to do & get the prices that he does." Clearly, Markus's strategy of marketing himself as an exotic outsider and his hats as marvelous imports from Paris had paid off, and within a few years the fact of having worked for Markus was being used by other credit reporters as a positive reference for young women setting up in business for themselves.[45] This surge to the top of a trade dominated by women puts female entrepreneurial efforts into perspective. No female entrepreneur entered Albany with anything like the financial backing or sophistication of Markus, and no businesswoman in any field managed such a spectacular opening. Indeed, there appears to have been a "glass ceiling" beyond which female-owned and -operated businesses in Albany did not reach—about $8,000 for single milliners, and approximately $100,000 for previously married businesswomen (for example, those involved in male-dominated trades such as hotel keeping, brewing, and plumbing, as previously discussed). The amount of capital needed to speculate and innovate was rarely available to Albany's women, and credit examiners rarely felt that even profitable businesses run by women required or deserved credit "away from home." Here we do, I believe, see the influence of nineteenth-century gender ideology. It certainly appears that native-born, single women who would have had enough personal or family resources to make a business splash did not attempt to enter the marketplace as female entrepreneurs. Whether this resulted from their personal prejudices or an inability to influence their relatives to support them in such ventures, or whether both were outgrowths of generally accepted (if not hegemonic) middle- and upper-class values, cannot be discussed based on available evidence for Albany.

Conclusion

Entrepreneurship is a term strongly associated with the most prominent nineteenth-century businessmen, and an entrepreneurial spirit clearly motivated much of the male business community of Albany, even those engaged in such a seemingly "feminine" trade as selling women's bonnets and millinery trimmings. However, this brief perspective on the potential for male entrepreneurship is meant to reinforce, not obscure, the central point of this chapter—that if we measure female success, enterprise, and entrepreneurship by "male" yardsticks, women's businesses will only look like pale echoes of male models. But if we measure female businesses against the experiences of female workers and businesswomen, we can begin to recognize new models, and formulate new yardsticks for achievement based on women's own experiences, while always realizing that women did not enter the mid-nineteenth-century marketplace as equals with men. As women are introduced into our picture of mid-nineteenth-century market activity in the United States, I believe that female entrepreneurs should be conceptualized as a distinctive segment within the overall group of business proprietors. More enterprising, ambitious, innovative, and risk-taking than their less entrepreneurial female counterparts, they nonetheless should be recognized as representing one end of a wide spectrum of women's business strategies and behaviors—rather than imagined as unique individuals who overcame overwhelming obstacles to succeed in a "male" business sphere.

And if Rebecca Lukens, the antebellum Quaker widow who became an iron manufacturer, was no Andrew Carnegie, we must admit that even Julia Ridgway, one of Albany's most entrepreneurial female proprietors, was no Rebecca Lukens. The stories of even the most entrepreneurial business-women in Albany tend to be "limited" success stories—limited especially in terms of capital. No doubt many more stories like those of Anderson, Tietz, Leask, Ridgway, Pohly, and Blake remain to be unearthed in other nineteenth-century American communities. Until these stories are told, we can only speculate on how exceptional, or representative, the entrepreneurial women of Albany described in this chapter may have been.

To return to the example of Bridget Murphy Kennedy, through her entrepreneurship and the contributions she made to the success of P. J., Bridget Murphy Kennedy surely influenced the lives of her great-grandchildren, John, Robert, and Edward Kennedy—and through them, American history. Yet, as noted by Laurence Leamer, author of *The Kennedy Women,* the story of this female entrepreneur has been lost not only to American history but "even in the oral history of the Kennedy family."[46] Surely the entrepreneurial businesswomen of Albany also contributed to their families' prosperity, class mobility, and—in the case of immigrant families—assimilation into the economy and culture of the United States. Much like the Kennedys, however, in most cases their descendants proba-bly have no idea that their great-great grandmothers were businesswomen. Finally, even if these great-great grandchildren know something of their family history, they would be more likely to think of these female propri-etors as "working women" than "entrepreneurs."

Clearly, Bridget Murphy Kennedy will never attain the historical stature of her grandson Joseph Kennedy, or her great-grandson President John Fitzgerald Kennedy. Indeed, there is little chance that the story of this "founding mother" will even become integrated into the mythology sur-rounding their family—both because the very concept of a female entre-preneur does not fit traditional ideas of how nineteenth-century women "should have" behaved and because her success was never spectacular. (Had she been the first Irish-American millionaire, one trusts that Bridget Kennedy would have been considered noteworthy). Business historians, however, have the responsibility of not only highlighting "great" individu-als and important firms but also describing the ways in which entrepreneur-ship operated on the day-to-day, street level in America's communities. As in the case of Bridget Kennedy, Albany's entrepreneurial female propri-etors may have measured their success less in terms of a single family firm passed down from generation to generation, and more in terms of an intergenerational transmission of capital and status gained through busi-ness endeavors.

CHAPTER EIGHT

Illicit Business

Shady Tradeswomen in Albany

> Grouped about a beer-keg that was propped on the wreck of a broken chair, a foul and ragged host of men and women, on boxes, benches, and stools. Tomato-cans filled at the keg were passed from hand to hand. In the centre of the group a sallow, wrinkled hag, evidently the ruler of the feast, dealt out the hideous stuff. A pile of copper coins rattled in her apron. . . .
>
> —Jacob Riis, 1890[1]

JACOB RIIS'S CLASSIC 1890 EXPOSÉ, *How the Other Half Lives,* illustrates through words, line drawings, and photographs the rampant poverty, overcrowding, crime, filth, and exploitation that confronted the immigrants who flocked to American cities toward the end of the nineteenth century, as well as Riis's prejudices toward different ethnic groups. Although known primarily for his campaign against tenement housing, Riis also paints a vivid—even lurid—picture of marginal urban microentrepreneurship. In his description of "'the Bend,' foul core of New York's slums," for example, he includes a passage on female street vendors:

> Along the curb women sit in rows, young and old alike . . . haggling over baskets of frowsy weeds. . . . Ash-barrels serve them as counters. . . . Hucksters and pedlar's carts make two rows of booths in the street itself, and along the houses is another—a perpetual market doing a very lively trade. . . . Two old hags, camping on the pavement, are dispensing stale bread, baked not in loaves, but in the shape of big wreaths like exaggerated crullers, out of bags of dirty bed-tick. . . . Stale bread was the one article the health officers, after a raid on the market, once reported as "not unwholesome." It was only disgusting.[2]

For Riis, this street scene represents the disgusting disorder of the slum just as evidently as the junk-filled alleys, grimy basements, and homeless children we more commonly associate with his muckraking journalism. He clearly considers the stale bread offered by "two old hags" as unwholesome, worthy of being condemned by health officers on a raid—though not as worthy as "a fish stand full of slimy, odd-looking creatures" or "loads of decaying vegetables." Even the shape of the bread—not formed in orderly loaves, but in the exotic shape of an exaggerated cruller—seems to offend him. Though Riis himself had been a homeless immigrant when he arrived in the United States from Denmark in the 1870s, by the late 1880s he viewed impoverished street vendors and hucksters through middle-class eyes. For himself and his readers, the squalor of the market marked it as unsavory, bordering on illicit and illegal. But for the women who sold goods on the street, this was a method of self-employment and survival.

As he traveled through the city slums as a police reporter and, later, a journalist, Riis discovered ventures far more illicit than those of female street vendors and hucksters. His narrative of a police raid on "The Stale Beer Dives" of lower Manhattan reeks of moral indignation. Yet while he catalogs a list of horrors, Riis also inadvertently describes a type of capitalist enterprise that could be practiced by the down and out. "The Stale Beer Dives," according to Riis, were basement "burrows" where men and women drank flat beer that had been previously been discarded—that is, left on the curb outside more reputable saloons. These unsavory dregs were simply "touched up with drugs to put a froth" on them by the operator of the "dive." Specifically, Riis saw "A room perhaps a dozen feet square, with walls and ceiling that might once have been clean . . . but were now covered with a brown crust that, touched with the end of a club, came off in shuddering showers of crawling bugs, revealing the blacker filth beneath." Once inside, Riis witnessed the scene described in the quotation that begins this chapter, an underground "dive" operated by an older woman whom he characterizes as "a sallow, wrinkled hag, the ruler of the feast," her apron full of "copper coins."[3]

Who was this "sallow, wrinkled hag"? The disapproving Riis could not conceive of her as an independent entrepreneur, nor could he appreciate the service she provided to her customers. Yet such "dives" not only dispensed cheap beer but also served as a kind of informal flophouse where the homeless could stay the night for the price of admission. As reported by Riis himself, such "two-cent restaurants" (as they were known to their patrons, since it was possible to purchase a stale roll for that price) were generally run by Italians, Negroes, or "occasionally" women—all of whom were among the least employable and most vulnerable members of the dregs of society. And, as even Riis was forced to admit, these social outcasts were really quite entrepreneurial. Their profits were "considerable" since, as he himself noted, "barring a slight outlay in the ingredients that serve to give life to the beer-dregs, it is all profit." But isn't providing a vital service, minimizing expenses, and maximizing profits exactly what an entrepreneur is supposed to do?

There are no nineteenth-century accounts of Albany's marginal micro-entrepreneurial ventures that can match the vivid detail Riis offers in his description of the stale beer dives of Manhattan. The seamier side of life in Albany appears to have been left to the pen of acclaimed writer William Kennedy. In a memorable scene from *The Flaming Corsage,* a novel in his ongoing series about Albany, William Kennedy imagines his heroine, Katrina Taylor Daugherty—a cultured, wealthy woman of mixed English and Dutch ancestry—attempting to enter an Irish saloon for the first time in her life. Her initial reception is frigid; Katrina is confronted by six men who stare as she makes the mistake of entering through the front door. The experienced bartender immediately informs her, "We don't have women at the bar, Ma'am." The year is 1903, a decade after the advent of "The New Woman," and a period when the roles of modern women were presumably changing. Yet both Anglo-Dutch and Irish Albany appear stuck in an old-fashioned, "traditional," nineteenth-century view of separate male and female spheres.[4]

There is no hint in Kennedy's novel, which spans the years 1884 to 1912, that women in Albany might not only have regularly frequented saloons (in his story, they must slip in and out through the side door, sit in the back room, and not stay long) but could actually have owned and operated establishments that served liquor. Yet Albanian women did engage in enterprises deemed illicit by their contemporaries. The anxieties of reformers such as Riis and the attitudes portrayed by novelist Kennedy are not identical to those expressed by Albany's nineteenth-century business community. Although the R.G. Dun & Co. credit reporters would undoubtedly have been equally disgusted by female peddlers selling stale bread or women operating unlicensed beer dives, in most cases they expressed their concerns in economic rather than moral terms. And, unlike the characters in Kennedy's Irish bar, they would not have been surprised to find women running a saloon.

Illicit Business

In addressing the subject of "illicit" tradeswomen in nineteenth-century Albany, New York, one immediately confronts the suspicion (based on assumptions about proper female behavior and the limits of possible female occupations) that most women who dared to carry on businesses in the face of contemporary attitudes about the vital link between separate spheres and female respectability must have been—by definition—disreputable. Wasn't all business carried on by women in the mid-nineteenth century subtly illicit, one wonders? Wasn't it considered less-than-respectable for women to be in Albany's marketplace at all?

In fact, the R.G. Dun & Co. credit investigators never allude to such concerns. Somewhat surprisingly, their tone (at least in Albany) is neither condemning of, nor condescending toward, women in the marketplace. Instead, the credit evaluations appear to have been eminently practical. The examiners were looking for women (or men) running successful, profit-making businesses based on a sound capital investment. What they could not approve of were businesses that they considered too small to deserve credit, or without any solid financial resources, whether run by males or females. The purpose of these credit reports was to identify those businesses to which it would be safe, and ultimately profitable, to extend credit for the purchase of goods—that is, businesses that would not fail and leave their creditors in the lurch. Thus, the credit reports looked at a number of factors: size, potential for growth, capital resources (personal property, cash, loans, savings, real estate), expertise in the trade, location and type of shop, local competition, the type of customer, plus—and this is what makes them an invaluable source for the historian—the character of the business owner and his or her family members. The central question was, would a business owner (whether male or female) be able, and willing, to pay for goods purchased on credit, or would this businessperson be a "slow pay," possibly requiring the supplier to resort to such legal methods as suing for payment? Or, worst of all, might this entrepreneur end up as a bankrupt business failure, settling his or her debts at a mere 25 cents on the dollar?

Somewhat surprisingly, most businesswomen in Albany were judged positively in terms of their character, if negatively in terms of the size of their operations and capital resources. As we've seen, typical descriptions contain phrases such as "small concern" and "small means." Nevertheless, individual entries abound with terms such as "industrious," "attentive," "prudent," "respectable," "honest," and "worthy."

"Illicit" female businesses made up a tiny minority—if a fascinating and revealing subset—of the more than 750 cases located in the credit reports on Albany between 1840 and 1885. Having acknowledged the respectability of the vast majority of women's businesses, however, it is illuminating to consider what characteristics those ventures deemed "illicit" appear to have had in common. If a woman's entering the marketplace was not, in and of itself, reason to question her respectability, what was? What types of women, and which sorts of endeavors, were considered disreputable by the credit examiners (and, by extrapolation, by the business community as a whole)?

For purposes of this discussion, "shady" businesswomen and their "illicit" ventures can be divided into four categories. First, some business-women were labeled notorious simply because they were reputed to have "bad" characters and habits; indeed, the characters of the women them-selves and their enterprises appear to have been considered virtually inter-changeable by mid-nineteenth-century standards. Second, women starting their own business ventures were sometimes tainted by an association with men who had a history of what were described as "tricky" business dealings. Third, female entrepreneurs were considered shady when they employed tricky business practices. (These categories tended to overlap; women of "bad" reputation were often accused of questionable business practices.) Fourth, a few women operated types of businesses—primarily brothels, but also some unlicensed saloons and gambling establishments—deemed illicit by their very nature. In making such judgments, it seems that the R.G. Dun & Co. credit reporters were reflecting minimum community stan-dards of middle-class morality (at least for the city of Albany).

Interestingly, neither saloons nor other establishments that sold liquor—including breweries and dealers in wholesale liquor—appear to have been considered disreputable by the R.G. Dun credit examiners or, by exten-sion, the local business community. I would argue that middle-class values in an urban center such as Albany, with a large Irish and German immi-grant population, would clearly not have been identical to the middle-class values of a small town during the same period. As Roy Rosenzweig points out in his study of Worcester, Mass., "Whereas Worcester officials viewed these female liquor dealers as disreputable and criminal, the Irish commu-nity apparently looked at them quite differently. In Ireland, the keeping of a shebeen [a home-based liquor shop] was a 'recognized resource of widows,' and they had a 'privileged' status in the liquor trade. . . . Almost invariably, a woman arrested for illegal liquor selling would plead . . . that 'she was compelled to sell a little beer and whiskey in order to make a liv-ing.'"[5] According to information gleaned from city directories, the federal census, and the credit ledgers of R.G. Dun & Co., it is evident that in the decade between 1875 and 1885 alone more than 350 Albany women were proprietors of saloons, breweries, wholesale liquor stores, small gro-ceries, and other types of businesses that produced or dispensed intoxicat-ing spirits. (Rosenzweig also found numerous Irish female keepers of grog shops and small saloons in Worcester, Mass., particularly in the early 1870s before the passage of the 1875 license law.) Single, married, and widowed, ranging in age from 17 to 79, most of these women—including numerous mothers of young children, including infants—not only sold "drink" but almost always did so out of their own places of residence. That is, they brought both the marketplace and alcohol into the very center of their family life.[6]

However, Albany's credit reporters did not automatically condemn such businesses or the women who operated them. They expressed no criticism at all for businesswomen who were running such establishments as home-based enterprises, even when (as we can learn from the manuscript census) those homes included young children. For instance, Mrs. George Elder was praised as "indust[rious]," "honest, saving," and "careful" in the running of her saloon from 1869 to 1876, and Mary Ronan, an "old lady" running "a living business" in groceries and liquors with stock worth about $50, was described as "well reg[arde]d" in 1879.[7] Mrs. Ed Ryan, who ran a small grocery and saloon in 1880, was characterized not only as "honest" but also as being of "good hab[it]s."[8] Indeed, many women who sold liquor out of their homes were neither desperate nor destitute, but were married to respectable working men, such as policemen, teamsters, moulders, machinists, or employees of the railroad.

"Bad Character & Habits"

In contrast, let us consider some examples of tradeswomen of "bad characters and habits" according to the credit reporters—known as either drunk, disorderly, "loose," as keeping low-class company, or as spendthrifts. Irish-born milliner Kate Corbally, for instance, earned the following series of negative assessments from credit examiners on the basis of her regular inebriation:

> 1858: . . . her landlord can't get his rent. she gets drunk & is not wo[rthy] of any cr[edit] at all
> 1859: poor concern. Drinks poor rum. Cant recomm[end]
> March 1861: Bad egg
> September 1861: Bad. Bad
> 1862: Out of business[9]

Note that Corbally's millinery enterprise was not really evaluated at all. Her character as a drunk was enough in itself to tarnish her prospects, and one is only surprised that her venture lasted as long as it did. It is important to recognize, however, that Kate Corbally was one of only two women accused of drunkenness in more than 700 entries located.[10] This contrasts dramatically with numerous examples of tradeswomen's husbands who were said to have been intemperate.

Credit reporters also criticized women who indulged in behavior they considered "disorderly." Mrs. Margaret Kivlin, for instance, was a sometime pawnbroker in the 1880s. A credit entry under her husband's name explained that "He & his wife are not living on good terms & either party has the other arrested for assault and battery about every three mon[th]s, no one here would care to give him cr[edit] and none is advised."[11] When Mrs. Kivlin began operating a shop in her own name in 1885, credit reporters did not even bother to investigate and assess her worth, and one can safely assume that her reputation within the business community, like that of her husband, would not have been high.

Interestingly, except for women who were running brothels, almost no tradeswomen were described as promiscuous. A rare exception was Julliette B. Straight, whose husband opened a boot and shoe store under her name in 1869, after having "failed & cheated his creditors" in a previous venture. According to the credit examiner's report of that year, "His wife Juliette B. is a loose character (or was, a short time ago. she may have reformed)." Regular entries over the next few years reiterated both the husband's untrustworthiness and his wife's notoriety, and even after their business failed in 1872, a report noted "standing weak morals said to be loose." Again, the comments make no explicit connection between Juliette Straight's loose morals and the boot and shoe business—for instance, there is no indication that the store was a front for a house of ill-repute—but Straight's reputation added a black mark that appears to have been considered of equal significance to her husband's previous commercial failure.[12]

A slightly different kind of character "flaw" was displayed by women whose reputations were not questioned but who consorted with what the credit reporters considered "low" company, especially at their place of business. Miss Ellen Carmody, for example, operated a small grocery in the 1880s. According to the credit examiner in 1881, "her place is a resort for a low class of people & she has hardly trade enough to make expenses."[13] Clearly, in the eyes of the R.G. Dun reporters, these situations were connected, and the problem was not so much the status of Carmody's companions, or her lack of taste in selecting them, as their poverty. With indigent clientele, it was unlikely that her business would make money or attract better-paying customers.

One might wonder how a grocery store could be described as a "resort" for any type of people, but in an analysis of business in the nineteenth century one discovers that small neighborhood grocery stores almost always sold liquor as well as food, a fact decried by early investigators and reformers such as Virginia Penny. According to Penny, "There are too many small groceries in New York for any to thrive. I have been told that in the majority (even when attended by women) liquor is sold. What a crime."[14] In

Albany, a terse description by a credit examiner of the grocery-saloon kept by Caroline Stein read in 1870, "Has a few vegetables and fruits and keeps a bar."[15] In numerous other cases, a venture described in city directories as a grocery is identified as a saloon or liquor store in the census or credit records, and vice versa, suggesting that there was little difference between such enterprises at the time.[16]

A final example of a businesswoman whose character was questioned by the credit reports (and thus, one suspects, by some of the local business community as well) was the "spendthrift" Mrs. Olive Blanchard. In cases of male and female proprietors, credit examiners often expressed suspicion about individuals who appeared to be extravagant or to be living what they called a "fast" lifestyle. For the purposes of the R.G. Dun & Co. credit reporters, it was good for a businessperson to be dependable and steady, whereas it was conceived of as dangerous for a man, woman, or entire family to live extravagantly, since too much personal spending could easily put the resources loaned by the creditor to a business venture in jeopardy.

This particular case is rather unusual, since Mrs. Blanchard was also acknowledged to be running a profitable and well-managed millinery establishment. The wife of wig maker James W. Blanchard, she was regularly characterized in far more positive terms than her husband, who was criticized as a "politician" and "unsafe without a backer"; even army service as a captain in the Civil War does not seem to have impressed the credit reporters at all favorably. A report of 1853 included the unusual praise "Mrs. B. is said to be the best man of the two & makes the most money." However, the same entry noted Olive Blanchard's "show of extravagance," and three years later credit reporters complained that Mrs. Blanchard was "all the time saucy and impudent" despite (or perhaps because of?) getting "the largest prices in town" and "making money." A series of entries under Olive Blanchard's own name added (in 1866), "Rather tricky & slow pay. . . . Is a gay woman and does a gay business. Husband is a fast man Ought to pay cash"; and (in 1871) "is a slow pay & has to be sued. . . . She & family live high & save 00." These brief glimpses into Olive Blanchard's personality reveal a fascinating tension between the credit examiners' admiration for her business acumen and disapproval of her general attitude—not least, perhaps, her rather flippant attitude toward *them*.[17]

Tainted by Association

Credit records reveal numerous cases in which a businesswoman was tainted by association with a shady male relative—husband, father, brother, son—or even a male employer. In 1842, for instance, Mrs. Gitty Walker (who had opened a dry goods store) was described in these words: "widow dau[ghter] of Jeremiah Smith, but I am not aware he has anything to do with her, if he has, it w[oul]d with me be suff[icient] of itself to deprive her of cr[edit]."[18] Similarly, in 1863 when Ann Smith took over the business previously run in her husband's name, the credit examiners reported: "she is the wife of Edward Smith (late of Smith and Owens) a tricky Englishman, he used to pay his debts when he could not help it. He is said to have money. She has nothing. The change of the business from his name to hers is evidently for dishonest purposes."[19] In 1870 credit investigators reported on the millinery goods business of Nora Halpin in these terms:

> she was a shopgirl for Isaac Hahn (a dead beat, whom we think you know) & when he made his assignment [that is, settled his debts at less than their full value] she left him & opened a store in South Pearl St. . . . & it was believed (& by some stated positively) that part of Hahn's stock found its way into that store. We have lost track of her for the last two months— don't know where she hangs out now—be it as it may, we must caution parties selling her or anyone who is at all connected with our friend Isaac Hahn.

Later that year, Halpin married another man of questionable character:

> lately married to "James Buggins," suppose she will call herself Mrs. James Buggins but the old sign is up yet. "Husband" not wor[th] anything. Formerly kept a low saloon. She was a shop girl for Isaac Hahn and was somewhat mixed up in his failure. advise C.O.D.[20]

The remainder of the entries on Nora Halpin all make this same suggestion of demanding cash on delivery, though Walker and Smith were eventually able to establish better reputations in their own right.

In the mid-nineteenth century, credit examiners often made specific negative comments about Jews and Jewish-run businesses—reflecting the prejudices of American society at large.[21] When Mrs. Lewis Lowenstein took over a clothing business after her husband's failure, the credit entry of 1860 read, "wife of 'Lewis L.' who failed some years since & says he cant pay but prob[ably] he is a dishonest Jew would not trust her or him." In 1864 the credit investigator stated, "Mrs. M. Lowenstein is supp[ose]d to be the wife of Lewis. . . . Lewis is a bust up Jew. . . . They have a g[oo]d store & st[oc]k do a g[oo]d retail bus[iness]. It no doubt belongs to the husband but is difficult to prove it."[22]

These several cases also illustrate a variation of illicit business—the practice of putting the business of a failed man into the name of a female relative in order to escape creditors and begin again. In such cases, it is difficult to assess the role of the wife in the endeavor. Some appear to have been figureheads, while others had clearly been involved in the ventures now operated under their names all along. Although the first credit entries under a female name often warned suppliers that she was not the "real" head of the concern, later reports often disclosed the wife's role as an active partner, as in the case of Sarah Guyer, whose husband Hugh opened a business selling window sashes, blinds, and doors in her name in 1875. The original credit entries explain that in 1869 his own business in the same line had been "Swallowed up by Judgements and mortgages." After about six months the credit examiners stated that her husband was "dishonest and untrustworthy," but that Sarah herself was "good" if a "slow pay." Instead of referring to "H" as conducting the business, the records now talk of "Sarah" and "her husband." Owning "consid[erable] p[ro]p[er]ty in her own name," Sarah seems to have been seen as a better risk than her spouse, and although the business was recorded as "out" in 1879, no bankruptcy or judgments were noted in the R.G. Dun records at that time.[23]

Shady Business Practices

As has been revealed by several entries so far, women seen as having "bad" characters and "shady" business practices such as slow payments tended to be associated. What upset credit examiners most were deliberate attempts to cheat creditors. Although one might assume that businesspeople who constantly disappointed their creditors would quickly have ended their careers in failure, some businesswomen managed to operate for decades despite a long history of credit problems. For instance, Anna Andrews was an Irish-born milliner married to an English-born produce dealer and was the mother of two sons (one born the year she originally entered business in her own name). Beginning in 1857 and continuing until 1882, Andrews's business practices regularly earned the censure of the R.G. Dun & Co. credit reporters. At first, entries were concerned with the size and scope of her venture, as in those of 1857, "has a small st[oc]k in a front room of a dwelling," and 1860, "buys goods only to make up." That same year, investigators advised "no credit," and entries for the following years began to be peppered with the unusually strong term "bad," as in:

61: "Better buy for cash." "Bad. Bad."
62: "No better." "Bad egg."
63: "Not good."

By the late 1860s Andrews's problem had been narrowed down: "has some means but is a little trickey" (1866), and in 1873 it was explained that "there are some houses here who sell her & call her good for wants, but as a rule her cr is none of the best, her morals are not said to be high toned & she is said to be tricky." In 1880 it was noted that "the trade at home do not regard her as a very desirable customer owing to unsatisfac[tory] settlements," although her estimated worth had risen to $3,000 to $4,000. Finally, in 1882 (when she was 52, after twenty-five years in business), Anna Andrews helped her son John open a fancy goods store. According to credit reports, "his mother supplies the capital—he himself is worth nothing . . . none of the family have the best of a reputation."[24] Nevertheless, the Andrews family provides a clear example of how some businesspeople with tricky business practices and shady reputations managed not only to survive but even to flourish over the years—and how businesswomen as well as men were capable of shifty dealings in the marketplace.

The most spectacular case of a female entrepreneur who tricked her creditors seems to have been that of Mary Sachs, who came from New York City to Albany in 1882 to take over the furniture business of Henry Freedman, putting her son Philip in charge. According to the credit report, "it is their intention to carry on under the same system as 'F' did, viz. the Installment plan. How well she will do no one can say, but none of the Israelites who have hitherto worked this class of business have succeeded & this party is not likely to fare any better." In fact, credit examiners soon discovered Sachs was a close relative of Freedman and "presumed to be a cover for his bus[iness]." Within a few months she also took over a company of the same kind in Troy, across the Hudson River. Shortly after, her Albany store was burned out, with only about half the value insured. In less than a year the business had failed—a failure that, according to the credit examiners, was "looked upon as a 'put up job,' and should be fully investigated by her creditors." Her liabilities were estimated at almost $10,000 (again, the equivalent of approximately $1 million in today's money, using the formula offered in chapter 3). In terms of an era in which women struggled for years to build up enterprises worth a few hundred or perhaps a few thousand dollars, managing to lose $10,000 of creditors' money within six months was a remarkable feat of illicit business activity.[25]

Infamous Businesses

Finally, we will consider women who were involved in trades that were by their very nature considered immoral by the credit examiners. Enterprises in this category appear to have been limited to low-class, unlicensed saloons, gambling houses, brothels, and their fronts. For instance, in the 1850s and '60s Mrs. Fantin Lawlor ran a provision store characterized as a "small Rum Hole," "a groggery," and "a Rum mill." Credit records also noted that she was "s[ai]d to have [been] indicted for selling liquor without a license," and (in another case of guilt by association) that her son had embezzled money from the St. Nicholas Hotel, in New York City. The suspect Mrs. Lawlor, however, continued to do an "average" business until her death around 1863—leaving debts that remained, according to the credit reports, unlikely to be paid.[26] Twenty years later, in the 1880s, credit examiners condemned a saloon run by Mrs. Leonard Reed in these terms: "The place is nothing more than a gambling establishment and does not bear a good reputation. The business is looked after by her husband, a disreputable sort of man."[27]

The boarding house and liquor store of Emma McGee were judged to be illicit because they simply provided the front for a brothel. As the credit entry noted in 1886, "She runs a house of ill-repute. do not believe any further information is necessary."[28] This brief comment suggests that once a business was identified as a house of prostitution, it would be regarded as beyond the pale, and that R.G. Dun reporters would not find it productive or necessary to investigate further. This, however, had certainly not been the case in previous decades. In the 1850s and '60s two female entrepreneurs—Sarah Creswell (discussed in chapter 1) and Elizabeth Hemstead—who ran houses of prostitution in Albany under the front of other business ventures, attracted a great deal of attention from credit investigators. Indeed, examiners appear to have visited these establishments again and again simply to make the same report.

Elizabeth Hemstead (or Hempstead) was a married madam who operated her brothel behind the front of a millinery shop. In 1843 it was said that she had been in business for five years, and the entry stated rather obliquely that her reputation was "not high." In 1849 a report included the blunt assessment, "her moral char[acter] is of the worst kind, her house s[ai]d to be one of ill-fame." (Interestingly, that same year Mrs. Hempstead advertised her business under the "Millinery and Fancy Goods" section of the city directory, directly beneath a series of respectable shops.) By 1850 investigators stated, "she is w[orth] ab[ou]t $4[000] but you c[oul]d not collect 4 c[en]ts from her, if she c[oul]d cheat you she w[oul]d do it." Later in 1850 an entry added, "tricky & belongs to a tricky fam[ily], bad moral char[acter] (well acquaint[e]d with a few Albanians besides her husb[an]d). Wont pay. Keep clear. Husb[an]d is a drunken loafer." (Despite such proclivities, her husband, Isaac Hemstead, was listed in city directories as a physician, and later as a Commissioner of Deeds). In 1851 the credit reports declared that she was "bad v[er]y bad"; in 1852 she was called a "Bad egg." In 1853 her entry asserted, "Engaged in more kind of bus[iness] than one, notorious bad char[acter], would not trust her 25 c[ent]s, bad as can be, if anybody trusts her they deserve to loose their money." In 1854 she was called "Dishonest, tricky, & unreliable, unworthy of cr[edit], does not pay when she can. Now do[in]g bus[iness] under cover of her foreman—'a regular blazer'—." In 1855 reports added in the same vein, "Hard case. One of those low 25¢ places!! Dirt cheap!!!" In 1868 investigators continued, "good for 00 don't credit," and finally in 1872 (after approximately 35 years in trade), "Out of business. Old prostitute, not in this line now."[29]

Finally, let us consider the story of a couple of flamboyant characters who appear to have stepped out of the pages of a novel by William Kennedy. The businesswoman, identified by credit examiners as "the old widow 'Dayton,'" was in "bad repute"—indeed, in 1857 it was said that her reputation was "bad eno[ug]h to sink" her new husband, one William Burnett. (In fact, the R.G. Dun & Co. reports added, "what she could not do her daughter would," and that her "first husband is s[ai]d still to exist"!) By 1865 their hotel was described as a "low crib" and a "haunt of the worst of depraved women." Credit reports explained that Burnett was "f[or]m[er]ly Pilot of a vessel who blew up" and that he had "Saved the life of a notorious woman named Elizabeth Dayton." It was she who owned "the hotel and grounds worth $20,000" for which she had paid cash. According to credit reports, the couple kept "a Bad house." Nevertheless, by 1870 they were said to be "d[oi]ng a v[er]y fair bus[iness]" and Burnett, though "not wo[rth] anything" on his own, was judged "g[oo]d [for credit] with wifes endorsement." Cases such as this one illustrate that it was perfectly possible for men and women to carry on illicit businesses in Albany despite bad reputations and adverse credit evaluations—if they had cash on hand or could get backing from a person with less-than-fastidious moral scruples. When Elizabeth Dayton Burnett died in 1871, she left her husband an estate worth $20,000—which he squandered (through bad habits and extravagance, according to reports) by 1876.[30]

Context and Conclusions

It is vital to remember that the women whose illicit businesses have been the subjects of this chapter represented only a tiny proportion of the population of women who conducted business enterprises in mid-nineteenth-century Albany. Here I must differ with Angel Kwolek-Folland, who suggests, "Before about 1880 brothel keeping and its related activities may well have been the single most important type of female proprietorship, surpassing in numbers and capital investment even millinery and dressmaking."[31] Accepting that existing sources for Albany may well undercount the number of brothels, even if we counted all female-run boarding houses in the city as houses of prostitution (an unlikely possibility), as well as all female-operated saloons (an impossibility if we can trust the credit examiners at all), there is no way that the number of female proprietors engaged in brothel keeping could have exceeded the number of dressmakers or grocers.

Yet the stories of illicit businesswomen raise complex and subtle issues with which neither women's history, business history, nor labor history have dealt. They suggest that businesswomen were not completely different from businessmen, and indeed that they did not practice a "kinder, gentler" version of male business culture. Nor do these "illicit" female proprietors appear either as victims of the marketplace or as heartless victimizers of their employees and customers (a view often reflected in popular and reform literature of the period). The women involved in "illicit" business appear once again as a diverse group of heterogeneous individuals, exhibiting a wide range of behaviors and motives.

Although the stories of Albany's illicit businesswomen may remind us of lurid characters—madams in particular—from the pen of William Kennedy, they challenge his image of a male-dominated world of work and leisure. Instead of his vision of sex-segregated spheres, within the shady world at the edges of the Albany business community we once again see men and women interacting in the marketplace. Not only did businesswomen serve male patrons in saloons and bordellos but these businesses required the same interaction with male suppliers, creditors, credit examiners, and sheriffs as other female-run ventures. Clearly, male relatives were often active partners and backers in women's concerns. Considering both licit and illicit marketplace activities, the case of Albany once again presents a challenge to the supposed hegemony of separate spheres based on gender differences.

CONCLUSION

●

Incorporating Businesswomen into History

> But it is obvious that the values of women differ very often from the values which have been made by the other sex; naturally, this is so. Yet it is the masculine values that prevail. Speaking crudely, football and sport are "important"; the worship of fashion, the buying of clothes "trivial." . . . This is an important book, the critic assumes, because it deals with war. . . . A scene in a battlefield is more important than a scene in a shop—everywhere and much more subtly the difference of value persists.
>
> —Virginia Woolf, *A Room of One's Own*, 1929[1]

DECADES BEFORE A WAVE of feminist historians tackled the project of integrating women into the mainstream of historical thought, writing, and analysis, Virginia Woolf raised a vital point about how this endeavor must be understood. Women's history is not only a matter of changing one's subject—adding female actors to preexisting narratives of politics, economics, culture, and society—but also of adjusting one's viewpoint and values. As Woolf understood quite well, though she was speaking of fiction rather than history, such narratives have traditionally privileged male actors, experiences, and values. Yet the novelist put it aptly when she added, "naturally, this is so." One need not assume a deliberate conspiracy on the part of men, even powerful men or influential male historians, to recognize that "the values of women differ very often from the values which have been made by the other sex." Nor need one imagine that all women partake in some universal "feminine" nature to accept the proposition that—across time, place, and culture—the attitudes and values of women have not been identical to those of men, even men of their own race, class, and ethnic background.

Gender theory postulates that the integration of women into scholarly analysis requires a reconsideration and reconceptualization of entire disciplines. Thus, seriously considering gender—maleness and femaleness—as valid categories of analysis will necessarily result not only in new research areas but also in a reconsideration of all aspects of mainstream history. Periodization and concepts of progress, for example, are two areas of "traditional" history that have been the object of notable challenges by feminist historians. Another way in which "adding" gender alters the standard approach to history is by opening up areas of investigation that seem to fall into the "cracks" between specialties within disciplines. (Indeed, "edges" or "boundaries" have been seen as particularly fruitful for gender analysis.)[2]

The subdiscipline of American women's business history is a relatively new field that can be seen either as falling into, or as bridging, the gaps between the histories of women, labor, and business. In the hands of the most sophisticated of its recent practitioners, this subspecialty has been conceived as both a discussion of "what women did" in American business (a subject that remains dramatically understudied despite recent efforts) and a consideration of what female business activities have meant to the economic, social, and cultural life of the United States.

Having reported on the presence of female proprietors in the marketplace of mid-nineteenth-century Albany; having envisioned these women within the context of their families, neighborhoods, and the communities of both working women and business owners; having then reconceptualized both the categories used to describe their enterprising activities and the yardsticks by which these activities might be evaluated; and having explored variations in female proprietorship, success, entrepreneurship, and respectability, what conclusions remain to be drawn? How might the results of this study be understood to impact the new subspecialty of "business and gender," as well as the fields of business history, labor history, women's history, urban history, family history, and the larger discipline of history itself?

To the lively subspecialty of "gender and business," the contribution of my research and analysis will be at least additive, and I hope it will be thought-provoking as well, contributing both to the project of presenting the basic evidence on which historical insights must be built, and to the more complex intellectual task of interpreting that evidence. New categories developed for the understanding of nineteenth-century businesswomen should be neither hierarchical, mutually exclusive, nor oppositional, since useful definitions ought to encompass complex patterns of business structure and behavior rather than simple dichotomies. Instead, the classifications developed for this project may be less useful in "defining" or "differentiating" between different types of female proprietors than in opening up our understanding of the variety that existed within the population of mid-nineteenth-century businesswomen.

This concluding chapter moves beyond the narrow scope of period and location that circumscribe my topic—beyond mid-nineteenth-century Albany—to draw some broader connections and insights. As business history continues to incorporate "gender" as a category of analysis, there is a potential for "substantially revising" not only the history of women, business, labor, and nineteenth-century industrializing cities but the mainstream of economic, social, and cultural history as well. Women's history has generated important insights into the history of both women and men. In the case of business history, an analysis of female microentrepreneurship and the family business economy provides a new angle for studying nineteenth-century businessmen, the majority of whom were also engaged in very small ventures.

Putting Small Business at the Center

It is clear that the study of businesswomen is currently poised on the brink of making an important contribution to the field of women's history. But can it make an equally important contribution to the study of business history? Or, as Joan Scott asked in her commentary at the 1996 Hagley Conference, "Conceptualizing Gender in American Business History," so what? "The history of women in business surely supplements an existing business history, but how does it substantially change it?"[3] What difference can the inclusion of women make to the business history field? When considering how to "fit" women into business history, it will clearly not be enough to simply locate their activities at the edges of traditional narratives, nor to just "insert" a few outstanding female examples into their rightful places. Instead, I would like to experiment with turning our conception of nineteenth-century business history inside out.

When one looks at the vast majority of women who were in business during the mid-nineteenth-century in the United States, one is faced with evaluating the importance of tiny, home-based, neighborhood enterprises—such as groceries, boarding houses, variety stores, saloons, liquor stores, fancy and dry goods stores—and the impact of these microentrepreneurial ventures on their communities and local business networks. Instead of thinking of these small businesses as located on the fringes of the real marketplace, we can consider the ways in which microentrepreneurial ventures provided an everyday, essential conduit for goods and services, and especially cash, throughout the economy of the working-class community. Suppose we reconceptualize microbusiness as being at the center of monetary exchange for the poor and working classes in the urban centers of the nineteenth century? What piece of the commercial and economic puzzle do such businesses, whether run by women or men, represent for a nine-teenth-century city? Where, in other words, did most of Albany's laboring class spend its money? In what ways did this network of small shops—even peddlers—provide the economic underpinning for Albany's wholesale houses and larger markets? Although big department stores did represent the most dramatic and visible shopping opportunities in a city such as Albany, many goods and services were still sold by neighbors to neighbors within the neighborhood.[4] Businesswomen in Albany were often provid-ing the "necessities of life"—that is, food, drink, clothing, and shelter—to working-class and poor people. Such "life-support" enterprises were vital to the economic life of the city. Small neighborhood businesses provided the "base of the pyramid" of nineteenth-century commercial interactions. As Wendy Gamber has recently argued in her work on boarding-house keep-ers, the market revolution, industrialization, urbanization, and the rise of a wage-earning working class "could never have been accomplished without boardinghouses and the labor of those who kept them."[5] In a similar way, the provision of cheap food, drink, and daily "necessaries" for workers, as well as fashionable clothes for a rising middle class that vied for status through dress, were also vital to this period.

Intersecting Spheres

Moving from economic and business to women's history, based on evidence about Albany's female proprietors, it is clear that the so-called separate spheres dear to the hearts of Victorian moralists and an earlier generation of women's historians had little relevance to the lives of businesswomen, especially the majority who came from working-class or immigrant backgrounds.[6] Yes, they occupied a segmented business sphere where the provision of female-associated goods, services, and food dominated their trades. Nevertheless, rather than inhabiting a sex-segregated, clois-tered world, most of Albany's businesswomen regularly interacted with the "male" world—that is, men as backers, suppliers, customers, competi-tors, and/or employees. Most of these women were also very closely tied to their families, neighborhoods, and local business networks, in which they provided a vital link. Indeed, for women in working-class families in mid-nineteenth-century Albany, especially Irish and German immigrants, the middle-class ideal of separate spheres would have been considered an impractical luxury. In Albany, the ability to separate home and business was clearly an upper-middle-class delineator. For the women in a family not to generate any cash income, to consume without producing, offers a perfect example of what Thorstein Veblen would later call "conspicuous leisure" and "conspicuous consumption."[7] Immigrant and native-born working-class women in Albany, in contrast, often worked for wages before marriage and motherhood, and many carried on small, home-based business ventures as wives, mothers, and widows—or assisted in such ventures as sisters and daughters.

Certainly, most businesswomen in Albany entered the marketplace with the full knowledge and support of their families. It appears that these female proprietors maintained a very different attitude toward home-based businesses than the middle-class women whose values and attitudes are sometimes taken as "culturally hegemonic" for this period. "Business" was hardly considered a male preserve; nor was the home viewed as a haven from the cutthroat marketplace. As we have seen, numerous women brought the marketplace—with its customers and cash transactions—into the heart of their family's homes.

Looking at the results presented in this study, it would be tempting to argue that mid-nineteenth-century women were actually more likely to become independent proprietresses than were women of the twentieth century.[8] After all, how many female grocers, saloon owners, and liquor store proprietors would we have found in Albany in 1950, 1980, or even today? Superficially, it appears that the mid-nineteenth century, with its proliferation of small commercial and industrial establishments, with its explosion in trade and manufactured goods, with its emphasis on small-business ownership and self-employment as ideals, and with its lack of positive alternatives for female employment, was actually a high point in female business ownership—followed by declension as small businesses were replaced by big business. In the case of the needle trades, for instance, business opportunities of the mid-nineteenth century were soon taken over by department stores and clothing manufacturers, both owned and managed by men.[9]

Such a "rise and fall" narrative would oversimplify the history of female proprietors as a group. Although individual female dressmakers and milliners, for instance, were certainly driven out of business by competition from mass production and department stores, other women found new business opportunities by opening, for example, beauty parlors. Envisioning the story of nineteenth-century female proprietors as one of rising, then declining, opportunity for women would also ignore a longer view of businesswomen from medieval times to the present.

Continuity over Time

And what of labor history—how might a study of female proprietors contribute to that field? The story of female penny capitalists and the mixed business/wage economy in which they operated also challenges our discrete and oppositional definitions of nineteenth-century class structure based on a dichotomy between capital and labor. In addition, a study of nineteenth-century businesswomen leads one to question the Marxist-derived, "stages of development" model—a model that has at times appeared to be as common for economic and labor historians as the "rise and fall" narrative is for women's historians, or the "grand narrative of progress" has been for business historians. Indeed, the very fact that female microentrepreneurs fall into the cracks between women's history, business history, and labor history can be interpreted as a sign that the fragmentation of history into discrete subdisciplines has outlived its usefulness in explaining historical phenomena. Is it time to delve more deeply into the continuous and simultaneous aspects of labor and economic history—the manner in which small-business-as-labor has remained similar over centuries, and the ways in which different "stages" or levels of development existed simultaneously—especially in the nineteenth century?

One remaining question is the extent to which the women described in my study—those individuals who were visible enough to be recorded in official records—may represent only the "tip of the iceberg" in terms of women's contributions to Albany's commercial economy and the economic welfare of their families. How many more women may have operated tiny business ventures part-time, or for a few months, or on-and-off, out of their own homes? Although impossible to quantify, the existence of such commercial exchanges cannot be doubted; both fictional and anecdotal sources for this period suggest a myriad of ways in which women engaged in business. As historians begin to study the entire scope of women's business activity, we may discover more continuity than change in the occupations of most businesswomen over time and across geographic location, and that small business has provided an occupation and source of cash income for a significant proportion of working women from medieval times to the present, as part of both the "visible" and the "hidden" economies.

Across the entire "Western World" of the later nineteenth century, women were involved in the same types of endeavors discovered by researchers of earlier eras. As Pat Hudson and W. R. Lee have observed, European women of the medieval, early modern, and modern periods have continued to be involved in "irregular, low-status employments which do not readily enter the historical record."[10] According to these scholars, "spinning, sewing, millinery, silkworking, laundering, nursing, and petty retailing, as well as dairywork, much food and drink preparation and low-status fieldwork seem to have been predominantly in female hands over many centuries even though the structure of the economy and market environment had changed dramatically."[11] What Hudson and Lee get exactly right here is the linkage between low-status employments and what they call "petty retailing," as well as the association of female business (and labor) with the preparation of food and clothing. By adding shelter, in the guise of hotels, inns, and boarding houses, to this list, one would have a fairly comprehensive representation of the trades in which the vast majority of Albany's businesswomen were involved in 1880.

Extensive evidence supports this claim of continuity. Fernand Braudel's work on commerce in the early modern era, for instance, includes numerous illustrations of female peddlers, fishwives, market women selling everything from vegetables to bread to dairy products, as well as a striking portrait of a Scottish female grocer from 1790.[12] As for the nineteenth century, recent scholarship by Béatrice Craig documents French women's continuing participation in retail food and textile trades, as wives, widows, and independent traders.[13]

One can find continuity as well in the involvement of a few, noteworthy women in more prestigious and lucrative endeavors over the centuries. Alice Clark, the pioneering historian of women workers who began her classic *Working Life of Women in the Seventeenth Century* with a chapter titled, "Capitalists," reported on numerous female merchants (including "the aristocracy and *nouveau-riche*") engaged in such fields as shipping, moneylending, contracting army and navy stores, and running collieries. Later scholars have uncovered evidence of women merchants in eighteenth-century Germany, and the Dutch colony of New Netherlands.[14] The work of Leonore Davidoff and Catherine Hall for early-nineteenth-century England, and of Bonnie Smith for nineteenth-century France, clearly documents the participation of middle-class women in family business as long as those businesses were located at home.[15] Even at the height of the Victorian era, while decrying the lack of opportunity for women in the United States, reformers Caroline Dall and Virginia Penny reported that female merchants prospered in England and France. According to Penny, "In Paris large stores are owned and conducted by women, and even the importing and exporting of goods is in the hands of some."[16] Although one may sometimes doubt Penny's accuracy on foreign lands, Craig's work on Lille confirms women's involvement in French retail stores, and research by Kolleen Guy has also uncovered a number of widows prominent active in the champagne industry.[17]

Contemporary Microentrepreneurship

Finally, I would like to propose that we look forward in time as well as backward, and consider similarities between patterns uncovered here—

self-employment, dual-income families, women's representation in trades related to the domestic concerns of food, clothing, and shelter, the location of businesses at home, microentrepreneurship—and the place of female workers in today's postindustrial economy. Clearly, small business and self-employment are vital economic engines of capitalism. Though historians have described history as the story of "change over time," history also requires an understanding of continuity over time. Refocusing attention on microentrepreneurship through history not only opens up the whole story of women's participation in the capitalist, cash economy from the Middle Ages to the present but also serves to enrich the linear narrative of history, adding complexity to a story line that has sometimes been conceptualized on "bigger-is-better" assumptions about modernization and progress that appear somewhat outdated in the service- and information-based economy of the postmodern world.

An understanding of the lasting place of microentrepreneurship in the lives of women throughout the world would have an important impact on public policy as well. Despite the attention paid to "microentrepreneurs" in the press over the past decade, I believe that the importance of home-based microentrepreneurship as a viable and valuable means of self-support for women is just beginning to be appreciated. Evidence on female proprietors from medieval times to the present, and across the world, can inform present understandings of women's place in the economy, as well as suggest changes in public policy to benefit female microentrepreneurs rather than mammoth corporations. The 2006 Nobel Peace prize awarded to Muhammad Yunus for his innovative program of microcredit in the developing world recognized the power of financial policies that assist microentrepreneurship. Perhaps even in the United States, tax relief for large companies could be replaced, or at least supplemented, by microloans to small businesswomen.

Female proprietorship is hardly a panacea for the multiple inequities that working women in the twenty-first century still face, such as the "glass ceiling" for female executives; labor-market segmentation for the mass of female wage workers; unequal pay; the devaluation of service occupations, particularly those associated with the care of children or the elderly; an inadequate minimum wage; and the lack of health insurance for part-time work. Nor can a home-based business eliminate such personal challenges as a mother's "triple-shift" of work, child care, and housekeeping. Nevertheless, microentrepreneurship has clearly provided an important option for women historically and around the globe, and although it need not be touted as the "only" or even "the best" route to independence and self-sufficiency, it should be recognized and valued as a proven contributor to those goals.

In conclusion, a careful consideration of both ordinary and "extraordinary" businesswomen, their opportunities and limitations, moves our conception of women's business and labor history out of narrow channels, and allows the simultaneity, continuity, multivalence, and nuance of women's experiences to shine through. I would also like to suggest a new "yardstick" by which women's endeavors in business and elsewhere might be judged—one of fulfillment and satisfaction, valuing pleasure as much as power. Within this reconceptualization, women's responsibility for family and community, and their interdependence, might be accepted as possible sources of comfort and strength instead of limits to an idealized freedom and autonomy. That is, instead of modeling our image of a successful life on the ideal of an "onward and upward" individual journey toward a clear and specific goal, we would make space in our success model for "redefinition," adjustments associated with life stages, and the "creative potential of interrupted and conflicted lives," as well as "lifelong learning and adaptation."[18] Instead of interpreting the demands of home and family on women (or men) as obstacles to be overcome and problems to be solved, such a redefinition of success would acknowledge that human relationships may require sacrifice but—along with a satisfying occupation—also provide a source of joy.

APPENDIX ONE

Types of Female Self-Employment and Proprietorship in Albany, 1830–85

The trades listed below are those defined and counted as business for purposes of this study; at least one female proprietor in each type of business was located in the Albany city directory, in the R.G. Dun & Co. credit ledgers, or in the federal manuscript census.

Artist
Baker
Bandbox manufacturer
Beds, spring beds
Blacksmith
Boarding-house keeper
Bookseller, bookstore
Boot and shoe dealer
Brewers, breweries
Candy store
Cigars/Tobacco shops
Cigar manufacturing
Chemicals
Cloaks & mantillas
Clothing, children's clothing
Cloths & cassimeres
Coal & wood dealer
Coffees
Collars, linen collars
Confectioner, confectionery manu-
   facturing
Corsets/corsetmaker
Costumier
Crockery dealer

Dressmaker
Dress patterns
Dry goods
Fancy goods
Fish, fish store
Florist
Forwarder of lumber
Fruit, fruit cellar/seller
Furniture
Furnishings
Furrier
Gentlemen's goods, gent's furnish-
   ing goods
Glove dealer
Grocer/grocery
Hair/hair goods
Hairdresser/hairdressing
Hair jewelry
Hay and straw dealer
Hats and caps
Hoop skirts
Hotel, hotel keeper
Ice cream dealer
Inks

Inn
Jeweler, jewelry & watches
Laces, lace store, lace manufacturing
Ladies furnishing goods
Laundry, commercial laundry
Linen goods
Liquor, retail and wholesale
Livery, livery stable
Meat, meat markets
Merchant
Milk, milk depots
Milliner/millinery
Millinery goods
News depot, newsroom
Notions, Yankee notions
Opera house
Painter (fine art)
Pawnbroker, pawn shop
Peddler
Pianos, piano dealer
Plumber, plumbing
Porter house
Printing and publishing

Provisions
Saloonkeeper
Saw manufacturer
Shirts & collars
Shopkeeper
Stationery
Store, storekeeper
Refreshment saloon
Restaurant
Root beer
Rubber goods
Tavern
Teas
Trimmings, tassels, fringes, cords
Toys
Umbrellas, umbrellas & parasols
Undertaker
Underwear
Variety, variety store
Vegetables
Wax flower maker
Wig maker
Worsted

APPENDIX TWO

•

Sources and Methods

City Directories

Albany city directories for the years 1830/31, 1840/41, 1850, 1860, 1865, 1870, 1875, 1880, and 1885 were studied in depth, and all females with occupations, especially businesswomen, were recorded in a series of databases in order to assess change over time.[1] In addition, city directories for 1875–80 and 1882–85 were used to identify all businesswomen active between 1875 and 1885, and these individuals were then traced backward and forward in time using the directories from 1840 to 1874 and 1886 to 1920.[2] Using this method, I located 1,507 individual female proprietors active between 1875 and 1885, plus 854 businesswomen from the selected directories of 1830/31–70.[3]

On the basis of this research, several databases were designed. A master database included all businesswomen active from 1875 to 1885 and recorded all information gleaned on each female proprietor and its source, except for the transcriptions of credit records (which were recorded in separate databases, as described below). In addition, less detailed databases were created for each selected year or period (1830/31, 1841, 1850, 1860 as compared to 1865, 1870, and 1875, as compared to 1880 and 1885). These databases listed all women identified by occupation in the city directories and made it possible to track changes in trades over time.

Credit Records

The R.G. Dun & Co. Collection, housed in the Archives of the Baker Library of the Harvard Graduate School of Business Administration, includes nine volumes on the city of Albany: eight volumes of entries, and a one-volume index. Each large ledger includes hundreds of pages (generally ranging from 200 to 300) of closely written entries on individuals and firms in the city, some cross-referenced to additional earlier or later entries on the same person. Every page of every ledger was searched for entries on women, and the index volume was then used to locate entries that might have been missed by the page-by-page review. Using this method, I originally located 132 female milliners evaluated for credit, plus 46 male milliners or millinery dealers; later, I identified 653 *more* businesswomen engaged in trades other than millinery. Entries for each female proprietor might be as short as a line, or long enough to fill most of a page; almost all of these entries were transcribed into one of two databases, one for milliners, and one for women engaged in other trades.[4]

The Manuscript Census of Population for 1880

For the federal manuscript census of 1880, all three microfilm reels were searched line-by-line for women identified as having business occupations, and photocopies were made for the household of each businesswoman.[5] In addition, a list of individual female proprietors was generated by using the master database for 1875–85, and the manuscript census was searched a second time to look for businesswomen previously identified in city directories or credit records, but whose trades were not recorded by the census enumerators. The addresses and information on family members in the directories and credit records made it easier to recognize such individual businesswomen and to distinguish between women with the same name. Once again, photocopies were made to record individual and household information on each female proprietor, whether or not she was identified as such in the census. Evidence from the photocopies was then entered into the master database for 1875–85. Finally, data on the 632 individuals located and their households were entered into SPSS to generate a statistical analysis.

In addition, the manuscript census of 1880 was used to record information on all female workers in two enumeration districts: the 8th and the 22nd. Here, I simply counted the number of women with occupations listed in the census (321 in the 8th district, and 231 in the 22nd) and analyzed the frequency of various female occupations and the ratio of business owners to other working women.

Anomalies between City Directories and Credit Records, 1840–85

During the research phase of this study, it became clear that there were significant anomalies between city directories and credit reports. In some cases, information presented in the sources proved contradictory (as when starting and ending dates varied, or the spelling of names varied wildly, or in the identification of trade or marital status). It was more common, however, for these sources to record information that represented a variation rather than a direct contradiction (for instance, each source presented a different population with a different proportion of each trade).

Although the range of trades for businesswomen represented in city directories and credit records match rather closely, the proportions of each trade do not. For instance, dressmaking proprietors are far more prevalent in city directories (at 22% of the total listings) than in the credit ledgers (where they make up only about 10% of the recorded businesswomen), as were female boarding-house keepers (who made up about 15% of city directory listings but less than 3% of credit entries). In contrast, dry and fancy goods dealers made up a larger ratio of female proprietors listed by credit examiners than in the directories—a full 15% of businesswomen evaluated for credit operated dry or fancy goods stores, as compared to only 6.5% of such women in city directories.

Similarly, female grocers made up a far larger share of women evaluated for credit between 1840 and 1885—more than 26%—than they did of the businesses appearing in city directories from 1841 to 1880—only 12%. Saloonkeepers were twice as prevalent in the credit records (at 10%) as they were in city directories (less than 5%). The type of business with the most similar proportions was millinery (with 18% of the R.G. Dun & Co. listings and 21% of city directory listings).[6]

How can the anomalies between these two primary sources—city directories and credit reports—be understood? Why, for instance, are more dressmakers and boarding-house keepers listed in the city directories, while one finds a larger proportion of female grocers, dry and fancy goods dealers, and saloonkeepers in the credit records? The obvious answer would be that dressmakers and boarding-house keepers bought less on credit than grocers, storekeepers, and saloonkeepers. Looking at the question from the other angle, it seems to have been less likely for small grocers or saloonkeepers to be listed in the business sections of city directories—even the individual listings for such women often give no indications of trades that are recorded in both credit records and the census. Assuming business directories charged for listing, women running neighborhood businesses may well have concluded it was not worth their while to pay for the advertising. Alternately, those compiling the directories may not have considered such small shops to be worth recording. Beyond such speculations, however, one can conclude that directories and credit records each represent a limited source of information on female proprietors, and that neither should be taken as an absolute indication of the parameters of women's participation in the marketplace.

Discrepancies between Sources, 1875–85

Intensive focus on the single decade from 1875 to 1885 made it possible to compare and contrast the evidence from all three sources—city directories, credit ledgers, and the federal population census—to each other, and to assess the ways in which each source may have under- or overrepresented specific types of business pursuits. Compared to the master database taken from linked sources, city directories alone for the years 1875, 1880, and 1885 provide fairly similar figures for needleworkers, dry and fancy goods dealers, grocers, saloonkeepers, bakers, confectioners, hairdressers and makers of hair products, and cigar dealers. Not surprisingly, however, city directories underrepresent peddlers and hucksters, who make up 1% of the businesswomen between 1875 and 1885 based on linked sources, but less than one-tenth of 1% of businesswomen listed in the city directories. Another trade underrecorded in city directories consisted of boarding-house keepers (representing 14% of businesswomen in the master database but less than 10% of female proprietors in city directories). Similarly, female liquor dealers make up some 4% of the female proprietors in the master database for this decade but less than 1% of businesswomen in city directories.

If instead one consulted the R.G. Dun & Co. credit ledgers alone, one would have a rather different view of female business activity in Albany between 1875 and 1885. The most striking discrepancy between the evidence of city directories and credit records is in the areas of dressmaking and millinery. While dressmakers made up 29% of all businesswomen listed in the directories of 1875, 1880, and 1880, they accounted for only 7% of all female proprietors reviewed for credit between 1875 and 1885 by R.G. Dun & Co. The proportions were reversed in the opposite direction for millinery proprietors, who represented only 5% of businesswomen in city directories but 16% of female proprietors in the credit ledgers. Figures for boarding-house and hotel keepers were also inverted in these two sources: in city directories, female boarding-house keepers outnumbered hotel keepers by a ratio of almost 10 to 1, while the credit records listed twice as many hotel keepers as women running boarding houses. Other areas of dramatic contrast include dealers in dry and fancy goods, who made up only 10% of all businesswomen listed in city directories but 20% of businesswomen evaluated for credit for this period. These discrepancies can be explained by the fact that milliners, hotel keepers, and dry or fancy goods dealers required more credit to operate their enterprises than did dressmakers and boarding-house keepers. In fact, the preponderance of milliners in the credit ledgers may be taken as proof that their businesses required more capital than those of dressmakers, as may the fact that of the very few women-owned enterprises listed in the census of manufactures for mid-nineteenth-century Albany, milliners were most likely to be included.

What were the characteristics of female proprietors whose trades were not listed in the census, but whom we know from other sources were engaged in business in 1880? What were the patterns in census underreporting? Of the 129 businesswomen located in the 1880 federal census for whom the census enumerators gave no trade or occupation, the largest group by far (46.5%) were boarding-house keepers. Most of these were women who were clearly keeping boarding houses, because there were several nonrelated boarders in the household (at least four), but who were identified only as "keeping house" rather than "keeping a boardinghouse." Female proprietors in the needle and clothing trades do not seem to have been significantly underrecorded. Purveyors of food and drink, on the other hand, were more likely to be reported by the census enumerators. While they made up 37% of all businesswomen located in the 1880 census, they make up only about 15% of female proprietors in business in 1880 whose trades were not reported. Looking specifically at saloonkeepers and women who sold liquor, these proprietors were far more likely to be recorded with their trades than might be predicted on the basis of their share of businesses. That is, while such liquor dealers and saloonkeepers made up more than 13% of the businesswomen in Albany who have been located in the census, they made up only 7% of those whose trades were not recorded. For storekeepers the discrepancy was not as great, but they also make up a smaller portion of women whose trades were not reported than they did of female proprietors as a whole.

Another variable significantly associated with underreporting was marital status. Married women made up more than 50% of the women whose trades were not reported, although they represented only 34% of the population of female proprietors located in the 1880 census. In contrast, single and widowed women were far less likely to be recorded without their business employments. It is difficult to determine whether it was census enumerators who automatically recorded married women as "keeping house," or whether female proprietors themselves reported that occupation. If so, it would still be hard to know whether such married women considered "keeping house" their primary duty and thus occupation, or whether they were trying to conceal their business involvement from census enumerators for some reason.

Did nativity have any impact on underreporting? In fact, female proprietors born in the United States were more likely to be recorded without trades as compared to Irish-born women, who were more likely to be recorded with their trades.[7] Women born in Great Britain or elsewhere in the British Empire were, like those born in the United States, more likely to be underrepresented as doing business by census enumerators, but only slightly; German-born women were slightly overrepresented as doing business in the census. Whether a woman's trade was recorded in the census seems to have been related to her status—with a hierarchy of American-born, then British, then

German, and finally Irish businesswomen in which the Americans were most likely to be identified as simply "keeping house" and the Irish most likely to be tagged with their trades.

Finally, just as city directories identified some female proprietors whose trades were not recorded in the census, so the census recorded some businesswomen who were never identified by trade in the city directories or evaluated for credit in the R.G. Dun & Co. records. Of the 632 businesswomen located in the federal manuscript census of 1880, for example, some 190 (or about 30%) have not been located in either city directories or credit reports. Of these female proprietors, more than 60% were immigrants, and another 15% were native-born children of immigrants. It is clear that the census records were more likely than city directories to record women with lower-status trades, such as grocery and saloonkeeping, and that they were also more likely to record the trades of women who were single or widowed than of those who were married.

Conclusion

What is the importance of recognizing such disparities? Rather than dwelling on the unreliability of these sources, we can recognize that each source underrepresents female proprietors, and that patterns of underrepresentation reflect the social and cultural values of the period. The recording of a woman's business occupation in the city directory, for instance, suggests relatively high status and high visibility in the Albany business community. Such women were less likely to be recorded as doing business in the census, especially if they were married or native-born. Conversely, the lack of a listing in the city directory, coupled with the recording of a woman's trade in the census, suggests lower status and visibility, with a higher likelihood of being Irish or German. In comparison, evaluation for credit was associated with size, visibility, and those trades in which credit was necessary to operate rather than status or social standing. However, by drawing on all of these sources, we are much more likely to capture the full range and diversity of businesswomen in nineteenth-century Albany.

NOTES

•

_____

Preface

1. Mary Field Belenky, Blythe McVicker Clinchy, Nancy Rule Goldberger, and Jill Mattuck Tarule, *Women's Ways of Knowing: The Development of Self, Voice, and Mind* (New York: Basic Books, 1986), p. ix.

2. Held at Russell Sage College in Troy, 1990.

3. Gerda Lerner, "The Lady and the Mill Girl: Changes in the Status of Women in the Age of Jackson, 1800–1840," *Mid-Continent American Studies Journal* 10 (1969): 5–15.

4. Susan Ingalls Lewis, "Milliners in Albany 1840–1880: Female Entrepreneurs, Artisans, and Workers" (paper presented at the 12th Annual North American Labor History Conference, Wayne State University, Detroit, Mich., October 1990).

5. A critique of this approach is well expressed by Wendy Gamber in the Introduction to *The Female Economy: The Millinery and Dressmaking Trades, 1860–1930* (Urbana: University of Illinois Press, 1997), pp. 3–4.

6. That is, I focused on female proprietors with relatively long careers and detailed entries. Susan Ingalls Lewis, "Female Entrepreneurs in Albany: 1840–1885," *Business and Economic History* 21 (1992): 65–73.

7. Susan Ingalls Lewis, "Beyond Horatia Alger: Breaking through Gendered Assumptions about Business 'Success' in Mid-Nineteenth-Century America," *Business and Economic History* 24, no. 1 (Fall 1995): 97–105.

8. Jürgen Habermas, *The Structural Transformation of the Public Sphere: An Inquiry into a Category of Bourgeois Society* (Cambridge, Mass.: MIT Press, 1989).

9. According to the *Encyclopedia of Feminism,* published in the late 1980s, false consciousness is a "concept adapted from Marxism" that "refers to any erroneous belief which keeps a woman from being aware of her own oppression in a sexist society"—thus, false consciousness can be "replaced by feminist consciousness" through consciousness-raising. However, as pointed out in the more recent *Concise Glossary of Feminist Theory,* "the presumption of a gap between a collective feminist consciousness

and individual women's consciousness" that "implies the existence of women's false consciousness" would seem to "contradict feminist respect for women's accounts of their own experience." Lisa Tuttle, *Encyclopedia of Feminism* (New York: Facts on File, 1986), p. 100; Sonya Andermahr, Terry Lovell, and Carol Wolkowitz, *A Concise Glossary of Feminist Theory* (London: Arnold, 1997), pp. 34–35.

Introduction

1. Here Bird was commenting specifically on the tiny proportion of women categorized as entrepreneurs (42 out of 1,359 entries) in the first three volumes of *Notable American Women;* interestingly, even most of these famous female entrepreneurs were ignored by women's historians in the 1980s. Caroline Bird, *Enterprising Women* (New York: W. W. Norton, 1976), p. 13; Edward T. James, Janet Wilson James, and Paul S. Boyer, eds., *Notable American Women 1607–1950: A Biographical Dictionary* (Cambridge, Mass.: Harvard University Press, 1971) 3:715.

2. New York, Vol. 7, pp. 7, 180, 219, R.G. Dun & Co. Collection, Baker Library Historical Collections, Harvard Business School.

3. Virginia Penny, *How Women Can Make Money, Married or Single, in all Branches of the Arts and Sciences, Professions, Trades, Agricultural and Mechanical Pursuits* (New York: Arno Press Inc., 1971; orig. pub. 1870, reprinted from *Employments of Women: A Cyclopedia of Women's Work*, 1863); *Think and Act, A Series of Articles Pertaining to Men and Women, Work and Wages* (New York: Arno & The New York Times, 1971; orig. pub. 1869); Caroline H. Dall, *Woman's Right to Labor, or Low Wages and Hard Work* (Boston: Walker, Wise, 1860); Helen Campbell, *Prisoners of Poverty: Women Wage-Workers, Their Trades and Their Lives* (Westport, Conn.: Greenwood Press, 1970; orig. pub. 1887); Charlotte Perkins Gilman, *Women and Economics: A Study of the Economic Relation Between Men and Women as a Factor in Social Evolution* (Boston: Small, Maynard & Co., 1898).

4. Bird, *Enterprising Women*, p. 13.

5. Wendy Gamber, "A Precarious Independence: Milliners and Dressmakers in Boston, 1860–1980," *Journal of Women's History* 4 (Spring 1992): 60, 81. Unfortunately, Dexter's research covers only the early years of the nineteenth century. Elisabeth Anthony Dexter, *Career Women of America, 1776–1840* (Clifton, N.J.: Augustus M. Kelley, 1972, orig. pub. 1950).

6. For a standard 1980s treatment of nineteenth-century businesswomen, see Julie Matthaei, *An Economic History of Women in America: Women's Work, the Sexual Division of Labor, and the Development of Capitalism* (New York: Schocken Books, 1982), pp. 51–74, 101–39.

7. Claudia Goldin, "The Economic Status of Women in the Early Republic: Quantitative Evidence," *The Journal of Interdisciplinary History* (1986), reprinted in Nancy Cott, *History of Women in the United States*, vol. 7, *Industrial Wage Work, Part 1* (Munich: K. G. Saur, 1993), pp. 3–32; Carol Groneman, "Working-Class Immigrant Women in Mid-Nineteenth-Century New York: The Irish Woman's Experience," *Journal of Urban History* 4 (May 1978), reprinted in Nancy Cott, *History of Women in the United States*, vol. 7, *Industrial Wage Work, Part 1* (Munich: K. G. Saur, 1993), pp. 145–63; Hasia R. Diner, *Erin's Daughters in America: Irish Immigrant Women in the Nineteenth Century* (Baltimore: The Johns Hopkins University Press, 1983), p. 96; Mary P. Ryan, *Cradle of the Middle Class: The Family in Oneida County, New York, 1790–1865* (Cambridge: Cambridge University Press, 1981), p. 205; Suzanne Lebsock, *The Free Women*

of Petersburg: Status and Culture in a Southern Town, 1784–1860 (New York: W. W. Norton, 1985), p. 185; Clyde Griffen and Sally Griffen, *Natives and Newcomers: The Ordering of Opportunity in Mid-Nineteenth-Century Poughkeepsie* (Cambridge, Mass.: Harvard University Press, 1978), p. 254; Jane H. Pease and William H. Pease, *Ladies, Women, & Wenches: Choice & Constraint in Antebellum Charleston & Boston* (Chapel Hill: The University of North Carolina Press, 1990), p. 53.

8. Griffen and Griffen, *Natives and Newcomers,* pp. 244–45.

9. As with Ryan, Lebsock, Pease and Pease, and, later, Gamber.

10. As in Sarah Stage, *Female Complaints: Lydia Pinkham & the Business of Women's Medicine* (New York: W. W. Norton, 1981); Christine Daily, "A Woman's Concern: Millinery in Central Iowa, 1870–1880," *Journal of the West* 21, no. 2 (1982): 26–32; Juliet E. K. Walker, "Entrepreneurs in Antebellum America," in Darlene Clark Hine, ed., *Black Women in America: An Historical Encyclopedia,* Vol. 1 (Brooklyn: Carlson, 1993); and Diner, *Erin's Daughters in America.*

11. Most notably in Alice Kessler-Harris's *Out to Work: A History of Wage-Earning Women in the United States* (Oxford: Oxford University Press, 1982).

12. Alice Kessler-Harris, "Women and the Work Force," in *The Reader's Companion to American History,* ed. Eric Foner and John A. Garraty (Boston: Houghton Mifflin, 1991), p. 1159.

13. Mansel Blackford, *A History of Small Business in America* (New York: Twayne, 1991), p. 124; and "Small Business in America: A Historiographic Survey," *Business History Review* 65 (Spring 1991): 25.

14. Wendy Gamber, *The Female Economy: The Millinery and Dressmaking Trades, 1860–1930* (Urbana: University of Illinois Press, 1997); Angel Kwolek-Folland, *Incorporating Women: A History of Women and Business in the United States* (New York: Twayne, 1998).

15. Wendy Gamber, "A Gendered Enterprise: Placing Nineteenth-Century Businesswomen in History," *Business History Review* 72 (Summer 1998): 188–217; Kathy Peiss, "'Vital Industry' and Women's Ventures: Conceptualizing Gender in Twentieth Century Business History," *Business History Review* 72 (Summer 1998): 218–241; and Joan Scott, "Comment: Conceptualizing Gender in American Business History," *Business History Review* 72 (Summer 1998): 242–249.

16. Mary A. Yeager, ed., *Women in Business,* vols. 1–3 (Cheltenham, UK: Edward Elgar, 1999).

17. Jeannette M. Oppedisano, *Historical Encyclopedia of American Women Entrepreneurs: 1776 to the Present* (Westport, Conn.: Greenwood Press, 2000).

18. Patricia Cleary, *Elizabeth Murray: A Woman's Pursuit of Independence in Eighteenth-Century America* (Amherst, Mass.: University of Massachusetts Press, 2003); Lynn M. Hudson, *The Making of "Mammy Pleasant": A Black Entrepreneur in Nineteenth-Century San Francisco* (Urbana: University of Illinois Press, 2003); Jane R. Plitt, *Martha Matilda Harper and the American Dream: How One Woman Changed the Face of Modern Business* (Syracuse, N.Y.: Syracuse University Press, 2000); Charles Slack, *Hetty: The Genius and Madness of America's First Female Tycoon* (New York: Harper-Collins Publishers Inc., 2004).

19. Harvard Business School, *Women, Enterprise, and Society* http://www.library. hbs.edu/hc/wes; Laura Cochrane, "From the Archives: Women's History in the Baker Library's Business Manuscripts Collection," 74 (Autumn 2000): 465–76.

20. Angel Kwolek-Folland, "Gender and Business History," *Enterprise and Society* 2 (March 2001): 1–10; D. M. Haftner, "Women in the Underground Business of Eighteenth-Century Lyon," *Enterprise and Society* 2 (March 2001): 11–40; L. J. Owen,

"Gender Differences in Labor Turnover and the Development of Internal Labor Markets in the United States during the 1920s," *Enterprise and Society* 2 (March 2001): 41–71; Béatrice Craig, "Petites Bourgeoises and Penny Capitalists: Women in Retail in the Lille Area during the Nineteenth Century," *Enterprise and Society* 2 (June 2001): 198–224.

21. Margaret Walsh, "Gendered Endeavours: Women and the Reshaping of Business Culture," *Women's History Review* 14, no. 2 (2005): 181–202.

22. Edith Sparks, *Capital Intentions: Female Proprietors in San Francisco, 1850–1920* (Chapel Hill: The University of North Carolina Press, 2006); Wendy Gamber, *The Boardinghouse in Nineteenth-Century America* (Baltimore: The Johns Hopkins University Press, 2007).

23. "Enterprising Women" opened at the National Heritage Museum in Lexington, Mass., in October of 2002 and traveled to the New York Historical Society, the Atlanta History Center, the National Museum of Women in the Arts in Washington, DC, the Women's Museum in Dallas, and the Los Angeles Public Library; it closed at the Detroit Historical Museum in January of 2005. The companion Web site, www.enterprisingwomenexhibit.org, is no longer active.

24. Virginia Drachman: *Enterprising Women: 250 Years of American Business* (Chapel Hill: The University of North Carolina Press, 2002).

25. Kenneth Lipartito, Foreword, in Kwolek-Folland, *Incorporating Women*, pp. ix–x.

26. Kwolek-Folland, *Incorporating Women*, p. 9.

27. Deborah Rosen, *Courts and Commerce: Gender, Law, and the Market Economy in Colonial New York* (Columbus: The Ohio State University Press, 1997), p. 109.

28. Mansel Blackford, *A History of Small Business in America,* 2nd ed. (Chapel Hill: The University of North Carolina Press, 2003), pp. 3, 201.

29. Rowena Olegario, *A Culture of Credit: Embedding Trust and Transparency in American Business* (Cambridge, Mass.: Harvard University Press, 2006), p. 109.

30. Kwolek-Folland, *Incorporating Women*, p. 56.

31. Pamela Walker Laird, *Pull: Networking and Success since Benjamin Franklin* (Cambridge, Mass.: Harvard University Press, 2006), pp. 1–10.

32. Scott A. Sandage, *Born Losers: A History of Failure in America* (Cambridge, Mass.: Harvard University Press, 2005); Edward J. Balleisen, *Navigating Failure: Bankruptcy and Commercial Society in Antebellum America* (Chapel Hill: The University of North Carolina Press, 2000).

33. Susan Yohn, "'The Apartments Are Suitable; The Location One of the Very Best': Mapping Women's Businesses in Brooklyn in the Nineteenth Century" (paper presented at the Annual Meeting of the Organization of American Historians, Washington, DC, April 2006); Barbara Balliet, "The Business of Art, Political Networks & Visual Culture in the Nineteenth Century City" (paper presented at the Annual Meeting of the Social Science History Association, Chicago, Ill., 2004).

34. Sparks, *Capital Intentions.*

Chapter One

1. Richard D. Heffner, ed., *Democracy in America* (New York: New American Library, 1956), p. 244.

2. See Laura Keene in Faye E. Dudden, "Managing: The Decline of Laura Keene," *Women in the American Theatre: Actresses and Audiences, 1790–1870* (New Haven: Yale

University Press, 1997), pp. 123–48; Mary Surratt in James M. McPherson's *Ordeal by Fire: The Civil War and Reconstruction*, 3rd ed. (New York: McGraw-Hill, 2001), p. 520; Elizabeth Keckley in reference works, including Marie Garrett, "Elizabeth Keckley," in Jessie Carney Smith, ed., *Notable Black Women* (Detroit: Gale Research, 1992), pp. 616–21; as well as Louise P. Maxwell in Jack Salzman, David Lionel Smith, and Cornell West, eds., *Encyclopedia of African-American Culture and History*, vol. 3 (New York: Macmillan, 1996), pp. 1529–30; and Kathleen Thompson in Darlene Clark Hine, ed., *Black Women in America: An Historical Encyclopedia*, vol. 1 (Brooklyn: Carlson, 1993), pp. 672–73.

3. Barbara Welter, "The Cult of True Womanhood: 1820–1860," *American Quarterly* 18, no. 2, part 1 (Summer 1966): 151–74; Gerda Lerner, "The Lady and the Mill Girl: Changes in the Status of Women in the Age of Jackson, 1800–1840," *Mid-Continent American Studies Journal* 10 (1969): 5–15; Nancy Cott, *The Bonds of Womanhood: "Woman's Sphere" in New England, 1780–1835* (New Haven: Yale University Press, 1977).

4. As in Edith Wharton's novella "Bunner Sisters," in which a pair of sisters run a small fancy goods shop; in Louis Auchincloss, ed., *The Edith Wharton Reader*, pp. 303–80 (New York: Charles Scribner's Sons, 1965, orig. pub. 1916); or in Anne M. Butler's study of prostitutes on the frontier, *Daughters of Joy, Sisters of Misery: Prostitutes in the American West, 1865–90* (Urbana: University of Illinois Press, 1985).

5. Anita J. Rapone, "Clerical Labor Force Formation: The Office Woman in Albany, 1870–1930" (PhD diss., New York University, 1981). Brian Greenberg's *Worker and Community: Response to Industrialization in a Nineteenth-Century American City, Albany, New York, 1850–1884* (Albany: State University of New York Press, 1985) makes no mention of female workers or businesswomen—indeed, the term "women" does not even appear in its index. Based on his study, one would assume that artisans and entrepreneurs in mid-nineteenth-century Albany were exclusively male.

6. Two of these studies focus almost exclusively on men: Paul Johnson's *A Shopkeeper's Millennium: Society and Revivals in Rochester, NY, 1815–1837* (New York: Hill and Wang, 1978) and Stuart Blumin's investigation of Kingston, *The Urban Threshold: Growth and Change in a Nineteenth-Century American Community* (Chicago: The University of Chicago Press, 1976). Other studies written at roughly the same time—Griffen and Griffen's *Natives and Newcomers: The Ordering of Opportunity in Mid-Nineteenth-Century Poughkeepsie* (Cambridge, Mass.: Harvard University Press, 1978), and Ryan's *Cradle of the Middle Class: The Family in Oneida County, New York, 1790–1865* (Cambridge: Cambridge University Press, 1981)—integrate women, even businesswomen, into their community models. Two studies that focus particularly on working-class women in the Hudson River region are Carole Turbin, *Working Women of Collar City: Gender, Class, and Community in Troy, New York, 1864–86* (Urbana: University of Illinois Press, 1992), and Christine Stansell, *City of Women: Sex and Class in New York, 1789–1860* (Urbana: University of Illinois Press, 1987).

7. J. Fry, *The Annual Register and Albany Directory for the Year 1816* (Albany: Packard & Van Benthuysen, 1816).

8. *The Albany Directory for the Years 1830–31* (Albany: Cammeyer & Gaw, E. B. Child, 1830).

9. Codman Hislop, *Albany: Dutch, English, and American* (Albany: The Argus Press, 1936).

10. Albany's population grew from less than 11,000 in 1810 to about 98,000 in 1884. The comparative size for Albany appears in Brian Greenberg, *Worker and Community*, p. 12.

11. Frances Wright, *Views of Society and Manners in America* (Cambridge, Mass.: Harvard University Press, 1963, orig. pub. London 1821), p. 79; Frances Trollope, *Domestic Manners of the Americans* (New York: Alfred A. Knopf, 1949, orig. pub. 1832), pp. 401–2; Charles Augustus Murray, *Travels in North America during the Years 1834, 1835 & 1836*, vol. 1 (New York: Da Capo Press, 1974, orig. pub. London, 1839), pp. 74–75; Isabella Lucy Bird, *The Englishwoman in America* (Madison: University of Wisconsin Press, 1966, orig. pub. London, 1856), pp. 328–29.

12. A. Bleeker Banks, *Albany Bi-Centennial Historical Memoirs* (Albany: Banks & Brothers, 1888), pp. 1, 3.

13. Henry P. Phelps, ed., *The New Albany: A Record of the City's Progress*, vol. 1–2 (Albany: Brandon Printing Co., 1892).

14. The relative size of the largest cities in the United States over time (1790–1990) is presented on the Web site of the U.S. Census Bureau. Albany's population/rank ranged from 3,498/nineteenth in 1790 to 94,923/twenty-ninth in 1890; Albany remained among the top 100 cities, however, until the census count of 1970. http://www.census.gov/population/www/documentation/twps0027.html

15. See Blackford, *A History of Small Business*, 2nd ed., pp. 1–2, for definitions of small business.

16. Joan Scott, "Comment: Conceptualizing Gender in American Business History," *Business History Review* 72 (Summer 1998), p. 247.

17. For example, both Catharine Beecher and Sojourner Truth promoted and sold their own books at public appearances as a means of self-support; Truth also sold photographs of herself. Kathryn Kish Sklar, Catharine Beecher: *A Study in American Domesticity* (New Haven: Yale University Press, 1973), pp. 120–24, 142, 215–16, 217; Nell Irvin Painter, *Sojourner Truth: A Life, A Symbol* (New York: W. W. Norton, 1996), pp. 110–11, 119, 129, 163, 198, 242, 259.

18. See Nancy Cott, ed., *History of Women in the United States: Historical Articles on Women's Lives and Activities, Vol. 1: Professional and White-Collar Employments* (Munich: K. G. Saur, 1994); Susan Coultrap-McQuin, *Doing Literary Business* (Chapel Hill: The University of North Carolina Press, 1990); Wendy Gamber, *The Boardinghouse in Nineteenth-Century America* (Baltimore: The Johns Hopkins University Press, 2007).

19. Angel Kwolek-Folland, *Incorporating Women: A History of Women and Business in the United States*, pp. 47–84 (New York: Twayne, 1998); Virginia Drachman, *Enterprising Women: 250 Years of American Business*, pp. 28–73 (Chapel Hill: The University of North Carolina Press, 2002).

20. William Cammeyer, Preface, *The Albany Directory, for the Year 1829–30* (Albany: H. D. Stone, 1829).

21. Women's historians generally agree that domestic service was the most common occupation for nineteenth-century women, although needlework, schoolteaching, and white-collar occupations are also recognized by most textbooks as offering employment for women. "For most of the nineteenth century the labor force was overwhelmingly male and women were limited to a handful of occupations, the most common being live-in domestic service." Mary Beth Norton and Ruth M. Alexander, *Major Problems in American Women's History*, 4th ed. (Boston: Houghton Mifflin, 2007), p. 260.

22. Alice Kessler-Harris, "Women and the Workforce," in Eric Foner and John A. Garraty, eds., *The Reader's Companion to American History* (Boston: Houghton Mifflin, 1991), p. 1159.

23. And, of course, most schoolteachers listed in the city directory during this period were running schools as small businesses rather than working as teachers for wages.

24. In 1885, the city directory listed 495 independent businesswomen versus 252 schoolteachers. Again, most music teachers during this period were actually independent and self-employed, rather than employees of any institution; however, for purposes of this argument, they have been counted as neither teachers nor businesswomen.

25. Female white-collar workers such as clerks, bookkeepers, and telephone operators made up less than 5% of the total number of business and professional women identified by name in the 1880 directory. Anita Rapone found a somewhat higher percentage for these groups in the 1880 census—a total of approximately 18% of the white-collar workforce reported in the census. Anita Rapone, "Clerical Labor Force Formation: The Office Woman in Albany, 1870–1930" (PhD diss., New York University, 1981).

26. For example, in the 8th enumeration district of the city of Albany in 1880, out of 321 women recorded as working, the most common occupations for female workers were as servants (29%), needleworkers not in business (23%), business proprietors (18%), laundresses—who may also have been self-employed—(9%), clerks in shops and stores (7%), factory workers (6.5%), and teachers (4.5%). In the 22nd enumeration district, with a female work force of 231, almost 30% of women listed with occupations were needleworkers, compared to one-quarter who were servants and other types of domestic workers, followed by laundresses (11%), businesswomen (10%), white-collar workers (9%), professionals—teachers and nurses—(8%), and workers in factories (6%).

27. Rapone, "Clerical Labor Force Formation," p. 59.

28. Mary Beth Norton's essay "The Paradox of 'Women's Sphere'" is an excellent example of this kind of critique. In Carol Ruth Berkin and Mary Beth Norton, eds., *Women of America: A History,* pp. 139–49 (Boston: Houghton Mifflin Company, 1979).

29. The selection of articles in Sklar and Dublin's reader focusing on issues of power, for example, encompasses all of these topics. Kathryn Kish Sklar and Thomas Dublin, *Women and Power in American History,* vol. 1 to 1880 (Upper Saddle River, N.J.: Prentice Hall, 2002).

30. New York, Vol. 7, p. 18M, Vol. 12, p. 344, R.G. Dun & Co. Collection, Baker Library Historical Collections, Harvard Business School.

31. New York, Vol. 7, p. 238K (Armstrong), and p. 238 (Doctor), R.G. Dun & Co.

32. New York, Vol. 10, p. 251, R.G. Dun & Co.

33. New York, Vol. 8, pp. 293, 408, R.G. Dun & Co.

34. New York, Vol. 9, p. 171, R.G. Dun & Co.

35. New York, Vol. 11, p. 1E, R.G. Dun & Co.

36. New York, Vol. 9, p. 82, R.G. Dun & Co.

37. New York, Vol. 9, p. 249, Vol. 9, p. 291, R.G. Dun & Co.

38. New York, Vol. 9, p. 112, Vol. 12, p. 106, Vol. 13, p. 196, Vol. 14, p. 75, R.G. Dun & Co.

39. For example, the advertisement for Cooke's Albany Lock Dispensary in 1830/31 announced its purpose as "established exclusively for the treatment and prevention of a certain class of diseases" and the ability to "suppress the most obstinate, malignant and doubtful Venereal cases." *The Albany Directory for the Years 1830–31. Containing a Concise Account of the City of Albany with an Alphabetical List of the Inhabitants, A Colored Map of the City,* . . . (Albany: Cammeyer & Gaw, 1830), unpaginated.

40. New York, Vol. 7, p. 193, R.G. Dun & Co.

41. An excellent discussion and critique of Victorian binary models of gender can be found in Mary Poovey, *Uneven Developments: The Ideological Work of Gender in Mid-*

Victorian England (Chicago: The University of Chicago Press, 1988), chapter 1, pp. 1–23, Conclusion, pp. 199–201.

Chapter Two

1. As quoted by Elisabeth Anthony Dexter, *Career Women of America, 1776–1840* (Clifton, N.J.: Augustus M. Kelley, 1972, orig. pub. 1950), p. 139.

2. Dexter, *Career Women*, p. 139.

3. Virginia Penny, *How Women Can Make Money, Married or Single, in all Branches of the Arts and Sciences, Professions, Trades, Agricultural and Mechanical Pursuits* (New York: Arno Press Inc., 1971; orig. pub. 1870, reprinted from *Employments of Women: A Cyclopedia of Women's Work,* 1863), pp. 98–120; Dexter, *Career Women*, chapters 6–8; Wendy Gamber, *The Female Economy: The Millinery and Dressmaking Trades, 1860–1930* (Urbana: University of Illinois Press, 1997), pp. 27–30; Angel Kwolek-Folland, *Incorporating Women: A History of Women and Business in the United States* (New York: Twayne, 1998), pp. 56–57.

4. The nineteenth-century female wage force has been characterized as young and single by Alice Kessler-Harris in *Out to Work: A History of Wage-Earning Women in the United States* (Oxford: Oxford University Press, 1982); Ellen Carol DuBois, *United States after 1865, in Women's and Gender History in Global Perspective,* a series by the American Historical Association's Committee on Women Historians, ed. Bonnie Smith (Washington, DC: American Historical Association, 2000), p. 5; and Linda Gordon, *U.S. Women's History,* in *The New American History, Revised and Expanded,* ed. Eric Foner (Washington, DC: American Historical Association, 1997), p. 16.

5. New York, Vol. 13, p. 117 (Held); New York, Vol. 9, p. 194 (Woods), R.G. Dun & Co. Collection, Baker Library Historical Collections, Harvard Business School.

6. Although she was listed in city directories from 1865 through 1871, and again from 1876 through 1880, Tygart's credit entries cover only the years from 1868 through 1874, and the entry for 1878 states simply "out." Thus, had one consulted only the credit records, one would have estimated Tygart's length of business at only 6 years; however, from the city directories one would have assumed a gap in business activity where there apparently was none. Combining these sources, one can deduce that this dressmaking establishment was actually in operation for at least 15 years.

7. New York, Vol. 9, p. 183, R.G. Dun & Co.

8. New York, Vol. 11, p. 268 (George Convery), R.G. Dun & Co.

9. It seems that James Lawrence must have been a son from a previous marriage and that Lamb had been widowed twice—unless she had changed her name for some other reason.

10. New York, Vol. 11, p. 196, R.G. Dun & Co.

11. New York, Vol. 8, p. 350, R.G. Dun & Co.

12. New York, Vol. 9, pp. 77, 78, R.G. Dun & Co.

13. See Appendix 2, "Sources and Methods."

14. The credit records use both spellings, Eagan and Egan; the spelling used in the text corresponds to that used in the cited entry.

15. New York, Vol. 11, p. 404, R.G. Dun & Co.

16. New York, Vol. 11, pp. 16, 98, R.G. Dun & Co.

17. Federal Manuscript Census of Population, Albany, N.Y., 1880, T9, reel 805, ED 3, p. 50, line 22.

18. New York, Vol. 13, p. 5, R.G. Dun & Co.

19. Federal Manuscript Census of Population, Albany, N.Y., 1880, T9, reel 805, ED 8, p. 66, line 2.

20. Wendy Gamber, *The Boardinghouse in Nineteenth-Century America* (Baltimore: The Johns Hopkins University Press, 2007), p. 7.

21. Federal Manuscript Census of Population, Albany, N.Y., 1880, T9, reel 805, ED 7, p. 20, line 5.

22. New York, Vol. 9, p. 210, R.G. Dun & Co.

23. Penny, *How Women Can Make Money*, pp. 121–22.

24. New York, Vol. 9, p. 32 (Burt); Vol. 9, pp. 133, 414 (McAneny), R.G. Dun & Co.

25. This larger point has been made convincingly by Lisa Christine Geib-Gundersen, whose 1996 dissertation in economics argues that "a large number of women were left out of the census count of gainfully occupied persons in 1880, 1900, and 1910" because "many women performing work in family-run businesses were overlooked, despite the fact that this work was of the type considered gainful by census definitions of employment." Although Geib-Gundersen's study defines these women as workers rather than businesspeople, and does not begin its analysis until 1880, her conclusions confirm that by including female participation in family business, their labor force participation for the years 1880–1910 becomes "as high or higher" than that after 1940. According to Geib-Gundersen, "Women were evidently not 'pushed' out of the labor force by industrialization. Instead, they were integrated as unpaid and largely unreported family laborers." Lisa Christine Geib-Gundersen, "Idle Observers or Productive Workers? An Analysis of Married Women's Involvement in Family Businesses and their Underenumeration in U.S. Censuses" (PhD diss, Department of Economics, University of California, Riverside, 1996), pp. vi–vii.

Chapter Three

1. Huybertie Pruyn Hamlin, *An Albany Girlhood* (Albany: Washington Park Press, 1990), p. 97.

2. Ibid., p. 97.

3. New York, Vol. 8, p. 500, R.G. Dun & Co. Collection, Baker Library Historical Collections, Harvard Business School.

4. New York, Vol. 11, p. 262, R.G. Dun & Co.

5. New York, Vol. 11, p. 70, R.G. Dun & Co.

6. For example, the Web site created and maintained by academic economists Laurence Officer and Samuel Williamson offers "Six Ways to Compute the Relative Value of a U.S. Dollar Amount" between 1790 and 2006, ranging from calculations based on the Consumer Price Index and Gross Domestic Product (and variations thereof) to one based on the unskilled wage. http://measuringworth.com.

7. New York, Vol. 7, p. 54, R.G. Dun & Co.

8. Armington's birth date was given as 1818 in the federal manuscript census of 1850, but as 1826 in the federal census of 1870, and as 1830 in the state manuscript census of 1875. However, her eldest son was recorded as having been born in 1838 or 1840, so she herself must have been born at the earliest date of 1818. Federal Manuscript Census of Population, Albany, N.Y., 1850, M432; 1870 M593, reel 898, ward 3; New York State Census of Population, Albany, N.Y., 1875, ward 5; New York, Vol. 8, p. 279, Vol. 11, p. 55, R.G. Dun & Co.

9. New York, Vol. 13, p. 284, R.G. Dun & Co.

10. New York, Vol. 8, p. 272, R.G. Dun & Co.

11. New York, Vol. 7, p. 18H (Jane Reagan); Vol. 13, p. 124 (John Reagan), R.G. Dun & Co.

12. New York, Vol. 7, p. 238L, R.G. Dun & Co.

13. New York, Vol. 10, p. 235, R.G. Dun & Co.

14. For instance, of 218 married women located in credit ledgers, only 3 entries specifically described their husbands as crazy, 3 as lazy or shiftless, 2 as invalid or sick (at the time the woman entered business), and 10 as drinkers or drunks.

15. New York, Vol. 8, p. 423, R.G. Dun & Co.

16. New York, Vol. 9, p. 15 (Keay); Vol. 8, p. 264, R.G. Dun & Co.

17. New York, Vol. 9, p. 1E, R.G. Dun & Co.

18. New York, Vol. 8, p. 433, R.G. Dun & Co.; remarkably, Mary E. Gillen is listed as a "Knit Goods Manufacturer" in the city directory of 1920, 57 years after she had entered business in 1863.

19. The R.G. Dun credit records employ a shorthand in which "c" stands for hundreds and "m" for thousands; thus this entry is actually written as "3m$–ho & lot 3m$–mtge 8c$;" New York, Vol. 19, p. 206 (Conroy), R.G. Dun & Co. A guide to common abbreviations used in the R.G. & Co. credit reports is available on the Web site of the Baker Library of the Harvard Business School: http://www.library.hbs.edu/hc/collections/dun/.

20. New York, Vol. 13, p. 95, R.G. Dun & Co.

21. New York, Vol. 10, p. 92, R.G. Dun & Co.

22. New York, Vol. 9, p. 365, R.G. Dun & Co.

23. New York, Vol. 7, p. 96Z; Vol. 11, p. 3 (Madame M. Duffy); Vol. 11, p. 276 (Ed Duffy), R.G. Dun & Co.

24. New York, Vol. 7, pp. 238H, 238I, Vol. 10, p. 302, R.G. Dun & Co.

25. New York, Vol. 7, p. 238L, Vol. 13, p. 4, R.G. Dun & Co.

26. New York, Vol. 7, pp. 225, 238N, R.G. Dun & Co.

27. New York, Vol. 7, pp. 26, 179, R.G. Dun & Co.

28. New York, Vol. 11, p. 387, R.G. Dun & Co.

29. New York, Vol. 11, p. 362, R.G. Dun & Co.

30. New York, Vol. 8, p. 493, Vol. 13, p. 254, R.G. Dun & Co.

31. New York, Vol. 11, p. 113, Vol. 13, p. 254, R.G. Dun & Co.

32. New York, Vol. 11, p. 299, New York, Vol. 13, p. 254, R.G. Dun & Co.

33. New York, Vol. 7, p. 54, R.G. Dun & Co.

34. Federal Manuscript Census of Manufactures, Albany, N.Y., 1860.

35. The quantitative analysis judged longevity only on the following rather conservative conditions: (1) when a business was listed in a woman's own name, or (2) if a woman was said to be "running" a businesses while her husband worked outside the home, or if the credit records made clear that husband and wife were both involved in the business venture. However, the method of tracing longevity through city directories and credit records probably results in cases with more than average longevity, since these sources tend to overrepresent more-established businesswomen.

36. New York, Vol. 12, p. 60, R.G. Dun & Co.

37. New York, Vol. 8, p. 264, R.G. Dun & Co.

38. New York, Vol. 11, p. 51, R.G. Dun & Co.

39. New York, Vol. 7, pp. 16, 27, Vol. 8, p. 344N, R.G. Dun & Co.

40. New York, Vol. 11, p. 325, R.G. Dun & Co.

41. New York, Vol. 12, p. 321, R.G. Dun & Co.

42. New York, Vol. 11, p. 311, R.G. Dun & Co.

43. New York, Vol. 8, p. 320J, R.G. Dun & Co.

44. New York, Vol. 12, p. 166, R.G. Dun & Co.

45. New York, Vol. 9, pp. 62, 185, R.G. Dun & Co.

46. New York, Vol. 7, p. 238K, R.G. Dun & Co.

47. New York, Vol. 10, p. 463, R.G. Dun & Co.

48. Federal Manuscript Census of Population, Albany, N.Y., 1880, T9 805, ward 1, p. 9, line 44.

49. New York, Vol. 8, p. 359, R.G. Dun & Co.

50. New York, Vol. 14, p. 105, R.G. Dun & Co.

51. New York, Vol. 14, p. 113, R.G. Dun & Co.

52. New York, Vol. 8, p. 378, Vol. 11, p. 129, R.G. Dun & Co.

53. That is, some 40 out of 635 credit entries for female proprietors who were not milliners suggested that these women were acting as legal agents for male relatives; similarly, 12 out of the 187 who were clearly identified as married were said to use their husbands as agents.

54. New York, Vol. 11, p. 273, R.G. Dun & Co.

55. New York, Vol. 14, p. 244, R.G. Dun & Co.

56. Edith Eleanor Sparks, "Capital Instincts: The Economics of Female Proprietorship in San Francisco, 1850–1920," Ph.D. diss., University of California, Los Angeles, 1999, p. 109.

Chapter Four

1. Pamela Sharpe, "Gender in the Economy: Female Merchants and Family Businesses in the British Isles 1600–1850," *Social History* 34, no. 68 (2001): 288, 306.

2. "Family Business," chapter 2 of Caroline Bird, *Enterprising Women* (New York: W. W. Norton, 1976), pp. 41–43.

3. Claudia Goldin, "The Economic Status of Women in the Early Republic: Quantitative Evidence," *Journal of Interdisciplinary History* 16 (Winter 1986): 375–404; Jennifer Reed Fry, "'Extraordinary Freedom and great Humility': A Reinterpretation of Deborah Franklin," *The Pennsylvania Magazine of History and Biography* 137, no. 2 (2003): 167–96.

4. "Astor, John Jacob," in William H. Harris and Judith S. Levey, eds., *The New Columbia Encyclopedia* (New York: Columbia University Press, 1975), p. 170.

5. According to Gordon: "The making of a great fortune was the aim and purpose of Astor's life, and he accomplished it by dominating the American fur trade and investing his profits in the real estate of burgeoning New York City. . . . Before long [after arriving in NYC] Astor was operating on his own account and prospered at once. He began putting his profits into Manhattan real estate." John Steele Gordon, "Astor, John Jacob," in Eric Foner and John A. Garraty, eds., *The Reader's Companion to American History* (Boston: Houghton Mifflin, 1991), p. 61.

6. See Pamela Walker Laird, *Pull: Networking and Success since Benjamin Franklin* (Cambridge: Harvard University Press, 2006).

7. Henry Pitt Phelps, *Players of a Century: A Record of the Albany Stage. Including Notices of Prominent Actors who Have Appeared in America,* 2nd ed. (New York: Benjamin Blom, Inc. Publishers; orig. pub. Albany, 1880), pp. 330–31, 359.

8. New York, Vol. 10, p. 152, R.G. Dun & Co. Collection, Baker Library Historical Collections, Harvard Business School.

9. The credit records on the Singer sisters are somewhat confusing and contradic-

tory, beginning in 1852 and lasting until 1878, but describing these women in very different ways—as married, then single, first old, then young. However, between 1870 and 1877, Hannah and Jane are listed as partners in the city directory. New York, Vol. 7, p. 287, R.G. Dun & Co.

10. New York, Vol. 12, p. 70, R.G. Dun & Co.

11. New York, Vol. 9, p. 77, R.G. Dun & Co.

12. New York, Vol. 9, p. 70, R.G. Dun & Co.

13. New York, Vol. 9, p. 193, R.G. Dun & Co.

14. New York, Vol. 9, p. 193, R.G. Dun & Co.

15. New York, Vol. 7, p. 222P, Vol. 9, p. 33, R.G. Dun & Co.

16. According to the "Products of Industry in Albany" of 1860, Theobald Youman (identified as Theodore Yauman in the credit records) was a hair jeweler operating with a capital of $4,000, whose materials included 150 oz. of gold (worth $2,700) plus 30 lb. of hair (worth $3,100); Federal Manuscript Census of Manufactures, Albany, N.Y., 1860, ward 5, p. 1, line 13. The work was done "by hand," with 1 male and 3 female employees producing $6,000 worth of hairpieces plus $1,500 of goods of "diff[erent] kinds." According to the credit ledgers, Mrs. Yaumans was a "hairdresser," while he was "the mechanical man"; New York, Vol. 7, p. 238E, R.G. Dun & Co.

17. New York, Vol. 8, pp. 290, 301, 454, R.G. Dun & Co.

18. New York State Census, 5th Ward, p. 34.

19. New York, Vol. 9, p. 6, R.G. Dun & Co.

20. New York, Vol. 12, p. 19, R.G. Dun & Co.

21. New York, Vol. 7, p. 43, R.G. Dun & Co.

22. New York, Vol. 7, pp. 27, 16 (Mrs. A. C. Roberts), R.G. Dun & Co.; Erastus Corning, Corning Family Papers, AP 166, 1940, Albany Institute of History and Art.

23. New York, Vol. 13, p. 151, R.G. Dun & Co.

24. Louise A. Tilly and Joan W. Scott, *Women, Work, and Family* (New York: Routledge, 1987), pp. 15, 20, 63, 104–6, 112–13, 123–36, 226.

25. Carole Turbin, "Beyond Conventional Wisdom," in *To Toil the Livelong Day, America's Women at Work, 1780–1980,* ed. Carol Groneman and Mary Beth Norton (Ithaca, N.Y.: Cornell University Press, 1987), pp. 47–67.

26. Sarah Deutsch, *Women and the City: Gender, Space, and Power in Boston, 1870–1940* (Oxford: Oxford University Press, 2000), p. 31.

27. New York, Vol. 10, p. 32, Vol. 12, p. 50, R.G. Dun & Co.

28. New York, Vol. 9, p. 1, Vol. 11, p. 224, R.G. Dun & Co.

29. New York, Vol. 8, p. 264, R.G. Dun & Co.

30. New York, Vol. 9, p. 193, R.G. Dun & Co.

31. New York, Vol. 11, p. 139, R.G. Dun & Co.

32. New York, Vol. 7, p. 222M, R.G. Dun & Co.

33. New York, Vol. 13, p. 285, R.G. Dun & Co.

34. New York, Vol. 13, p. 107, R.G. Dun & Co.

35. New York, Vol. 14, p. 188, R.G. Dun & Co.

36. New York, Vol. 9, pp. 274, 224, R.G. Dun & Co.

37. New York, Vol. 12, p. 241, R.G. Dun & Co.

38. New York, Vol. 9, p. 342, R.G. Dun & Co.

39. New York, Vol. 10, p. 315, R.G. Dun & Co.

40. New York, Vol. 14, p. 26, R.G. Dun & Co.

41. New York, Vol. 11, p. 201J, R.G. Dun & Co.

42. New York, Vol. 9, p. 26, R.G. Dun & Co.

43. New York, Vol. 7, p. 67, R.G. Dun & Co.

44. New York, Vol. 8, p. 527, R.G. Dun & Co.
45. New York, Vol. 9, p. 177, R.G. Dun & Co.
46. New York, Vol. 9, p. 367, R.G. Dun & Co.
47. New York, Vol. 10, p. 271 (Jane Davey); New York, Vol. 8, p. 248 (Phoebe Earl), R.G. Dun & Co.
48. New York, Vol. 9, p. 179, R.G. Dun & Co.
49. New York, Vol. 7, p. 198 (Lawlor); Vol. 10, p. 401 (Sill); Vol. 10, p. 100, R.G. Dun & Co.
50. New York, Vol. 12, p. 94 (Beck); Vol. 12, p. 198 (Paulus), R.G. Dun & Co.
51. New York, Vol. 12, p. 344, R.G. Dun & Co.
52. New York, Vol. 12, p. 87, R.G. Dun & Co.
53. New York, Vol. 11, p. 202, R.G. Dun & Co.
54. New York Vol. 12, p. 33 (Ferguson/Hodges), R.G. Dun & Co.
55. New York, Vol. 10, p. 462, R.G. Dun & Co.
56. New York, Vol. 14, p. 82, R.G. Dun & Co.
57. New York, Vol. 9, p. 33, R.G. Dun & Co. In New York State, a woman could legally own her own property from 1848. According to what is known as the first of the "Married Women's Acts," women would retain the right to property owned both when they were married and acquired thereafter, including "rents" and "profits." However, as has been noted by scholars in the field, there was often a discrepancy between the law and common practice; see Kwolek-Folland's discussion "Changes in Women's Status: Law" in chapter 3, "Mills and More: Women's Business and the First Industrial Revolution, 1830–1880," *Incorporating Women: A History of Women and Business in the United States* (New York: Twayne, 1998), pp. 44–54; and Norma Basch, *In The Eyes of the Law: Women, Marriage, and Property in Nineteenth-Century New York* (Ithaca, N.Y.: Cornell University Press, 1982), p. 9.
58. Basch, *In the Eyes of the Law,* pp. 212–13.
59. Ibid., p. 213.

Chapter Five

1. Helen Campbell, *Prisoners of Poverty: Women Wage-Workers, Their Trades and Their Lives* (Westport, Conn.: Greenwood Press, 1970; orig. pub. 1887), p. 19.
2. Ibid., pp. 55–65.
3. Louisa May Alcott, "May Flowers," in *A Garland for Girls,* pp. 1–47 (New York: Grosset & Dunlap, n.d.).
4. Christine Stansell, *City of Women: Sex and Class in New York, 1789–1860* (Urbana: University of Illinois Press, 1987), p. 120.
5. New York, Vol. 12, p. 93, R.G. Dun & Co. Collection, Baker Library Historical Collections, Harvard Business School.
6. Wendy Gamber, *The Female Economy: The Millinery and Dressmaking Trades, 1860–1930* (Urbana: University of Illinois Press, 1997), p. 107.
7. New York, Vol. 9, p. 177 (Dunn); Vol. 10, p. 259 (Murphy), R.G. Dun & Co.
8. New York, Vol. 12, p. 282, R.G. Dun & Co.
9. New York, Vol. 7, p. 238E (Rockwell); Vol. 14, p. 58 (Scott), R.G. Dun & Co.
10. *Hoffman's Albany Directory, and City Register, for the Years 1849 '50* (Albany: L. G. Hoffman, 1850), p. 13.
11. New York, Vol. 11, p. 325, R.G. Dun & Co.
12. New York, Vol. 7, p. 230, R.G. Dun & Co.

13. New York, Vol. 7, p. 238M, R.G. Dun & Co.

14. New York, Vol. 11, p. 293, R.G. Dun & Co.

15. Franklin Mendels, "Proto-Industrialization: The First Phase of the Industrialization Process," *Journal of Economic History* 32, no. 1 (1972): 241–61; Jean Quataert, "A New View of Industrialization: 'Protoindustry' or the Role of Small-Scale, Labor-Intensive Manufacture in the Capitalist Environment," *International Labor and Working-Class History* 33 (Spring 1988): 3–22; Maxine Berg, Pat Hudson, and Michael Sonenscher, eds., *Manufacture in Town and Country before the Factory* (Cambridge: Cambridge University Press, 1983); Hans Medick, "The Proto-Industrial Family Economy: The Structural Function of Household and Family during the Transition from Peasant Society to Industrial Capitalism," *Social History* 1 (1976): 312–13; D. C. Coleman, "Proto-Industrialization: A Concept Too Many," *Economic History Review* 36 (1983): 435–48.

16. Alcott, "May Flowers," p. 22.

17. Ibid., p. 12.

18. Federal Manuscript Census of Population, Albany, N.Y., 1850, M432, ward 5, household #283, line 9 (Roberts); 1860, M653, reel 719, ward 5, p. 247, line 16 (Blanchard).

19. New York, Vol. 8, p. 320O (Bernhardt), R.G. Dun & Co.; Federal Manuscript Census of Population, 1870, Albany, N.Y., M593, reel 898, ward 1 (Cornock).

20. Federal Manuscript Census of Population, Albany, N.Y., 1870, M593, reel 898, ward 4, p. 13, line 18.

21. New York, Vol. 9, p. 175 (Cochrane); Vol. 9, p. 180 (Lagrange); Vol. 9, p. 173 (Lewis); Vol. 9, p. 194 (Smith), R. G. Dun & Co.

22. New York, Vol. 9, p. 365, R.G. Dun & Co.

23. New York, Vol. 7, p. 239L (Robb); Vol. 8, p. 290 (Bateman), R.G. Dun & Co.

24. New York, Vol. 7, p. 238E, R.G. Dun & Co.

25. Melinda Talbot, "Mary Anne Warriner, Rhode Island Milliner," *Annual Proceedings, Dublin Seminar* 24 (Boston, 1999), pp. 69–83.

26. Metta Victoria Fuller Victor, "Miss Slimmens' Window," *Godey's Ladies Magazine* 57: 40–45, 147–52, 233–38, 337–42, 425–31, 524–29.

27. Fanny Fern, *Rose Clark* (New York, Mason Brothers, 1856), p. 63.

28. Julie Jones-Eddy, *Homesteading Women: An Oral History of Colorado, 1890–1950* (New York: Twayne, 1992). The story of the often lent-out wedding dress, also set around the turn of the century, appears in Carrie Young, *The Wedding Dress: Stories from the Dakota Plains* (New York: Dell, 1996).

29. New York, Vol. 7, p. 52, R.G. Dun & Co.

30. Edith Wharton, *The House of Mirth* (New York: Berkley Books, 1981, orig. pub. 1905), pp. 282–85.

31. Edith Wharton, "Bunner Sisters," *The Edith Wharton Reader* (New York: Charles Scribner's Sons, 1965, orig. pub. 1916), p. 304.

32. Ibid., p. 303.

Chapter Six

1. The phrase "A small but safe business" was used in the 1870s and '80s by the R.G. Dun & Co. credit examiners to describe the concerns of Emma Dennstead, who

sold cords and tassels; Catherine Sill, who dealt in gentlemen's furnishing goods; Mrs. C. W. Spawn, a milliner; and Mrs. W. G. Terry, a confectioner.

2. Virginia Penny, *How Women Can Make Money, Married or Single, in all Branches of the Arts and Sciences, Professions, Trades, Agricultural and Mechanical Pursuits* (New York: Arno Press, 1971, orig. pub. 1863), p. 125.

3. Virginia Penny, *Think and Act. A Series of Articles Pertaining to Men and Women, Work and Wages* (Philadelphia: Claxton, Remsen, & Haffelfinger, 1869), pp. 22, 281–82.

4. [Metta Victoria Fuller Victor], "Miss Slimmens' Window," *Godey's Lady's Book* 57 (1859), pp. 40–45, 147–52, 233–38, 337–42, 425–31, 524–29. The writer of the story remained anonymous, identified in *Godey's* simply as "the author of 'The Tallow Family,'" but scholars have identified Metta Victoria Fuller Victor as the author of this serial novel and its sequel. See Katharine A. Parkham, "Metta Victoria Fuller Victor (1831–1885)," in Denise D. Knight, ed., *Nineteenth-Century American Women Writers: A Bio-Bibliographical Critical Sourcebook,* pp. 433–37 (Westport, Conn.: Greenwood Press, 1997).

5. Metta Victoria Fuller Victor, the author of "Miss Slimmens' Window," published stories, poetry, and even a novel while still in her teens. After her marriage in 1856 to Orville James Victor, a prominent journalist and editor, Metta Victoria also became an editor and continued writing and editing until her death in 1885, in addition to bearing and raising nine children. Parkham in *Nineteenth-Century American Women Writers,* p. 433.

6. We know quite a bit about Hogeboom and her small millinery shop, since the business is recorded in three sources: city directories, the R.G. Dun & Co. credit ledgers, and the 1860 Federal Manuscript Census of Manufactures. Mary Hogeboom herself can be located in the federal population census of 1870. Federal Manuscript Census of Manufactures, Albany, N.Y., 1860, ward 4, p. 4, line 7; Federal Manuscript Census of Population, Albany, N.Y., 1870.

7. New York, Vol. 8, p. 344L, R.G. Dun & Co. Collection, Baker Library Historical Collections, Harvard Business School.

8. The manufacturing census gives Hogeboom's invested capital at $1,000; according to the credit ledgers, Hogeboom's business was worth about $800 in 1868, and her personal property was valued at $1,000 in the population census of 1870.

9. New York, Vol. 7, p. 60, R.G. Dun & Co.

10. *The Albany Directory for the Year 1877, Containing a General Directory of the Citizens, A Business Directory, Record of the City Government, its Institutions, &c., &c.* (Albany: Sampson, Davenport, 1877), p. 407.

11. Even soap operas have been analyzed as feminist narratives: "As the Dissertations Churn: Academe Has the Hots for TV Soaps," *The New York Times,* 25 September 1994, sec. 4, p. 9.

12. Mary Catherine Bateson, *Composing a Life* (New York: Plume, 1990), pp. 9–13.

13. As in my own early work; see Susan Ingalls Lewis, "Female Entrepreneurs in Albany, 1840–1885," *Business and Economic History* 21 (1992): 65–73.

14. See Pamela Walker Laird on the importance of mentoring for American businessmen: *Pull: Networking and Success since Benjamin Franklin* (Cambridge: Harvard University Press, 2006).

15. New York, Vol. 9, p. 1A (Hart); Vol. 11, p. 273 (Loveday), R.G. Dun & Co.

16. New York, Vol. 10, p. 32 (Laitz); Vol. 12, p. 198 (Paulus), R.G. Dun & Co.

17. New York, Vol. 9, p. 77 (Hayes); Vol. 8, p. 566 (Davis), R.G. Dun & Co.

18. New York, Vol. 9, p. 197, R.G. Dun & Co.

19. New York, Vol. 11, p. 185, R.G. Dun & Co.

20. New York, Vol. 11, pp. 31, 185, R.G. Dun & Co.

21. New York, Vol. 7, p. 222E, Vol. 11, p. 5, Vol. 13, p. 254, R.G. Dun & Co.

22. New York, Vol. 7, p. 107, R.G. Dun & Co.

23. New York, Vol. 8, pp. 385, 437, Vol. 9, p. 198, Vol. 11, p. 397, Vol. 14, p. 36, R.G. Dun & Co.

24. These percentages add up to more than 100% because some businesswomen were described with more than one "small" term. However, there is also some under-counting here because of variations in wording—this search would not have picked up "small retail store," for instance, or "means and capital are small."

25. These figures add up to less than 100% (actually, to 94%) because they were de-termined by looking at each entry and selecting the first term associated with "small," rather than searching for each term (say, "small business") in all entries.

26. New York, Vol. 9, p. 432 (Kappes); Vol. 11, p. 379 (Mann), R.G. Dun & Co.

27. New York, Vol. 7, p. 205; Vol. 9, p. 185 (Donn, Don, or Dunn); Vol. 9, p. 185 (Crew), R.G. Dun & Co.

28. Donn is listed until 1895, Crew until 1897.

29. New York, Vol. 9, p. 275; Vol. 13, p. 2 (Maggie Manifold); Vol. 11, p. 147 (Charles Torrey), R.G. Dun & Co.; Federal Census of Manufactures, Albany, N.Y., 1860.

30. Penny, *How Women Can Make Money,* pp. xiii, 107, 109, 112, 126.

31. Carole Turbin, *Working Women of Collar City: Gender, Class, and Community in Troy, New York, 1864–86* (Urbana: University of Illinois Press, 1992), p. 52.

32. New York, Vol. 11, p. 267, R.G. Dun & Co.

33. New York, Vol. 9, p. 174, R.G. Dun & Co.

34. Federal Manuscript Census of Population, 1860, Albany, N.Y., M653, reel 719, ward 1.

35. New York, Vol. 9, p. 269, R.G. Dun & Co.

36. New York, Vol. 9, p. 215 (Schwarzman); Vol. 11, p. 173 (Barrett), R.G. Dun & Co.

37. Such were the conclusions reached in Clyde Griffen and Sally Griffen, *Natives and Newcomers: The Ordering of Opportunity in Mid-Nineteenth-Century Poughkeepsie* (Cambridge, Mass.: Harvard University Press, 1978), who judged that in both the eighteenth and nineteenth centuries "women's participation in business was sporadic and unusual"; and that although clothing firms (milliners, dressmakers, and fancy goods shops) represented the most common avenue for businesswomen, "most of these shops remained small and vanished quickly" (pp. 244–45).

38. Federal Manuscript Census of Population, 1860, Albany, N.Y., M653, reel 719, ward 3.

39. Thomas Dublin, *Transforming Women's Work: New England Lives in the Indus-trial Revolution* (Ithaca, N.Y.: Cornell University Press, 1994), p. 134.

40. Wendy Gamber, "Gendered Concerns: Thoughts on the History of Business and the History of Women," *Business and Economic History* 23 (Fall 1994): 137.

41. Helen Campbell, *Prisoners of Poverty: Women Wage-Workers, Their Trades and Their Lives* (Westport, Conn.: Greenwood Press, 1970, orig. pub. 1887), p. 106; Chris-tine Stansell, *City of Women: Sex and Class in New York, 1789–1860* (Urbana: University of Illinois Press, 1987), p. 133.

42. The 1860 federal population census entry on Neville lists three children born in

the 1840s, the same period when credit records describe her as running a canal grocery; Federal Manuscript Census of Population, 1860, Albany, N.Y., M653, reel 719, ward 7; New York, Vol. 8, p. 413, R.G. Dun & Co.

43. Federal Manuscript Census of Population, 1860, Albany, N.Y., M653, reel 719, ward 5; New York, Vol. 8, p. 358, R.G. Dun & Co.

44. New York, Vol. 7, pp. 126O, 158, R.G. Dun & Co.

45. New York, Vol. 9, p. 70 (Owen); Vol. 9, p. 178 (Henry); Vol. 10, p. 77 (Roseboom); Vol. 7, p. 96C (Blanchard), R.G. Dun & Co.

46. New York, Vol. 8, p. 378, Vol. 12, p. 129, R.G. Dun & Co.

47. The famous phrase "ladders on which the aspiring can rise" was used by Andrew Carnegie in a different context (his discussion of philanthropic contributions to educational institutions such as libraries) in his famous 1889 essay "The Gospel of Wealth," originally published in 1889 in the *North American Review* and republished in 1900 as "Wealth," the title essay in *The Gospel of Wealth and Other Timely Essays* (New York: The Century Co., 1900).

48. See Gamber, *The Female Economy: The Millinery and Dressmaking Trades, 1860–1930* (Urbana: University of Illinois Press, 1997).

49. New York, Vol. 7, p. 238L, Vol. 13, p. 4, R.G. Dun & Co.

50. New York, Vol. 7, pp. 238Y, 238Z6, R.G. Dun & Co.

51. New York, Vol. 12, p. 94, R.G. Dun & Co.

52. New York, Vol. 10, p. 253, R.G. Dun & Co.

53. New York, Vol. 7, pp. 54–55, 96C (J. W. Blanchard and Mrs. Olive Blanchard), R.G. Dun & Co.

54. New York, Vol. 10, p. 466, R.G. Dun & Co.

55. Gough was said to have inherited $10,000 from her husband in 1847, but the estimate was adjusted downward to $5,000 or $6,000 later that year; by 1852–53 she was reported to be "insolvent." New York, Vol. 7, p. 105, R.G. Dun & Co.

56. New York, Vol. 11, p. 109, R.G. Dun & Co.

57. New York, Vol. 7, p. 238L, R.G. Dun & Co.

58. New York, Vol. 8, p. 316, R.G. Dun & Co.

59. New York, Vol. 11, p. 1J, R.G. Dun & Co.

60. New York, Vol. 7, p. 238L, R.G. Dun & Co.

61. New York, Vol. 11, p. 149, R.G. Dun & Co.

62. New York, Vol. 11, pp. 201, 1J, R.G. Dun & Co.

63. New York, Vol. 7, p. 37, R.G. Dun & Co.

64. New York, Vol. 7, p. 238L, R.G. Dun & Co.

65. New York, Vol. 11, p. 70, R.G. Dun & Co.

66. [Metta Victoria Fuller Victor], "Miss Slimmens' Boarding House," *Godey's Lady's Book* (January–June 1860); reprinted as a book, *Miss Slimmens' Boarding House* (New York: J. S. Ogilvie, 1888).

Chapter Seven

1. Angel Kwolek-Folland, *Incorporating Women: A History of Women and Business in the United States* (New York: Twayne, 1998), p. 84.

2. The story of Bridget Murphy Kennedy's entrepreneurship is summarized from Laurence Leamer's popular (rather than scholarly) group biography of women in the Kennedy family. However, notes for the chapter on Bridget Murphy Kennedy demonstrate that Leamer consulted historical sources such as tax assessments, census records,

vital records, and church records. Laurence Leamer, *The Kennedy Women: The Saga of an American Family* (New York: Villard Books, 1994), pp. 6–24.

3. Andrea Tone, *Devices and Desires* (New York: Hill and Wang, 2001), pp. 33–34.

4. Mansel G. Blackford and K. Austin Kerr, *Business Enterprise in American History* (Boston: Houghton Mifflin, 1986), p. 2.

5. New York, Vol. 7, p. 238, R.G. Dun & Co. Collection, Baker Library Historical Collections, Harvard Business School.

6. New York, Vol. 9, pp. 193, 205, 420, R.G. Dun & Co.

7. New York, Vol. 14, p. 335, R.G. Dun & Co.

8. New York, Vol. 7, p. 218, R.G. Dun & Co.

9. New York, Vol. 10, p. 279, R.G. Dun & Co.

10. New York, Vol. 8, p. 359, R.G. Dun & Co.

11. New York, Vol. 9, p. 365, R.G. Dun & Co.

12. New York, Vol. 10, p. 391, R.G. Dun & Co.

13. New York, Vol. 13, p. 2 (Maggie Manifold), R.G. Dun & Co.

14. New York, Vol. 14, p. 99, R.G. Dun & Co.

15. New York, Vol. 10, p. 466, R.G. Dun & Co.

16. New York, Vol. 9, p. 196, R.G. Dun & Co.

17. New York, Vol. 8, p. 290, R.G. Dun & Co.

18. New York, Vol. 10, p. 92, R.G. Dun & Co.

19. New York, Vol. 11, p. 72, R.G. Dun & Co.

20. New York, Vol. 7, p. 54 (Harris); Vol. 11, p. 299 (Devilin), R.G. Dun & Co.

21. Businesswomen did advertise in the newspapers, but these advertisements were so extensive that they were not analyzed for this study but remain to be explored in the future.

22. *Hoffman's Albany Directory and City Register, for the Years 1844–5* (Albany: L. G. Hoffman, 1844), p. 9.

23. *Munsell's Albany Directory and City Register for 1854* (Albany: J. Munsell, 1854), p. 441.

24. New York, Vol. 7, p. 90, R.G. Dun & Co.

25. Federal Manuscript Census of Population, 1880, Albany, N.Y., T9, reel 805, ward 5, page 23, line 36; New York, Vol. 8, pp. 297, 377, 582, R.G. Dun & Co.

26. *The Albany Directory for the Year 1880, Containing a General Directory of the Citizens, a Business Directory, Record of the Government, its Institutions, &c., &c.* (Albany: Sampson, Davenport, 1880), p. 421.

27. New York, Vol. 9, p.112, Vol. 14, p.75, R.G. Dun & Co.

28. New York, Vol. 8, p. 314, R.G. Dun & Co.

29. Listed as part of the New Hampshire Newspaper Project by the New Hampshire State Library: http://www.nh.gov/nhsl/nhais/project_title_list.html.

30. New York, Vol. 11, p. 71, R.G. Dun & Co.

31. This advertisement appears on the inside cover of Colt's own *The tourist's guide through the Empire State: Embracing all cities, towns, and watering places, by Hudson River and New York Central Route* . . . (Albany: Mrs. S. S. Colt, 1871).

32. Trimble Opera House Programme, *The Colleen Bawn* (Albany, 1870). Manuscripts and Special Collections of the New York State Library.

33. Trimble Opera House Programme, *Kenilworth!*, The Orchestra, A Daily Journal Devoted to Music and the Drama for the Week Ending January 14th (Albany: Colt Publishing Co., 1871). Manuscripts and Special Collections of the New York State Library.

34. For instance, Mrs. Sincimer, a bonnet maker, paid four female employees a total of $48 a month, Miss Simmons, a milliner, paid eight employees $100 per month, Mrs. Matchin paid eight employees $100 per month, Mrs. Hogeboom paid five employees $60 per month, and Miss Newton paid one employee $11; the highest rate recorded was for Mrs. Wood, who paid two employees $40 per month, or an average of $5 a week; Federal Census of Manufactures, Albany, N.Y., 1860.

35. New York, Vol. 7, p. 51, R.G. Dun & Co.

36. *Munsell's Albany Directory and City Register for 1852–53 with Map and Index* (Albany: J. Munsell, 1852), p. 433.

37. New York, Vol. 7, p. 221, Vol. 9, pp. 73, 442, R.G. Dun & Co.

38. *The Albany Directory for the Year 1877, Containing a General Directory of the Citizens, A Business Directory, Record of the City Government, its Institutions, &c., &c.* (Albany: Sampson, Davenport, 1877), p. 376.

39. *The Albany Directory for the Year 1889, including Bath, East Albany and Greenbush, also a Business Directory and Records of the City and Village Governments, their Institutions, &c., &c.* (Albany: Sampson, Murdock, 1889), p. 491.

40. New York, Vol. 7, p. 55 (Blanchard); Vol. 7, p. 225 (Hunt); Vol. 9, p. 219 (Denmead); Vol. 8, p. 437 (Martineau), R.G. Dun & Co.

41. New York, Vol. 9, pp. 83, 90, Vol. 12, p. 257, R.G. Dun & Co.

42. New York, Vol. 7, p. 106, R.G. Dun & Co.

43. New York, Vol. 7, p. 173, R.G. Dun & Co.

44. New York, Vol. 7, pp. 211, 18C, Vol. 11, pp. 1A, 227, R.G. Dun & Co.

45. New York, Vol. 9, p. 195, R.G. Dun & Co.

46. Leamer, *The Kennedy Women,* p. 19.

Chapter Eight

1. Jacob Riis, *How the Other Half Lives* (Dover; originally published 1891), pp. 61–62.

2. Ibid., p. 50.

3. Ibid., pp. 61–62.

4. William Kennedy, *The Flaming Corsage* (New York: Penguin Books, 1996), p. 87.

5. Roy Rosenzweig, *Eight Hours for What We Will* (Cambridge: Cambridge University Press, 1983), p. 43.

6. Ibid., pp. 40–45.

7. New York, Vol. 9, p. 207 (Elder); Vol. 10, p. 466 (Ronan), R.G. Dun & Co. Collection, Baker Library Historical Collections, Harvard Business School.

8. New York, Vol. 13, p. 153, R.G. Dun & Co.

9. New York, Vol. 8, p. 344L, R.G. Dun & Co.

10. The other was the brothel keeper Sarah Creswell, discussed in chapter 2.

11. New York, Vol. 14, p. 13, R.G. Dun & Co.

12. New York, Vol. 10, p. 100, R.G. Dun & Co.

13. New York, Vol. 13, p. 348, R.G. Dun & Co.

14. Virginia Penny, *How Women Can Make Money, Married or Single, in all Branches of the Arts and Sciences, Professions, Trades, Agricultural and Mechanical Pursuits* (New York: Arno Press, 1971, orig. pub. 1863), p. 122.

15. New York, Vol. 9, p. 210, R.G. Dun & Co.

16. It is also very difficult to determine from these three sources which businesses

identified as saloons or groceries were family ventures selling beer to the people of the neighborhood and which might have been gathering places for "depraved" individuals; even the credit records do not really make this distinction clear except in a few cases. I am assuming that except for those businesses the credit records identify clearly as brothels or disreputable "hangouts," businesses that appear in the credit reports were generally considered respectable. A really cheap "beer-dive," for instance, would have no reason to ask for credit and thus no reason to appear in the credit reports or even the city directories.

17. New York, Vol. 7, pp. 54–55, R.G. Dun & Co.

18. New York, Vol. 7, p. 37, R.G. Dun & Co.

19. New York, Vol. 8, p. 398, R.G. Dun & Co.

20. New York, Vol. 10, pp. 186, 223, R.G. Dun & Co.

21. See Rowena Olegario on the immigrant Jewish community and credit reports: "'That Mysterious People': Jewish Merchants, Transparency, and Community in Mid-Nineteenth Century America," *Business History Review* 73 (Summer 1999): 190–220.

22. Lewis Lowenstein appears to have been the same individual identified in some sources as Lewis Levenstein and even Dennis Livingston: New York, Vol. 7, pp. 193, 195, Vol. 8, p. 352, R.G. Dun & Co.

23. New York, Vol. 9, p. 141 (Hugh Guyer), R.G. Dun & Co.

24. New York, Vol. 7, p. 230, Vol. 11, p. 315, Vol. 13, p. 350, R.G. Dun & Co.

25. New York, Vol. 14, p. 72, R.G. Dun & Co.

26. New York, Vol. 7, p. 198, R.G. Dun & Co.

27. New York, Vol. 14, p. 330, R.G. Dun & Co.

28. New York, Vol. 14, p. 17, R.G. Dun & Co.

29. New York, Vol. 7, p. 52, R.G. Dun & Co.

30. New York, Vol. 7, pp. 84–85, 96L, R.G. Dun & Co.

31. Angel Kwolek-Folland, *Incorporating Women: A History of Women and Business in the United States* (New York: Twayne, 1998), p. 65.

Conclusion

1. Virginia Woolf, *A Room of One's Own* (New York: Harcourt, Brace & World, 1957, orig. pub. 1929), p. 77.

2. Joan Kelly, *Women, History & Theory, The Essays of Joan Kelly* (Chicago: The University of Chicago Press, 1984), especially chapter 2, "Did Women Have a Renaissance?"; Joan Scott, "Gender: A Useful Category of Analysis," *American Historical Review* 65 (1986): 27–90.

3. Joan Scott, "Comment: Conceptualizing Gender in American Business History," *Business History Review* 72 (Summer 1998): 242.

4. I am indebted here to the sophisticated conceptualization developed by Elizabeth Ewan in her paper "Hucksters in the High Street: Petty Retailers in late Medieval Scotland," delivered at the Exeter Conference on "Women, Trade, and Business from Medieval Times to the Present," July 1996.

5. Wendy Gamber, *The Boardinghouse in Nineteenth-Century America* (Baltimore: The Johns Hopkins University Press, 2007), p. 3.

6. Or, as Joan Scott stated in her comment on papers presented at the 1996 Hagley Symposium on *Conceptualizing Gender in American Business History*, studies of businesswomen "enlarge our sense of the scope of women's activities in nineteenth and twentieth century America, placing them outside exclusively domestic locations,

and thus adding another nail to the coffin of 'separate spheres' as a way of conceiving women's experience in the past." Joan Scott, "Comment: Conceptualizing Gender in American Business History," *Business History Review* 72 (Spring 1998), p. 243.

7. Thorstein Veblen, *The Theory of the Leisure Class* (New York: Penguin Books, 1979; originally published 1899).

8. In fact, this argument has been made for Canadian women by Peter Baskerville, who found, based on statistical analysis, that "working women's self-employment was a more common fact of life at the century's commencement, than it is at the century's close." Peter Baskerville, "Gender, Family, and Self-Employment in Urban Canada: 1901 and 1996 Compared" (paper presented at the Fifth Canadian Business History Conference, McMaster University, Hamilton, Ontario, October 1998), p. 23.

9. See Wendy Gamber, *The Female Economy: The Millinery and Dressmaking Trades, 1860–1930* (Urbana: University of Illinois Press, 1997).

10. Pat Hudson and W. R. Lee, "Women's Work and the Family Economy in Historical Perspective," in Pat Hudson and W. R. Lee, eds., *Women's Work and the Family Economy in Historical Perspective* (New York: Manchester University Press, 1990), p. 2.

11. Ibid., p. 5.

12. Fernand Braudel, *The Wheels of Commerce* (Berkeley: University of California Press, 1992); see especially chapter 1, "The Instruments of Exchange," pp. 25–137; portrait of the eighteenth-century female grocer, p. 66.

13. Béatrice Craig, "Petites Bourgeoisies and Penny Capitalists: Women in Retail in the Lille Area during the Nineteenth Century," *Enterprise and Society* 2 (June 2001): 198–224.

14. Daniel A. Rabuzzi, "Women as Merchants in Eighteenth-Century Northern Germany: The Case of Stralslund, 1750–1830," *Central European History* 28, no. 4 (1995): 435–56.

15. Hall, Davidoff, and Smith all document declension, but here I believe their declension should be associated primarily with family mobility rather than a shift in societal values. That is, as families became more successful and the workplace and homeplace became separated, it is true that upper-middle-class women no longer participated in family business—but during the same period, lower-middle-class women remained engaged in home-based family ventures. Leonore Davidoff and Catherine Hall, *Family Fortunes: Men and Women of the English Middle-Class, 1780–1850* (Chicago: The University of Chicago Press, 1987); Bonnie G. Smith, *Ladies of the Leisure Class: The Bourgeoisies of Northern France in the Nineteenth Century* (Princeton: Princeton University Press, 1981).

16. Virginia Penny, *How Women Can Make Money*, p. 105.

17. Kolleen M. Guy, "Drowning Her Sorrows: Widowhood and Entrepreneurship in the Champagne Industry," *Business and Economic History* 26 (Winter 1997): 505–14.

18. Mary Catherine Bateson, *Composing a Life* (New York: Plume, 1989), pp. 6–14.

Appendix Two

1. For the earlier years, before directories by trade appeared at the back of the book, these volumes were scanned line by line. For the years from 1859 forward, when the back-of-the-book business directories were introduced, business directories were used but then checked against a line-by-line search.

2. Special Collections at the SUNY Albany Library does not have a copy of the 1881 directory, and since more than 1,200 individual female proprietors had been identified using the available directories, it did not seem necessary to consult the directory for this year. This decision resulted in an undercount of both active businesswomen in the early 1880s and an underestimation of the number of years that a few businesswomen remained active (that is, women who began or ended their careers in 1881 would be recorded with careers a year shorter than they actually lasted). However, since city directory listings by themselves cannot provide a truly exact and accurate count of businesswomen's ventures, this undercount seemed acceptable.

3. Some of these 854 entries overlapped; that is, since some female proprietors who had been in business in 1831 were still operating their concerns in 1841, their names were repeated, and so on for following decades up to 1870; I have not attempted to determine how many of these 854 names were repeats. However, I clearly missed numerous businesswomen who operated in the years in between 1831 and 1841, or 1850 and 1860.

4. Because I began my project with milliners, that database had already been designed when I decided to expand my subject, and I found that other types of businesswomen required a slightly different database format.

5. Microfilm reels T9 805, T9 806, and T9 807.

6. Here the city directory for 1830/31 has been eliminated and a comparison drawn between credit entries (dated 1840–85) and city directories from 1841, 1850, 1860, 1870, and 1880.

7. Women born in the United States made up about 44% of the 510 women we know were doing business in Albany in the year 1880 (and thus should have been recorded in the census as doing business in that year), while women born in Ireland made up 34%, women from Germany 14%, and women from Great Britain and elsewhere in the British Empire, 7%. In contrast, of those businesswomen whose trades were not recorded in the census of 1880, 56% were born in the United States, 23% were born in Ireland, 15% were born in Germany, and 5% were born in Britain or its empire. Thus the discrepancies for the United States and Ireland are in the range of 10% or more, while the discrepancies for Germany and Britain are in the range of 1% to 2%.

INDEX

●

advertising/advertisements: for businesswomen, 11, 31 36, 64, 88, 98, 124–34, 153, 179n39, 190n21, 190n31; for businessmen, 33, 138

African-American businesswomen, 3, 5, 39, 119, 177n2; as laundresses, xv, 39

age of businesswomen, 22–23, 38, 41–44, 54, 104, 110, 121, 131, 146

Albany, New York: history and description of, 17–19; population of, 18; selection of, 17, 19

alcoholic husbands of businesswomen, 1, 16, 55–56, 107, 153, 182n14

Alcott, Louisa May, 86–88, 90, 94, 185n3, 186n16

Alger, Horatio, as hero, xiii, 67, 97, 100

Anderson, Grace, 72, 125–26 [fig. 7.1], 136

Anderson, Sarah, 31, 124

Andrews, Anna, 89–90, 151–52

apprentices, millinery, 60, 88, 90, 93, 96, 111

artisans: businesswomen as, 12, 13, 19, 25–26, 58, 88, 90, 92, 173n4; husbands of businesswomen, 40, 56, 75

artists as businesswomen, 11, 88, 91

Astor, John Jacob and Sarah Todd, 66–67, 82–83, 183nn4–5

average proprietresses, 41–45

Baker Library, Harvard University Graduate School of Business Administration, xviii, 6, 23, 167, 175n19

bakers, female, 16, 26, 36, 39, 40, 49, 50, 51–52, 61, 62, 69, 71, 72, 125, 165, 169

Balliet, Barbara, xviii, 11, 176n33

bankrupt businesswomen, 60, 74, 80, 113–15, 151–52; male relatives of businesswomen, 22, 56, 63, 68–69, 79–80, 148, 150. *See also* failure

bankruptcy, 10, 23, 81, 113, 145, 176n32

Barnes, Lucien, 68, 128

Basch, Norma, 81–82, 185nn57–58

Bateson, Mary Catharine, 99, 187n12, 193n18

Bird, Caroline, 1, 3–4, 7, 66–67, 82, 119, 174n1, 174n4, 183n2

Bird, Isabella, 18, 178n11

Blackford, Mansel, xviii, xx, 5, 9, 120, 175n13, 176n28, 178n15, 190n4

Blake, Adam, 135

Blake, Catharine, 39, 130, 135–36, 141

Historical Perspectives on Business Enterprise
Mansel G. Blackford and K. Austin Kerr, Series Editors

The scope of this series includes scholarly interest in the history of the firm, the history of government-business relations, and the relationship between business and culture, both in the United States and abroad. Included are histories of individual companies and biographies of business people. For a complete list of titles in this series, visit www. ohiostatepress.org.